Corporate Social Responsibility in Emerging Economies

Over the last few decades, emerging mar[illegible] their share in world GDP and have come to play a prominent and growing role in global business. Their period of impressive growth was triggered by major global advances such as economic liberalization and governance reforms and deregulation.

As governments and policy makers have permitted global competition from the more advanced, developed world, the prospect of millions of consumers in developing countries not only encourages locals to start businesses, but also appeals to multinational enterprises overseas. The growing presence of emerging markets on the world stage has not been left unnoticed and many investors have contributed significant amounts of capital with the hope of receiving major financial gains. In this context, emerging markets are particularly facing sustainability challenges due to their fast growing pace and fuzzy or inexistent sustainability regulations.

Corporate Social Responsibility in Emerging Economies represents a realistic critical overview of the state of affairs of CSR in the context of an emerging economy. It is an accessible and comprehensive diagnostic point of reference for the academic world as well as for policy makers. The topic of CSR is highly relevant for the business world and a challenging subject for the theory and literature.

This is a unique book that offers new empirical insights for policy makers and scholars of the fields of CSR, Business Ethics, Organizational Studies, and related disciplines.

Cosmina Lelia Voinea works as Assistant Professor of Strategy and Sustainable Management at the Faculty of Management, Science and Technology, Open University, the Netherlands.

Cosmin Fratostiteanu works as Associate Professor at the University of Craiova Faculty of Economics and Business Administration, Craiova, Romania.

Routledge Studies in Business Ethics

Originating from both normative and descriptive philosophical backgrounds, business ethics implicitly regulates areas of behaviour which influence decision making, judgment, behaviour and objectives of the leadership and employees of an organization. This series seeks to analyse current and leading edge issues in business ethics, and the titles within it examine and reflect on the philosophy of business, corporations and organizations pertaining to all aspects of business conduct. They are relevant to the conduct of both individuals and organizations as a whole.

Based in academic theory but relevant to current organizational policy, the series welcomes contributions addressing topics including: ethical strategy; sustainable policies and practices; finance and accountability; CSR; employee relations and workers' rights; law and regulation; economic and taxation systems.

Mismanagement, "Jumpers," and Morality
Covertly Concealed Managerial Ignorance and Immoral Careerism in Industrial Organizations
Reuven Shapira

Restructuring Capitalism
Materialism and Spiritualism in Business
Rogene A. Buchholz

The Ethics of Neoliberalism
The Business of Making Capitalism Moral
Peter Bloom

Integrity in Business and Management
Edited by Marc Orlitzky and Manjit Monga

Corporate Social Responsibility in Emerging Economies
Reality and Illusion
Cosmina Lelia Voinea and Cosmin Fratostiteanu

For a full list of titles in this series, please visit www.routledge.com

Corporate Social Responsibility in Emerging Economies

Reality and Illusion

Cosmina Lelia Voinea and
Cosmin Fratostiteanu

Routledge
Taylor & Francis Group
NEW YORK AND LONDON

First published 2019
by Routledge
605 Third Avenue, New York, NY 10017

and by Routledge
2 Park Square, Milton Park, Abingdon, Oxon, OX14 4RN

First issued in paperback 2020

Routledge is an imprint of the Taylor & Francis Group, an informa business

Library of Congress Cataloging-in-Publication Data
Names: Voinea, Cosmina Lelia, author. | Fratostiteanu, Cosmin, author.
Title: Corporate social responsibility in emerging economies : reality and illusion / Cosmina Lelia Voinea & Cosmin Fratostiteanu.
Description: New York : Routledge, 2018. | Series: Routledge studies in business ethics | Includes bibliographical references and index.
Identifiers: LCCN 2018015647 | ISBN 9781138082601 (hardback) | ISBN 9781315112411 (ebook)
Subjects: LCSH: Social responsibility of business—Developing countries. | Business ethics—Developing countries.
Classification: LCC HD60.5.D44 V65 2018 | DDC 174/.4091724—dc23
LC record available at https://lccn.loc.gov/2018015647

ISBN 13: 978-0-367-73407-7 (pbk)
ISBN 13: 978-1-138-08260-1 (hbk)

Typeset in Sabon
by Apex CoVantage, LLC

Contents

Preface

Emerging economies offer companies great opportunities, which simultaneously translates into a continuous intensification of business activities and a fast economic growth at the great compromise regarding sustainability. While ideas of sustainability and corporate social responsibility (CSR) have a relatively long history in developed economies due to well-established values of business standards, stable socio-economic, and political conditions and strong legal systems, in practice, however, it is the emerging economies who are most in need of sustainable ways of conducting business. CSR is believed to be useful in promoting social justice, equality, transparency, and accountability by holding organizations liable for their actions. Considering today's growing attention for environmental preservation and global poverty, it comes as no surprise that the increased need for social considerations is also necessary in emerging markets.

In contrast to the developed countries, emerging countries often have to deal with problems such as poverty, human rights violation, corruption, inequalities, and social exploitations. Organizations operating in emerging markets have the responsibility to address some of these issues. The purpose of the book is to give an overview of the state of affairs and developments of CSR in emerging economies by focusing on the hard reality instead of the idealistic and positive side portrayed by CSR enthusiasts.

Furthermore, given that the concepts of sustainability and CSR research have been conducted almost in a complete vacuum that is developed, economies, CSR models, and theories fail to account for the sustainability challenges in emerging markets. Through this book, we aim to expand the existing knowledge base on CSR models and practices to a different business environment of emerging markets.

Acknowledgments

We would like to express our special gratitude to Chiributa Ramona Alexandrina for her valuable role and support in the translation process. Without her great assistance, our work would not have been possible.

This book benefited from the great contributions of Ana Cristina Campos Marques, Bas Romein, Sabine Kester, Iris Braun, and Stefan Weijers. We would like to thank them all for their valuable input.

1 International Organizations Increasing Awareness on Social Responsibility

1. Introduction

Corporate social responsibility (CSR) is an outlook referring to the contributions that companies need to make toward the development of a modern society. As the states and international institutions became aware of adopting the CSR principles by companies and the sustainable development objectives, there also came the need for international standards to define a desirable corporate behavior.

The failure of some big corporations emphasized the importance of social responsibility and proved that an inadequate corporate administration, even in terms of a developed market economy, could seriously affect shareholders, creditors, state, investors, contractors, consumers (shareholders' assembly), and people (welfare-employees, depositors, retirees). It is noteworthy that the emerging problems would have had less negative consequences if more efficient methods of control and survey instruments for corporate management responsibility and transparency of their activity had existed.

The social responsibility originated in the nineteenth century. At that time, some employers were already behaving in a socially responsible manner toward their employees, offering several benefits, such as taking the responsibility for their children's education, social services, and so on. This responsible consciousness was far from being carried unanimously at that period. Only at the end of the twentieth century, the new concept of CSR started to develop and to be accepted.

Until the beginning of 1970s, the companies were concerned only with their economic performance, the satisfaction of shareholders being prioritized. CSR has its roots in an array of different factors such as the 1970s social movements, the Vietnam War, the political impact from South Africa, and the environmental disasters and climate phenomena which effects were felt in every country caused by environmental problems. In addition, the overall output gave birth to a thorough reflection regarding the social responsibility as well as for the environment, convincing some companies to adopt policies by the end of 1990 to become active in the direction of an increased social responsibility.

Not so long ago, only few were concerned about the social responsibility issue, which was perceived, generally speaking, as a major stage only for the companies listed on the stock exchange. On the other hand, the companies that are not listed on the stock exchange hesitate regarding the necessity of introducing the standards of social responsibility into their activity, justifying their reduced number of shareholders, and therefore, introducing the principles of social responsibility is expensive. Thus, it becomes clear why the developing countries don't attach the importance to matters concerning social responsibility and why the implementation of the respective principles barely unrolls.

Although the financial crises pointed out convincingly to the necessity of promoting the social responsibility, only in few developing countries, this matter is brought to the attention of the decisive factors. It is to be mentioned that inefficient procedures of social responsibility present a great danger not only to companies, but also to the entire society.

The investors become more and more demanding with regard to the quality of social responsibility information, the manner of revealing it, and to the implementation of leadership standards in companies where they are interested to invest their capital.

The promoting of some efficient measures of social responsibility and the implementation of business principles constitute efficient measures to foreworn and struggle against the corruption acts; the business principles are meant to guide in practice the small, medium, and large companies facing the struggle against corruption and bribery, promoting the advantages of a continuous business.

At first, social responsibility embodied the relations between managers and shareholders. Meanwhile, other aspects related to social responsibility appeared—mutual relations between the company and its management and interest parties: employees, creditors, contractors, and civil society.

Promoting the social responsibility principles, as well as the efficient measures for corporative administration, became the basic problem of reforms and economies both for developed countries, and for those in development.

The countries in transition began to show their interest in social responsibility, because many companies emerged after privatization, and some of them own a quota from the state. To provide proper standards of social responsibility, public's trust in the rightfulness of the privatization process grows in these domains, and it contributes to obtaining the maximum efficiency of national investments.

The international business environment is going through the process of a long-term structural change. Once with the appearance of highly qualified services industry, the companies that provide services and technology penetrated the international market. Large-scale companies are still responsible for the main part of international investments, and it is making an entry the tendency of wide range fusions. At the same time, the level of foreign investments made by medium- and small-size companies also increased, and these companies play a significant role on the international scene. Multinational corporations, as their equivalents, developed themselves to comprise a wide range of business arrangements and systematization. Strategic alliances and friendly relations with suppliers and contracting parties tend to erase the limits of a corporation.

The rapid evolution of the structures of multinational companies is mirrored also in the transactions displayed in the developing world, where the direct level of foreign investments has grown rapidly. In developing countries, the multinational corporations varied their production, exceeding the primary production phase and extractive industry by developing manufacture, assembly lines, markets, and autochthonous services.

The nature, goal, and speed of the economic change brought new strategic changes to corporations and their capital owners. Multinational corporations have the opportunity to implement the best practical politics and durable development that seek to ensure the coherence between social, economic, and environment goals. The ability of multinational companies to promote a durable development is achieved considerably when trade and investments are performed in open, adequately regulated competitive markets. Many multinational companies proved that showing respect for maintaining high standards in managing businesses can improve the economic growth. The existing competition is sharp, and multinational companies are confronted with staff variety. Within this context, some companies may be tempted to neglect their standards or principles, trying to achieve advantages, but not in a proper way.

2. International Organizations That Have Contributed to the Social and Governmental CSR Awareness

Many international organizations have contributed globally to the CSR development.

The United Nations (UN), the European Union, and the Organisation for Economic Co-operation and Development (OECD) are the three most important institutions involved in the elaboration of a frame to define and establish the indicators through which any social responsibility program can be transparently evaluated.

The United Nations Organization (UNO) is the most important international organization in the world. It has the mission to ensure the global peace, the compliance of human rights, international cooperation, and compliance of the international law UNO provides the food supply for 90 million people from 80 countries; co-operates with 193 countries to combat the climate change and support sustainable development; offers help for the improvement of health and lifestyle of millions of poor people from the rural areas; protects and promotes human rights; and uses diplomacy to prevent conflict.

During 2004–2005, Romania was a non-permanent member of the UN Security Council. From this position, it contributed to the application of the provisions of Carta UNO regarding the regional organizations, by promoting a resolution project concerning the UNO cooperation with regional organizations in maintaining peace and international security, a project that was adopted on October 17, 2005.

Through its presence in various UN bodies, Romania has the opportunity to participate in the decision-making process of global institutions, having international influence globally and in the neighboring geographical regions. In addition, its participation in the peace-keeping UNO operations highlighted the efficiency of Romanian army and its political availability to participate in multinational military activities to sustain the international stability.

The United Nations Development Programme (UNDP), as a subsidiary organ (specialized program) of the UN, was established in 1965. It represents a global UNO network in the development field, aiming to support the developing countries to attract and use appropriately the development assistance. The program has identified and is active in four main fields: poverty reduction and fulfilling of the Millennium Development Goals; democratic governance; preventing crises and helping reconstruction; and environment and sustainable development.

The UNDP office in Bucharest was opened in 1972. On February 1, 1972, it was already running six major projects, with a budget of 41.1 million USD. During this collaboration, the UNDP offered technical assistance and organized training programs for experts from different domains of activity.

The UNDP run a valued assistance and cooperation activity for development, with an inclusive impact on concrete sustainability of Romania joining the EU and the North Atlantic Treaty Organization (NATO). The UNDP was the main partner of the Govern at the elaboration of the National Strategy for Sustainable Development (2010–2030), an essential document for planning of sectorial politics, as well as in relation with the EU arrangements.

3. OECD Principles for Social Responsibility

To coordinate the actions of companies to achieve a sustainable development worldwide, in 1976, the OECD developed the Guidelines for Multinational Enterprises: a series of directives that need to be taken into consideration by any company regardless of their field of action having in sight the human rights, the protection of the environment, consumer interests, corruption, and competition.

Those who are engaged in politics in both economies, in the developed countries as well as those who tend to the market economy, direct their steps to ensure a good corporatist administration. The OECD principles of corporatist administration set the frame for favorable practices, approved by the governments of the 30 OECD member countries. They were conceived to assist the governments and regulation organisms both in the OECD countries and from other parts in outlining and applying the effective rules, regulations, and conduct policy. Simultaneously, they provide effective methods to follow for exchanging actions, investors, companies, or tertium quids, which play a role in the developing process of social responsibility. The OECD principles were used as reference points to accomplish national codes concerning management corporations.

The OECD principles of social responsibility include the following:

1) *Shareholders' rights*. Social responsibility has to ensure the frame for shareholder's right protection provided by the law and to verify its observance.

2) *Impartial treatment of all shareholders*. The frame of social responsibility has to ensure an impartial treatment of all shareholders, including those who are minority or foreign. All shareholders have to be effectively protected when their rights are not respected.

3) Disclosure and transparency of information and exchanges. The social responsibility frame has to ensure transparency, opportunity, and accuracy of all materials and documents related to company, including its financial condition, performances, patrimony, and management.

4) *Responsibilities of the company's board*. As part of social responsibility, the board has to ensure the strategic orientation of the company, the effective survey of the management, and their responsibility concerning the society its and shareholders.

5) *Interested Parties' Role (Stakeholders—employees, clients, creditors, government, civil society) in promoting social responsibility*. Hereby, social responsibility needs to acknowledge the interested parties' rights, as stipulated by law, and to encourage active cooperation between the company and interested parties to create welfare and jobs and to ensure financial stability of the company.

The principles were revised to take into account recent developments and experiences of the OECD member or non-member states. Those who make politics are now more aware of the contributions of a good social responsibility, which leads to balance on the financial market, to investments, and further economic growth. The companies have a better understanding of how social responsibility contributes to their competitiveness.

The principles are a vivid instrument, offering non-obligatory standards and favorable practices as an implemented guide that can be adjusted according to specific circumstances in individual countries or regions. The OECD offers a forum for informal dialogue and exchanging experience between the member and non-member countries. To handle changing circumstances, the OECD will look up closely the social responsibility development, identifying tendencies and foreseen remedies for future challenges.

The OECD efforts will also increase the culture of value for an ethical and professional conduct, with trust and integrity playing an important role in economic life for a healthy business environment and future prosperity.

The principles are not obligatory because their implementation needs to be adjusted according to different legal, economic, and cultural circumstances. This is a significant key of principles, which makes them a useful tool for the entire world, on developed markets or those being in transition to market economy. The governments also need to find a balance between the rules and regulations on one side and flexibility on the other side.

Because multinational companies operate worldwide, the international cooperation in this field needs to be extended to all countries. The governments that adhere to the OECD principles encourage companies that operate on the territory of their states to respect the provisions, considering the specific context of every host country.

The governments have the right to set the terms of internal jurisdiction in which the multinational companies will function, under the influence of international legislation. The entities of multinational companies from different countries are liable to legislation in force from those countries. When the multinational companies face contradictory demands imposed by adhering countries, the governments will cooperate with good faith concerning the solution to the issues.

The use of adequate international mechanisms, including arbitration, is encouraged to solve the conflicts and to enable decision making in case of legal differences that appear between the national governments and companies.

The OECD will continue its analysis of investment political fields, including the measure of maximizing the benefits of liberating the investments, social dimensions, and environmental impact.

The role of principles is to assist the governments of OECD and other member countries in their effort to estimate and improve the legal, institutional, and regulatory frame of social responsibility, and to provide the right paths and suggestions for the stock markets and other participants who play a role in the process of developing an efficient social responsibility.

The principles represent a mutual base that OECD member countries consider essential to improve the beneficent practices of social responsibility. They don't plan to serve as substitutes for government, semi-governmental initiatives, or the private sector to develop a more elaborate model of "the best practices" in social responsibility.

Social responsibility is the key element in improving efficiency and economic development, and also in increasing investors' trust. Social responsibility implies a set of relations between the company management and the board council, their shareholders, and others. It also provides a structure through which the objectives of a company are set, and the necessity of setting these objectives, to accomplish them, and to survey the performances.

Social responsibility should provide specific stimuli to the boarding council and management to obtain favorable objectives for the company and for its shareholders, and it should enable the survey. The presence of an effective system of social responsibility, within a company and in an economy as a whole, helps to deliver a confidence level necessary for good functioning of a market economy. Social responsibility is just a part of a wider economic context in which the firms operate. The social responsibility frame depends on a legal, regulatory, and institutional environment. In addition, factors such as business ethics and community social interests where the company operates can also have an impact on its reputation and long-term success.

The degree to which every company observes the basic principles of social responsibility is a growing factor, extremely important in making decisions and investments. Of a particular relevance is the relation between the social responsibility practice and the increasing of international character of investments. The international stream of capital entitles companies to obtain financing from a wide range of investors. If countries try to gain total profit from global capital markets, and if they try to bring long-term capital, the social responsibility arrangements need to be credible, well understood, within council, and in conformity with the accepted international principles.

The principles are not obligatory, and they try to set objectives and to suggest different ways of accomplishing them. Their purpose is to serve as a reference point. They can be used by those who politicize to examine and develop the law and regulatory frame of social responsibility to reflect their own social, economic, legal, and cultural circumstances.

To remain competitive in a changing world, the companies need to innovate and to adapt their social responsibility practices to greet new requests and to gather new opportunities. Similarly, the governments have a significant responsibility to form an efficient regulation frame to provide enough flexibility to allow markets to function effectively and to acknowledge shareholders' experience. It is at hand of governments and participants on the market to decide how to apply these principles to develop their own contexts of social responsibility.

The EU is interested in CSR, seeing it as a mean to attain the objective of becoming a competitive and dynamic system, capable of sustaining the economic development through more and better jobs and a greater social cohesion.

4. Social Responsibility: Analysis at the EU Level

CSR represents the involvement of the business environment in the improvement of the community's life quality that it belongs to and in which it runs its activities. To carry out these activities, it contributes to the creation of a direct channel between the society and organizations. Furthermore, through such a channel, any organization that develops social responsibility campaigns can realize that the good of the community represents in fact the good of the whole company.

The equilibrium between ethics and personal interest is not just possible but necessary for the long-term development of a company. On the other hand, in business, there is a need not just for financial capital, but also the assets, human resources, as well as a social capital created through reputation and trust. From the beginning of 1990s, the European Commission (EC) stated an active interest regarding the CSR. In 1993, the EC president, Jacques Delors, asked the business community from Europe to adopt a more active position against social exclusion.

The concept of CSR was gradually developed, which was manifested for example through establishing a common Declaration against social exclusion in 1995, or through launching of the European Business Network for Social Cohesion in 1996 (which became CSR Europe in 2000). The CSR Europe is a business network that comprises over 70 of the biggest multinational companies as direct members and other 3,000 companies through 31 National Partner Organizations. The goal is to support the companies in obtaining profit, sustainable increase, and social progress through the incorporation of CSR in the center of business practices.

In 2001, the launch of the first sustainable development strategy took place based on the idea that, in the long term, the economic increase, social inclusion, and environment protection are interdependent.

The regulations of the Parliament and the European Council from March 19, 2001, allowed the voluntary participation of the organizations from community schemes of management and environment audit. Over 4,500 organizations are currently part of it, out of which 23% are micro enterprises, 33% are small enterprises, 25% are medium enterprises, and 19% are large enterprises.

At the EU level, a Multi-Stakeholder Forum has been founded, chaired by the EC and made of the employee organizations, business networks, syndicates, and representatives of the civil society. The objective is to support the CSR practices, promote innovation, transparency, and instruments through the improvement of knowledge, and the exploration of stability possibilities of common guiding principles at the European level. In 2003, the European Council Resolution was signed, regarding CSR.

A special attention is given to the CSR within SMEs, along with the implementation of the Pan-European Campaign of Awareness of CSR by SMEs, including numerous events across the entire Europe and the foundation of an informative website. The European Council recommends the member states to encourage the companies to implement social responsibility. Thus, in 2010, the international standard ISO of social responsibility was launched, addressing all kinds of organizations, from multinationals, to SMEs, to public authorities, to unions, and nongovernmental organizations (NGOs).

Through other important initiatives in the CSR field, there can be named various international certificates for the quality management system or environment; international initiatives of equitable commerce or environment; the Global Reporting Initiative whose mission is to develop and disseminate guiding references in the sustainable development field that can be applied worldwide; instruments such as Europe 2020 strategy or the Universal Declaration of Human Rights.

These initiatives as a goal have the strengthening of the leadership role in the CSR field of the EU globally. The representative instruments of CSR politics play a fundamental role concerning the assurance of a proper frame for sustainable corporative performances development. The EU owns an important role in promoting and developing the social responsibility, promoting transparency, and coherence.

To guide the companies in CSR implementing, the EU also elaborated a series of principles. The EU recommends that the companies integrate these principles in their behavior codes and to report on how they applied them.

Nowadays, it is perfectly normal among businesspeople to talk about social responsibility and the civic role of the companies. Many businessmen confess the necessity of taking some responsibilities not only toward investors but also toward the nearby communities and to other involved groups, or those affected by their activities. Various programs aimed at these increased moral obligations have been summed up under a larger equation, that being the CSR.

The social responsibility of the companies became in the last years a very interesting subject for the private environment, authorities, and society. If the social responsibility of a company in the past was just a correction tool with a negative impact on the environment and communities, in the meantime, it became increasingly outlined, and it took a different perspective, as a responsible way of administrating the business, combining the well-being of the company with the communities, and also preserving of the environment.

At the European level, the reports regarding the social responsibility programs became mandatory; therefore, all companies from the EU must present the annual reports of their CSR activities.

In Europe, the most important body that promotes the activities of social responsibility is CSR Europe. It includes 60 multinational companies among which are ABB, Accor, BASF, BP, BT, Citigroup, Coca-Cola, Danone, Deloitte, Epson, France Telecom, HP, IBM, Intel, Johnson & Johnson, KPMG, Lloyds, L'Oreal, McDonald's, P&G, Nike, Nestle, Toyota, Unilever, Vodafone, and so on.

To better understand the impact it has on the society, we highlighted the CSR priorities of the EU member states:

> *Respecting the human rights in the business environment and the responsible management of the supply chain:* The Danish state choose to give the right to take action in the case of conflicts regarding the conformation of human rights, of an institution which has as a goal the mediation and conflict management.

Supporting the CSR development in SMEs: The initiative of Britain state encourages businessmen to develop CSR programs in the following areas: the creation of workplaces, supporting the local communities, SMEs development, employees' life improvement, and the reduction of carbon footprint. Germany had a praiseworthy initiative, financing with 36 million euros 73 CSR projects of the SMEs.

Social and professional inclusion of disadvantaged people: In Austria, the government created certification for the companies that choose to promote the advantages of working with elders and which ensure a proper working environment to everyone regardless of their age. The Spanish state tries to integrate the youth into labor, among who the unemployment rate is high, working out a strategy to educate and integrate young people in the labor market, granting certificates for the companies that help doing that.

Encouraging the consumption of responsible products by informing consumers and promoting the advantages of this kind of consumption: The Council for the Sustainable Business Development from Croatia published a dictionary with the necessary terminology, so the opinion leaders could understand what CSR means, in this way ensuring the understanding of CSR concepts by practitioners. The Estonian government tries promoting the sustainable businesses directly among consumers

Reference to CSR: In some states, reference to CSR performances is mandatory for certain companies. One of those states is France, where the stock-listed companies were forced to report non-financial information following social, environmental, and governmental corporative indicators.

CSR education and trainings: One of the countries where CSR became a field of study in the public education is France. The research national agency finances research programs in CSR, the objective being to offer the possibility for developing methods through which the transition to lifestyles and sustainable consumption can be accelerated. Another country in which the CSR education is delivered in a formal frame is Finland. Here, there is a NGO that offers to their members CSR consultancy.

Politics responsible with public acquisition: In 2008, Italy adopted an action plan for the consumption providing environment friendly products in the administrative sector. After that, there were also adopted other responsible acquisition plans, through which the state institutions committed to buy only from the suppliers who made sure that the employees' rights were respected, that they were offering adequate work conditions, and that their health and security were not endangered, or to facilitate the integration of people with disabilities.

Social responsible investments: CSR Netherlands is an organization in the Netherlands that offers to the CSR-interested entrepreneurs a platform where they can find the associations, the companies, the NGOs, the research institutions and other sustainable authorities, in which they can invest. In France, the support given to the sustainable businesses is going even further. The government established in 2012 an investment fund amounting to 42 million euro for sustainable SMEs.

Financial obligations and anti-corruption politics: In Sweden, the state implemented a remuneration scheme for those in charge of the state companies, through which the received wages and bonuses were limited. Among the taken measures we can find a fixed wage system, establishing the age of retirement to over 62 years old, the limitation at 6 months of the period for compensation salary, and so on.

The terms imposed by the EU caused institutional changes also regarding the contents of economic policies at the member states level to the extent that between the norms, the adoption frame and the policies contents at national level and the European frame there are no disparities. These adjustments imply costs for the member states, and the resulting benefits for the EU member state can be highlighted and maximized only if there is a high level of compatibility/convergence between polices and the institutional frame of adopting these policies at a national level.

One of the most important treating elements with obvious implications on cost and benefit report is the one expressed through legal criteria, respectively, the assume of relevant community acquis in the adoption of sector policies and with implications toward the competitiveness of the national companies. The importance of this criteria, besides the economic one, is justified by the following elements: the adoption of the norms and objectives as the EU institutional model for the elaboration of sector policies, the European factor prevailing upon the national elements; the adoption and transposing in the national legislation of the European regulations; European norms that have an impact on the competitiveness of the enterprises and the CSR activities, creating new conditions for their ongoing activities.

The main objective of the European economic policy endorses a faster economic increase that can create various workplaces and preserve the social protection system. The increase of the growing potential of the European economies will be a major challenge—a challenge that the EU faces through the triple objective of an intelligent growth, sustainable, and favorable inclusion.

The commerce encourages the EU growth, by encouraging the efficiency and the innovative spirit. The open commerce offers, as well, to the EU consumers' access to a large variety of products at lower prices. The opening of Europe to foreign direct investments strengthens the competitiveness. Also, the capacity of community society to invest abroad allows them to acquire a global dimension and to create new jobs locally as well as abroad.

EU is facing rapid changes of the world in full globalization process, in which it wants to change the course of international events, in such a way that the beneficiaries will not be found only among the rich countries but also the poor ones, a power searching for a moral frame, on which globalization process can be based through the solidarity principles and the ones of a sustainable development.

In this context, the coordination of the economic environment takes place, as well as the financial and fiscal one, which contributes as a role model for the rest of the world, which offers precise results regarding Europe's implication in the global business field through new opportunities and not by imposing restrictions. This means the encouragement of external exchanges (commerce, investments, information, citizens' travels, and so on), the creation of new jobs, the development of education, of the services in general, especially of the medical ones, and the improvement of the life quality. All these prove that the EU follows a path of renewing and reforming, that this represents a stability factor and a role model in today's multipolar architecture of the world.

The commerce should bring improvements regarding the social inclusion in the world as well in the EU. The developing countries that entered the world trade and the world production chains participated in the rapid growth of the incomes and the workforce, as well as in a significant reduction of poverty. The EU trade policy helps the poorest economies by giving them at the same time generous unilateral commercial preferences. Generally, the EU uses a careful differential approach depending on the level of development of the partners and gives systematically attention to the coherence with the development policies, such as diminishing the poverty.

At the same time, opening the trade continues to raise the level of well-being and the number of workplaces, and it determines an increase of the wages in the developed economies, including the EU. The opening creates jobs. But we admit at the same time that in some fields or sectors, the adjusting costs may, sometimes, be high; which is why there are needed social policies also in the workforce area adequate nationally and at the European level to help the workers and the companies to adapt.

In the future, the economic business environment within the EU has to count on maintaining competitive advantage for innovative and high value products, which generates workplaces well paid in a long term.

In addition, the EU has in sight the need for regulation services to be open in all countries, as well as nondiscriminatory, transparent, and in the public interest, so that all suppliers could run their activities better. Finally, being that the technological changes created new services and consolidates the cross-border exchange possibilities of services; the trade agreements of the EU should find a way of preventing the appearance of new obstacles in the path of trade with these services.

The barriers in terms of regulation for merchandise trade, services, and investments bring mainly damages to the EU exchanges with its main commercial partners, considering the intensity of the commercial and investment relations with them.

The strengthening of the cooperation in the field of regulation both for the equivalence and convergence progress (of norms, standards, tests, and certification practices) internationally, as for minimizing the useless costs regarding the regulation worldwide, it represents an important aspect in the EU commercial relations, especially with its main partners, as well as some free exchange agreements or similar negotiations. The EU invites its main commercial partners to join the existing initiatives in terms of sector convergence regulation, such as regulations regarding automobiles of the EC for the Europe of UNO and to actively participate in the development of some international standards or regulatory approaches in a large range of sectors. The experience reflects, indeed, that the well-established industrial EU sectors such as the automobile sector, machine tools, and chemicals, but especially in the emerging sectors with a fast progress such as online services or biotechnologies, it's easier to approach the potential barriers before the consolidation of regulations practices.

In an economy in the process of globalization, the elaboration by the EU of its regulatory norms has to be increasingly sensitive to the international context and to the necessity of helping the companies to stay competitive. Indeed, the connection between the trade opening to the outside and the inside market reforms is most of the time a two-way street, but giving the fact that in both cases the EU objective is to reduce the cost of useless regulation barriers that are against the circulation of goods, services, and investments.

Trade opening creates, generally, more jobs, but a strong growth requires a resource transfer to the most performing sectors, and it can bring job losses in some sectors. The market opening has to be accompanied by policies that offer the citizens necessary means to adapt to these changes.

While the responsibility of the member states is to establish proper enclosed measures regarding the social policies, as well that regarding the educational and the labor force, the EU also contributes to these measures through different instruments, including structural funds.

The EU is hired to promote sustainable development, international work standards, and proper work. The integration of developing countries in the global economy contributes to the poverty abolishment and benefits better work conditions. This is the favored approach by the EU concerning the partnership economic agreements with African countries, the Caribbean, and the Pacific: encouraging the development through regional integration promotion, creating opportunities for trade and investments, complying with the social responsibility principles, and improving the economic governance.

The EU suggested a reform of the EU generalized system of preferences. The goal was, among others, to favor countries with the most acute needs and the ones that apply efficiently the international standards of work and human rights and environment protection principles.

The EU trade policy encourages the rising ecological and climate change objectives, mainly the reduction of carbon emissions. The EU must be sure that the European industry is competitive in the sustainable economy of the future, including the fishing and agricultural sector.

Regarding the climate change, the priority is to close a global agreement that would impose the objectives of reducing the emissions in all countries. Trade policy supports the battle against the climate change through the abolishment of the obstacles from the path of trade with ecological products and services.

Broadly, trade policy has to continue to sustain and promote ecological growth all over the world also in the fields such as energy, resource efficiency, and biodiversity protection. In this way, the EU will also continue to give a special attention in applying the chapters of sustainable development from the commercial agreements, as well as the establishment of a tight cooperation with the civil society.

5. Greenpeace and Other NGOs

It says that people create NGOs when they cannot fight alone anymore against different problems in the society. One of the most influential organizations is Greenpeace. This organization fights for the environment protection and social equity, having over 2.8 million of supporters worldwide. Therefore, any newbie NGO planning its long-term activities can become an important vector in decision making in the activating field.

Greenpeace was founded in 1971 in Canada, and it is a NGO that militates for environment protection, having the headquarters in Amsterdam. By the end of 2008, Greenpeace developed so much that it came to own offices in 41 different countries, being globally present. Greenpeace has existed in Romania since 2007.

The difference between Greenpeace and other NGOs is given by the fact that they don't take donations from corporations, legal people or any kind of country, but just from natural people, proving even more the fact that it doesn't want to be associated with anyone.

Whether talking about soil, air, or water pollution, or even mining exploitation (an example in this context is the mining exploitation from Rosia Montana, Romania), the Greenpeace activists have stated their opinion and achieved on a long term or even definitely to eliminate the pollution outbreaks. Through the art of communication, the organization made a slogan "Think locally, act globally," and the majority of people who know it understand the aim and the objectives Greenpeace wants to attain.

Greenpeace has a series of objectives and principles and focuses its energy to remove the main danger that threatens our planet: environmental changes, protecting the oceans, restricting the useless and destructive fishing, and creating a global network of maritime reserves; protecting the forests of the world and the animals, plants, and the people who depend on them, working hard for peace through attacking of the conflict causes and calling for the elimination of all nuclear weapons; creating a non-toxic future with safer alternatives against dangerous chemicals; militating for sustainable agriculture through the collapse of genetically modified organisms; biodiversity protection; and socially responsible forms. Greenpeace puts a great effort into changing some ideas and customs in accordance to the environment and to highlight certain ecological sensibility.

In the Greenpeace activities, we can notice two types of direct action: either through the exposure of some secret actions (reporting of nuclear test from hidden places, poaching, revealing of certain documents that could prove that the way the waste was discharged by a factory into a river destroys flora and fauna in the region, and so on), or through taking the responsibility of direct risks by activists to shed light on the importance of a non-ecological measure. The aim of these two types of involvement is to change the attitude of state institutions, economic actors, and everyday people.

Another organization that has succeeded in changing the face of society is Habitat for Humanity. The foundation has as an objective dealing with improper living conditions and the absence of housing. Therefore, over 5 million people from 90 countries have benefited from decent livings. One of the greatest accomplishments was building of homes for 50.000 families from Haiti affected by the earthquake in 2010.

Habitat for Humanity was founded in 1976 in the United States, and in Romania, it has lead an ongoing complex program since 1997, with the objective of giving people a chance to have a simple, decent, and affordable house.

In addition, the foundation militates for women's right to property in the developing countries. Another successful example was Bolivia, one of the poorest countries in South America. Habitat for Humanity supported women by giving them trainings about their rights and offering solutions to improve their life quality.

Amnesty International is an organization which goal is to help create a world in which each person will enjoy all rights from the Universal Declaration of Human Rights and other international standards from the field of human rights protection. Until today, it has developed programs in over 70 countries requesting the freeing of political prisoners, the abolishment of death penalty, supporting gender equality and sexual rights, protecting the rights of refugees and migrants, as well as changing the oppressive laws. The activists group “Amnesty International Bucharest” is on the first locations in East Europe and Central Asia, having the best results in the global campaign “Write for Rights 2014.”

If at the beginning these organizations weren’t heard in the communities where they have their roots, some of them are now influencing the world.

6. The Diffusion of CSR in Romania

Turning our attention toward Romania, we can state the fact that the social responsibility was rightfully understood and well implemented by the companies that are active in the national business environment. The companies understood what the society needs, starting actions with the aim to contribute to the rapid growth of society. CSR companies, which imply the firms, focus on problems such as helping children, education, and environment protection.

A priority, before and after joining the EU for Romania was the improving of the business environment. So, Romania was interested in attaining a more attractive frame for investments, which would increase the interest of foreign investors. Lately, the collaboration with the international organizations from the World Bank Group helped it to strengthen its position in the region and to start to disseminate its experience with other countries. The planned objectives reflect these concerns, structured on different levels:

> Improving the quality of the administrative act, of the decisional process, and of the management and horizontal coordination of public policies.
>
> Creating a business environment that stipulates firms’ competitiveness and the development of abilities and high entrepreneurship skills, capable to face the competition on the single European market, as well as outside the EU.

Stimulating the firms’ capacity to create, add, capture, and retain values in the national productive chain, based on processes, products, and services.

Increasing the consumers trust, based upon an efficient protection and consistent rights.

These action directives aim to achieve the following results: simplifying and improving the legislative and administrative frame, diminishing bureaucracy and corruption, the administrative, fiscal, and par fiscal burden; reducing the number of administrative procedures, the time to obtain the authorization, advice, licenses, funds for these procedures, and implicitly the reduction of corruption; accelerating precompetitive reforms and promoting a honest competitive environment; elaborating and implementing an integrated and transparent strategy for improving and developing the business environment, based on the evaluation and the valorization of the factors with an impact on the firms' competitiveness and on the advertisement of the measures of improving the legislative and organizational frame; development in the educational field and of the specialized training programs, entrepreneurial culture, strengthening managerial performances and encouraging the innovative spirit. In this context, it is necessary to be aware of the importance of intellectual property rights of the quality management in the Romanian business environment, facilitating the access of the enterprises to European structural funds and to the financing mechanism and ensuring a high level of consumer protection through the effective appliance of the legislation; the consumer protection against wrong commercial practices, as well as risks which can disturb their life, health, security, and economic interests; developing the cooperation with the EU organs, with member states, as well as the civil society; and stimulating the individual associative self-protection capacity of consumers in the fulfilling of direct protection given by the state institutions.

The business environment and the public authorities will have to understand the role of the Competition Committee in maintaining a functional market economy, to know the ways through which this works and the goal of applying consequently the competition rules: the creation and development of a competitive environment that would protect its consumers in a way that they would benefit from the advantages offered by a right competition.

At the same time, the business community must be informed and know the ways through which it is protected by a legislation in the case where it could be the victim of non-competitive practices, but also the risk to which it is exposed if it breaks the rules. The economic agents must be aware that a profound knowledge of the legislation could give protection in the eye of the law. It must be known that promoting the values of competitive culture and applying sequent of its principles gives disadvantages just for inefficient companies, while, for the economy as a whole and for the consumers, the effects proved in tens of countries are those of promoting the technological progress, efficient allocation of resources, private sector development, and social well-being.

For the economic future, the development and the entrepreneurship education for youth are absolutely necessary, and for this reason, well-directed stimulants are needed from the authorities as well as from the business environment.

The competition gets permanently more difficult, in some sectors being truly fierce, which is why the companies must evolve from the entrepreneurship level to professionalism to be able to face it. This involves the bettering of entrepreneurs and professionals in the key areas of the organization. The professionalization requires a certain kind of management, different from the one applied until now. The success belongs to the ones who know what they want, who have long-term objectives for them and for the organization they run and who channel all their available resources in attaining those goals. The evolutions from the outside environment need to be taken into consideration-macroeconomic factors, as well as technological, political, and sociological; the industry evolutions—customers, suppliers, and competition; the ones inside of the organization—resources, especially the human ones and their characteristic skills, structure, systems, and the culture. The companies should be capable not only to define a coherent and valid strategy, but also to be able to apply that strategy.

Romania's Strategy for the improvement and development of the business environment approaches a medium and long-term vision through the implementation of an action package:

1. Promoting the economic development based on investments and optimizing the investment climate
2. Promoting transparency in the decisional process of public policies through the promotion of responsible behavior and business integrity
3. Developing the business environment and encouraging feminist entrepreneurship through rising of the entrepreneurs' access and liberal professions to quality consulting and through the improvement of consulting services
4. Increasing the administrative capacity of the central unity responsible for realizing and applying public policies with impact on the business environment, to improve the strategic planning processes, analysis, supervising, and evaluation

Promoting the responsible behavior in businesses is to be conducted through a series of measures: strengthening the administrative capacity of the institutions to abolish the tax evasion and corruption by promoting a prevention and control policy coordinated by specialized state organs; simplifying, transparency, and efficiency in public acquisitions; adopting the Integrity Codes at the level of all contracted authorities; adopting a normative act that could offer a proper and transparent regulation frame for lobby activities in Romania, respecting the democratic principles and the free association rights and the representation of legitimate interests regarding the legislative and executive central at a regional and local level; introducing the periodic mechanism of evaluation of the impact for all public policies; increasing the self-regulation role in the integrity field and the ethical conduct through the adoption of the Integrity Codes on a large scale.

The self-regulation and conglomerate initiatives of liberal professional bodies represent themselves under the form of ethical conduct development, of professional standard, of practice norms, and of agreements, which cannot argue against the general or specific legislation adopted, but rather complement it.

To be a responsible company means not only to fulfill the applicable legal obligations in the own field of activity, but also to continue by investing even more in the human capital, in the environment, and in the relationships with the interested groups, on one side, because the social problems exists and will always exist and, on the other, because more and more international bodies and private companies militate to what in the Western countries is known as the CSR.

The arrival of these concepts and practices associated with them to Romania has at least two important causes:

First, the economic development and the entry on the market of multinational companies determined a kind of pressure regarding the identification of some proper consolidation activities of the corporatist image and reputation. This gathered increasingly sophisticated strategies as consumers learned by themselves to make choices by following their knowledge and not their instinct.

Second, the withdrawal from the market of the big donors and diminishing the financial resources that came from the international bodies determine another kind of pressure, in reverse, the part of nonprofit organizations that diversify their financial attraction strategies from sources like the private sector, business sector, or citizens.

Nowadays, Romania is in a continuous ascending line regarding the social responsibility. The social practices of the companies are noticed through an increasing number of initiatives. There are corporatist foundations, corporatist volunteer programs, marketing initiatives, donation programs. There are more debates and seminars and competitions between the big corporations concerning the social responsibility projects.

The concept of CSR first started in 1990 with the appearance of various NGOs, mostly the humanitarian ones, founded with the support of public and private international institutions. This phenomenon was followed by major reforms in 2000s, as part of the process of integration in the EU, reforms that influenced the implication of large and small companies in CSR activities that were mostly concerning the restructuring/replacement of the production technologies with more friendly ones, with social measures regarding the employees and society.

The multiplication of the social responsibility implementation practices began to be more pronounced after the EU integration. The main engine was the multinational companies, which transferred the culture and the organizational practices from the central headquarters to a local level and afterwards the need to access the European funds. Following the EU integration, the responsible industries were also developed. These types of companies that have developed a business objective from the activities that bring a benefit to the environment and the communities and their responsibility indirectly results from their products and services. After the EU integration, an industry of renewable energy and waste management, rural tourism, and eco-tourism was born, as well as the commercialization of ecological and organic products.

The most common fields of the CSR initiatives in Romania are the well-being and education of children, arts, religion, environment, and sports. The CSR initiatives are not limited to the community investments, but also involve the responsibility regarding the supply chain, customer relations, customer satisfaction, as well as the well-being of employees.

2 Nonmarket Diffusion of CSR in Emerging Economies

1. Introduction

Corporate social responsibility (CSR) has been an issue in the literature for decades as a concept whereby companies on a voluntary basis integrate social and environmental concerns in their business operations and in their interactions with stakeholders (Wood, 1990; European Commission, 2000). The fundamental idea of CSR is that business corporations have an obligation to work for social betterment (Davis, 1973). CSR differentiates from the notion that businesses are only concerned with profit, but that organizations are also concerned with social ends such as pollution avoidance, discrimination elimination, and improving employment conditions. Nowadays, an increasing number of organizations are undertaking actions to become more socially responsible (Portney, 2008). These CSR activities are being increasingly adopted and diffused. However, why would organizations behave in a social way? Do they really feel the need to behave in social responsible ways? If the raison d'être of organizations is to make a profit and deliver shareholder value, then how can we explain organizations engaging in social activities since they could spend their money otherwise? This question can be answered in the light of an institutional perspective. According to Meyer and Rowan (1977), "organizations have to adopt products, services, techniques policies and programs which are institutionalized." This means that these products and services are taken for granted and can be maintained over long periods of time without further justification or elaboration (Zucker, 1987, in Oliver, 1992). Organizations are being pressured by different institutions to engage in CSR activities (Aguilera et al., 2007). Stating this, organizations do not engage in CSR activities because of their own intentions, but they are pressured to adopt CSR activities because of institutional forces. The diffusion of CSR activities is in this sense stimulated by exerted pressure from the institutional environment, instead of adopting these activities on a voluntary basis. Margolis and Walsh (2003) argue that the past literature ignored factors other than corporate financial performance that might affect CSR. Others argue that there is a need to "pay more attention to the institutional mechanisms that may influence whether corporations act in socially responsible ways or not" (Bühner et al., 1997; Doh & Guay, 2006; Orlitzky et al., 2003; Walsh et al., 2003).

Institutional theory can be useful in understanding the adoption and implementation of CSR activities (Campbell, 2006). Institutions can be market- or nonmarket-based. *Nonmarket* is an umbrella term applicable to a variety of intraorganizational and interorganizational as well as institutional phenomena (Boddewyn, 2003). Lyon and Maxwell (2008) argue that there is a growing attention toward market forces that are drivers for CSR initiatives, but what about nonmarket forces? Campbell (2006) contends that recent institutional theories are useful for understanding how institutions beyond the market contribute to enabling corporate social activities. These nonmarket forces can be very powerful in their influence on organizations like the government, collectives, and the media (Aguilera et al., 2007; Silverblatt, 2004). In this research, the institutional perspective will be the central rationale with its nonmarket institutions influencing the diffusion of CSR activities. Many forces from nonmarket institutions impinge on organizations to engage in CSR activities. However, relatively few studies have investigated how different types of nonmarket institutions may influence the development and the diffusion of CSR practices (Jones, 1999; Stanwick & Stanwick, 1998, in Jackson & Apostelakau). More attention should be paid to the institutional mechanisms that may influence whether corporations act in socially responsible ways or not (Bühner et al., 1997; Doh & Guay, 2006; Orlitzky et al., 2003; Walsh et al., 2003, in Campbell, 2007). Furthermore, this study will give insight to policy makers about the mechanisms that are likely to be effective in influencing the diffusion of CSR activities among organizations.

2. Nonmarket Institutions

The environment of organizations is composed of market and nonmarket components (Baron, 1995). The market environment consists mainly of market institutions such as suppliers, customers, and competitors, and interactions typically involved in voluntary economic transactions and the exchange of property. The nonmarket environment can be characterized as "the social, political, and legal arrangements that structure interactions outside of, although in conjunction with, markets and private agreements" (Baron, 2003). Furthermore, Doh et al. (2012) argue that in the market environment, firms typically compete for resources, revenues, and profits, while the nonmarket environment considers broader dimensions of impact and performance such as ethical behavior, policy attainment, and social responsibility. Thus, where market institutions try to get a profit, nonmarket institutions such as activists or nongovernmental organizations (NGOs) try to affect company and industry practices using the arena of public sentiment and the media (Baron & Diermeier, 2007). Boddewyn (2003) refers to the nonmarket as to the internal and external factors that provide order to markets, firms, and other types of institutions and organizations. This attribute of nonmarket institutions providing order might be the result of market failures. Arrow (1963) argues that nonmarket institutions might arise due to market failures. He states that if the market fails to achieve an optimal state, the society will, to some extent at least, recognize the gap, and nonmarket social institutions will arise attempting to bridge it (Carson et al., 2006). Nonmarket institutions can also arise and take action when certain issues arise. Issues are the basic unit of analysis and the focus of nonmarket action (Baron, 2003). Different nonmarket institutions like NGO's might feel concerns with respect to the organizations that do not operate in a social responsible way, which can be recognized as an issue. Therefore, these nonmarket institutions take action to let organizations behave more socially responsible by making use of different means such as regulation or by challenging the legitimacy of those organizations. There are different nonmarket institutions, and in literature, often mentioned nonmarket institutions are the government, collectives like NGO's and interest groups, the media, and the public (Aguilera et al., 2007; Silverblatt, 2004; Baron, 1995). These nonmarket institutions regulate exchanges between economic actors in the market system.

2.1. The Government

The government is a powerful nonmarket institution, which has the power to affect the legal and economic environment (Shenkar & Luo, 2008). It can enact and enforce laws, thereby influencing the legal environment, and with its coercive power, it can influence organizations to adopt certain practices or policies (Shipan & Volden, 2008). In some cases, markets are unlikely to achieve efficient solutions. In this case, the government can step in and try to improve efficiency and to fix market failures.

Governments also maintain laws and rules applicable in a specific market. For instance, a government could send out clear signals to businesses of the necessity to rid of the practices that are in contravention of social benefit (Porter, 1990, in Qu, 2007).

Furthermore, governments can play a large role in the diffusion process of organizational practices (Perrini, 2007) by affecting the rate of this diffusion process (Guler et al., 2002) due to the authorized coercive power of the government. This regulatory pressure of a government can thus have impact on a company's operations (Delmas & Toffel, 2004). A good illustration is adoption of standards. Governments have for example played an important role in firms' decisions to adopt ISO 14001 (Delmas, 2002), which is an environmental management standard (www.iso14000.nl). This shows their power with which they can influence organizations.

2.2. Collectives

The term *collectives* is an umbrella denotation for different interest-driven groups or organizations such as NGOs, activist groups, and professional associations. Collectives share some common characteristics in a way of expressing their meaning and thoughts about issues that they would like to change. Furthermore, they are referred as pressure groups or lobby groups. Of these collectives, NGOs can be considered as large structured nonprofit organizations striving to achieve their interests. Besides NGOs, professional associations as a collective can also influence the behavior of organizations. These professional associations act as negotiating or representative agencies, shaping and redefining appropriate practices of interaction for their respective memberships. They act as the means whereby communities represent themselves to others in the field (Greenwood et al., 2002). They play an important role in monitoring compliance with normatively and coercively sanctioned expectations. This corresponds to watchdog NGOs. Both are ensuring that the requirements of the system are met by various organizations.

Finally, activist groups can also influence organizational activities. According to Den Hond and De Bakker (2007), activist groups are presenting themselves as legitimate claimants in matters such as natural environment and, accordingly, put pressure on firms to address such issues, occasionally with considerable success. Also, as the activities of corporations have become matters of public debate, pressure from activist groups has become more prevalent (Klein et al., 2004).

2.3. *The Media*

The media encompasses all goal-oriented technical means or instruments for the procurement of information in print, visual, or auditory forms, as well as the organizational and institutional entities behind them that generate and provide this information. The information is directed, in a traditional manner, at a broad and public audience (Wirtz, 2011). There has been a dramatic rise in the public exposure of business via television, radio, newspapers, magazines, films, books, and social media (Fombrun & Shanley, 1990; Wood, 1990, in Greening & Gray, 1994).

The media can exert pressure on organizations, and according to Campbell (2007), the media plays an important role in that it monitors and reports on corporate behavior in ways that discipline corporations by subjecting them to the constant threat of public exposure. Furthermore, organizational reputation can be ruined due to negative attention drawn from the media, and organizations try to avoid scrutiny from it. Gamson and Modigliani (1989) state that the role of the media is believed to be central in framing issues for the attentive public, thereby pressuring organizations to conform. This is in line with Mitroff et al. (1989) who argue that the media can influence society's perception of a company, especially when environmental crises occur. Some organizations are for instance adopting green management practices because they do not want to be ousted by the media in that they are not doing the right thing (Babiak & Trendafilova, 2011).

Nowadays, the concept of CSR has become a hot topic in media circles. Journalists often provide free publicity of a firm's commitment or lack of commitment to CSR (McWilliams et al., 2006). This media attention toward CSR informs the public with access to new information regarding social attributes and methods of production. This free publicity, whether positive or negative, helps heighten the public awareness of CSR, reduces information asymmetry, and thus, influences demand for CSR (McWilliams, 2006).

2.4. *Society*

Society can be defined as a collection of individuals united by certain relations or mode of behavior that mark them off from others who do not enter into these relations or who differ from them in behavior (Ginsberg, 1931). Societies can differ in norms, values, habits, and ideas. Therefore, due to these differences, societies may differ in their expectations regarding the behavior of organizations. DiMaggio and Powell (1983) argue that formal and external pressures are exerted on organizations by cultural expectations in the society where they are operating in. The pressures stemming from society are not the same as other nonmarket institutions, since they are of more general nature (Lépineux, 2004).

Society can be an important player in the nonmarket environment with respect to the behavior of organizations. An organization may comply with external pressures because the approbation of society enhances its legitimacy, increases its stability, or sustains the logic of confidence necessary to conduct organizational activities in good faith (Meyer & Rowan, 1977 in Oliver, 1999). This is also in line with institutional theory, which asserts that firms adopt initiatives to gain legitimacy or acceptance within society (Zhu & Sarkis, 2007). Furthermore, Bansal and Roth (2000) found out that companies go green due to pressures such as society's wishes.

The first ideas and thoughts about CSR started to rise several decades ago (Bowen, 1953). This issue has become commonplace among business, political leaders, and business press (Buhr & Grafström, 2004). Also in literature, a lot of attention is drawn on CSR (Wood, 1990). The evolution of the CSR construct began in the 1950s (Carrol, 1990). In these early writings about CSR, Bowen (1953) mentions in his book: What responsibilities to society may businessmen reasonably be expected to assume?

Karnani (2010) stated that the idea that companies have a responsibility to act in the public interest and will profit from doing so is fundamentally flawed (Karnani, 2010). Also, as was stated before, Marquis et al. (2007) do not take up the argument that corporations have a responsibility to engage in social behavior. Most organizations do not engage in CSR because their inner needs tell them to behave in a responsible way. However, they might still engage in certain CSR activities, not because they feel responsibility for it, but because they are pressured to behave that way or think that benefits can arise for the organization itself. This way of thinking differs from the notion that organizations engage in CSR on a voluntary basis. This is in line with King et al. (2005), who argue that the fundamental idea of organizations adopting certain practices is that institutions drive adoption and diffusion (Campbell, 2007; Delmas & Toffel, 2004; Aguilera et al., 2007). The institutional perspective plays a central role within this field by explaining that the force of institutions influences the diffusion of CSR activities by organizations.

3. Diffusion of CSR

Diffusion theories describe how ideas and practices become established among a population of organizations, groups, or individuals (Haberberg et al., 2008). The diffusion of CSR in particular is taking place on a global scale (Matten & Moon, 2008). An increasing attention is being paid to CSR in many different countries on different continents. This has been shown in studies that found that CSR is gaining momentum in different geographical areas (Matten & Moon, 2005; Peinado-Vara, 2004). According to Lee (2008), the "idea of CSR became almost universally promoted by all constituents in society from governments and corporations to nongovernmental organizations and individual consumers." To give a comparison with Fortune 500 companies, less than half of those companies mentioned CSR in their annual reports in 1997. By the end of 1990s, close to 90% of Fortune 500 firms embraced CSR as an essential element in their organizational goal and actively promoted their CSR activities in annual reports (Boli & Hartsuiker, 2001, in Lee, 2008).

The widespread of CSR occurs on a global scale; however, the CSR activities that are diffused may differ across countries due to different institutional environments (Dobers & Halme, 2009). These institutional environments have different governmental, legal, and social operating actors, which causes different pressures on organizations. Strong institutional environments exist in developed countries in which organizations can face strong pressures to adopt CSR activities. Besides these pressures, these institutional environments also provide better guidance for organizations to engage in CSR. For instance, the Dow Jones Sustainability Index provides a list of the degree to which organizations engage in CSR activities, whereby organizations can distinguish themselves from others (Chapple & Moon, 2005). In developing countries, there is often a weaker institutional environment where according to Dobers and Halme (2009) "non-compliance, tax evasion, and fraud are a norm rather than an exception." Thus, the institutions in developing countries are often less developed and weaker than in developed countries. Therefore, their influence on organizations to let them behave in responsible ways is also diminished. This difference is also made clear by this quote from Kemp (2001):

> There are numerous obstacles to achieving corporate responsibility, particularly in many developing countries where the institutions, standards and appeals systems . . . are relatively weak

However, the differences between institutional environments are shrinking. For instance, Davies (2000) reported on the growth of Asian consumer expectations of socially responsible businesses. Furthermore, Chapple and Moon (2005) state that "business watchdogs, be they ethical investment organizations or NGOs, are increasingly active in monitoring and reporting on the behavior of multinational corporations (MNCs) in Asia."

These institutional environments can enforce pressures on organizations to adopt CSR activities, thereby facilitating the diffusion of CSR activities. Different nonmarket institutions bring different pressures. These pressures may vary due to the differences between the nonmarket institutions. Scott (1995) divides institutions into three pillars, which are widely known as the regulative, normative, and cognitive pillar. He defines them as "regulative, normative and cognitive structures and activities that provide stability and meaning to social behavior." The diffusion of CSR is stimulated by pressures stemming from the nonmarket institutions, and these are based on the three pillars from Scott (1995).

First, institutional pressures can be coercive in nature. Coercive pressures are defined as formal or informal pressures exerted on organizations by other organizations upon which they are dependent (DiMaggio & Powell, 1983). Coercive pressures can be conceived as either governmental regulations or sanctions, such as imposed fines or lawsuits (Dacin, 1997; Siegel et al., 1997). *Coercive regulative pressures* consist of laws, rules, and regulations that stem from the government, a nonmarket institution. The government can enforce their regulative power on organizations to adopt certain CSR activities, which can lead to a widespread of these activities. These pressures might be felt as force or as persuasion, and organizational change is a direct response to government mandate (Dimaggio & Powel, 1983). These authors give as an example in their article that manufacturers adopt new pollution control technologies to conform to environmental regulations.

Besides regulatory coercive pressures, *sanctioning coercive pressures* might also be exerted on organizations due to sanctioning forces like lawsuits. According to Hoffman and Ventresca (2002), lawsuits are used as a proxy for coercive pressure because they indicate the degree to which lawyers, regulators, and other external stakeholders, concerned with firm behavior, are watching an industry. If organizations do not obey the coercive regulations, they enlarge the possibility of getting sued. Organizations try to prevent becoming criticized, due to unsocial behavior for example, by different collectives such as interest groups and NGOs, because they have the ability of lawsuit tightening. For instance, Doh and Guay (2006) stated that Chiquita declared bankruptcy in 2001 after it was the subject of lawsuits and other negative reactions to its reputation as a cold, uncaring, and indifferent company with mediocre returns, a lack of innovation, and a demoralized workforce.

3.1. Professional Normative Pressures

Normative pressures are based on norms, implying how things should be done. The legitimacy and reputation of organizations can be questioned if they do not operate in the way "it should be done." Normative pressures can be brought forward by different kinds of institutions such as a society, government, or different kind of professions. They can impose stimulating pressures on a certain professional industry that may influence working activities or behavior in an industrial field. Preuss et al. (2006) state that a particular role has been identified for educational and professional bodies, which directly or indirectly set standards for "legitimate" organizational practices. They give an example that the master of business administration is increasingly becoming the standard formal qualification for corporate decision makers across the industrialized world. Matten and Moon (2004) also state that with the foundation of the European Academy of Business in Society (EABiS) in Europe and with similar initiatives at the national level, a growing number of professional associations exert normative pressures on businesses to adopt CSR activities.

3.2. Social Normative Pressures

The normative pillar of the institutional environment consists of values and beliefs, as well as the informal and diffuse rule systems that structure expectations and enforce mutual obligations between actors in an organizational field. Scott (1995), in Trevino et al., 2008) argues that these normative components of institutions define what is appropriate and what is "right" for a society's members. These normative pressures can guide organizations to engage in organizational practices, which are perceived to be legitimate. These normative pressures can come from collectives like NGO's, interest groups, and the media. They can highlight certain issues and bring them under public attention whereby the public opinion in a society is getting influenced. If the public opinion doesn't strike with what they expect from the business community, then the pressures brought forward by, for example, NGOs are reinforced on organizations to behave in a way that satisfies the public, or otherwise, legitimacy or corporate reputation might be lost.

3.3. Mimetic Pressures

Finally, the cognitive pillar refers to taken-for-granted beliefs and values that are imposed on, or internalized by, social actors (DiMaggio & Powell, 1983, in Peng, 2003). According to DiMaggio and Powell (1983), the isomorphic mechanism that better captures the cognitive institution is imitation. Since organizations prefer to act in conventional ways, they imitate those peers that seem to be more successful and legitimate. This mimetic behavior has a ritual aspect: Companies imitate to enhance their legitimacy, to demonstrate they are at least trying to improve, for instance, working conditions (DiMaggio & Powell, 1983). If a company is being pressured by nonmarket institutions to engage in a certain CSR activity, then this CSR activity might also be imitated by other related companies to prevent that they are drawn from negative attention and lose legitimacy.

4. Nonmarket Institutions and CSR Diffusion

It can be stated that the nonmarket institutions that we are going to analyze here are all expected to have a certain degree of influence on the diffusion of CSR activities. However, to what extent is still not thoroughly investigated.

As stated before, the government is a powerful nonmarket institution due to its influence on the legal and economic environment. It can influence organizations via different social normative pressures. Government initiatives can stimulate the diffusion of CSR activities by encouraging organizations to adopt them (Nidasio, 2004). Also, the government can give recommendations that are intended to have a guiding effect but have no legal standing (Buhmann, 2006). Furthermore, the government obtains different modes of coordination to diffuse CSR activities (Gond et al., 2011). These authors argue that CSR activities can be facilitated by the government through endorsement in the forms of speeches and other means of giving their imprimatur to business contributions to society. In this way, the government is not obligating organizations to engage in CSR, but putting social normative claims on them to adopt CSR activities. Besides facilitating, the government can also engage in partnerships with organizations to stimulate the diffusion of CSR activities (Gond et al., 2011). These partnerships can be established to address local issues, national issues (e.g., to improve SME's understanding of CSR in home country), and even global issues. Besides these social normative pressures, coercive pressures can also be initiated by the government. CSR activities can be mandated by the government, which is very important to let organizations behave in a social responsible way (Campbell, 2006). Campbell gives an example in which governmental deregulation during the 1980s and 1990s created an environment where US corporations began to act in more socially irresponsible ways than they would have otherwise. This implies that regulations are necessary to force organizations to engage in the right and desired behavior. Regulation can be viewed in a variety of ways, which may fall short of coercion and sanctions or punishments (Ayres & Braithewaite, 1992). Regulative coercing pressures arise through obligating organizations to obey to implemented rules. For instance, the UK government mandated the adoption of CSR policies by major companies (McBarnet, 2007). Steurer (2010) also argues that the government has a large role in influencing organizations with respect to their environmental activities and behavior. Besides these regulative coercing pressures, the government can also influence organizations trough sanctioning coercive pressures like lawsuits or by means of fines. These negative sanctions can discourage organizations from acting in socially irresponsible ways (Campbell, 2006).

It becomes evident that the government can influence the diffusion of CSR activities by making use of these different kinds of pressures. Therefore, we formulate the following hypothesis:

> Hypothesis 1: The government has a positive influence on the diffusion of CSR activities through social normative, regulatory coercive, and sanctioning coercive pressures.

Collectives may also influence the diffusion of CSR activities. It is argued that collectives like NGOs, which are seeking to promote what they perceive to be more ethical and socially responsible business practices, are beginning to generate substantial changes in corporate management, strategy, and governance (Doh & Teegen, 2003). This means that collectives influence organizations to behave in a more social and ethical way. Moreover, pressures are also stemming from unions, environmental activists, and professional associations. Their influence can be accomplished by, for instance, either issuing threats (such as boycotts, negative media campaigns, and lawsuits), or promise rewards (such as endorsements) (Lyon & Maxwell, 2008). Organizations are more likely to engage in CSR activities if pressured by collectives, because then, collectives will not inflict harm anymore on those organizations. This kind of social normative pressure can result in a loss of legitimacy or reputation for organizations. Social normative pressure arises when collectives engage in boycotts and campaigns where they accuse other organizations for their behavior or activities. Especially large organizations are likely to engage in social responsibility activities; otherwise they will be scrutinized by collectives since they have a reputation to maintain for a lot of stakeholders (Roberts, 1992).

Organizations do not want to lose their legitimacy and are inclined to do "what is desired from them." Once an organization is scrutinized in the public by collectives, competitors might prevent themselves from being scrutinized as well by collectives if their behavior is also "wrong." This is a form of mimetic pressure whereby organizations mimic other organizations if they are perceived to be more legitimate or to avoid negative attention drawn on them by collectives.

In addition to social normative and mimetic pressures, collectives can also bring forward sanctioning coercive pressures. Collectives can enforce lawsuits and thus punish organizations for their irresponsible behavior (Lyon & Maxwell, 2008). This gives collectives more influential power over organizations, who might be afraid of being caught up in an expensive and long-term lawsuit.

Finally, professional normative pressures can also be brought forward by collectives. These pressures occur when collectives pressure a certain profession or type of industry. For instance, the activist groups have targeted the pharmaceutical industry in Switzerland, accusing organizations like Monsanto and ADM of "preparing to unleash a horde of genetically modified organisms and food products across an unsuspecting world" (Spar & Mure, 2003). Matten and Moon (2004) argue that there is a growing number of professional associations exerting professional normative pressures on business to adopt CSR. Galaskiewicz (1991, in Campbell 2005) showed that corporations tend to act in socially responsible ways if normative or cultural institutions, like professional associations, are in place that create the proper set of incentives for such a behavior. For instance, when corporations or their managers belonged to business or professional associations dedicated to charitable giving, these corporations were more likely to engage in philanthropy.

Collectives are influential when it comes to the diffusion of CSR activities, and it is expected that they stimulate the diffusion of CSR positively through these different pressures. Therefore, we formulate the following hypothesis:

> Hypothesis 2: Collectives have a positive influence on the diffusion of CSR activities through social normative, mimetic, sanctioning coercive, and professional normative pressures.

The media is a powerful source since it can influence and reach a lot of people. According to Buhr and Grafström (2004), the attention of the media influences both the public opinion and general awareness of companies and the specific attributes associated with an organization. It can inform and frame people about which activities are carried out by organizations. The media can be crucial in mobilizing social movements such as environmental interest groups (Nikolaeva & Bicho, 2011). CSR is becoming increasingly reported by the media. For instance, in the financial times until 1998, referrals to CSR were rarely made. However, in 2002, interest in CSR was peaking with publishing over 100 articles about CSR (Buhr & Grafström, 2006). General sentiments of the society are reflected by the media. Therefore, companies pay close attention to the media to respond to society. This means that the media functions as a nonmarket institution pressuring organizations to behave in a manner which is legitimate in society, which is a form of social normative pressure. Gulyás (2009) found out in a survey that almost 80% of the surveyed organizations said that they felt an increased pressure of the media to improve their CSR performance. Also, the rate of adoption of CSR activities can be sped up by the media, which functions as a diffusion source (Strang & Soule, 1998). In addition to these social normative pressures, the media can also induce mimetic pressures. It can draw many attention to reports in which figures are announced about the sustainability and "greenness" of organizations or other rating systems (Schultz & Wehmeier, 2010). It is becoming increasingly desirable to provide insight in the social performance of organizations, and Brammer and Millington (2003) argue that "there is a growing institutional pressure on companies to provide detailed disclosures concerning their social performance." It means that organizations that are performing well in these reports receive positive media attention.

However, organizations performing bad are likely to imitate the successful organizations to evade large negative media attention. This leads us to the following hypothesis:

> Hypothesis 3: The media has a positive influence on the diffusion of CSR activities through social normative and mimetic pressures.

Organizations are expected to be good corporate "citizens" and good "neighbors." Furthermore, it is expected from them that they take care of the effects that their economic activities may have on the community and the environment (Figar & Figar, 2011). CSR is often associated with society, and it is often assumed that CSR should benefit the society (Dahlsrud, 2006). As was stated, Carroll (1999) identified four components of CSR; economic, legal, ethical, and philanthropic. The last two components go beyond obeying the law. He argues that "the ethical responsibility represents the kind of behaviors and ethical norms that society expects business to follow." Philanthropic responsibility represents voluntary roles that business assumes to be a good corporate citizen. According to this view, organizations have more responsibilities than just the provision of goods and services stemming from the economic responsibilities. Expectations from society can pressure organizations to behave in a more social way by being ethical and being a good corporate citizen. These expectations to fulfill a social role can for instance be met with engaging in CSR activities, thereby creating the possibility to contribute to society (Carroll, 1979). If organizations engage in the CSR activities that are widely accepted by the society, legitimacy might be enhanced. Therefore, the influence of society can be a driving force in the CSR activity diffusion. These expectations stemming from society function as a social normative pressure, and organizations that meet social desires might enhance their widespread approval (Maignan et al., 2005). Furthermore, these societal expectations can, besides a single organization, also be directed toward a certain profession or industry. If the behavior of organizations in a type of industry or profession is not accepted within a society, societal pressure can be put on them to behave in the way that is perceived as legitimate.

Finally, mimetic pressures can also be brought forward through society. Organizations that are performing well, following the society expectations, may be imitated by other organizations to be more successful as well. This is due to the fact that the fit between societal expectations and a firm's actions is very important for organizations to be successful (Zenisek, 1979). The behavior or activities from successful organizations in a society are likely to be imitated by other organizations, who also want to benefit from this success.

This leads us to the final hypothesis:

> Hypothesis 4: Society has a positive influence on the diffusion of CSR activities through social normative, professional normative, and mimetic pressures.

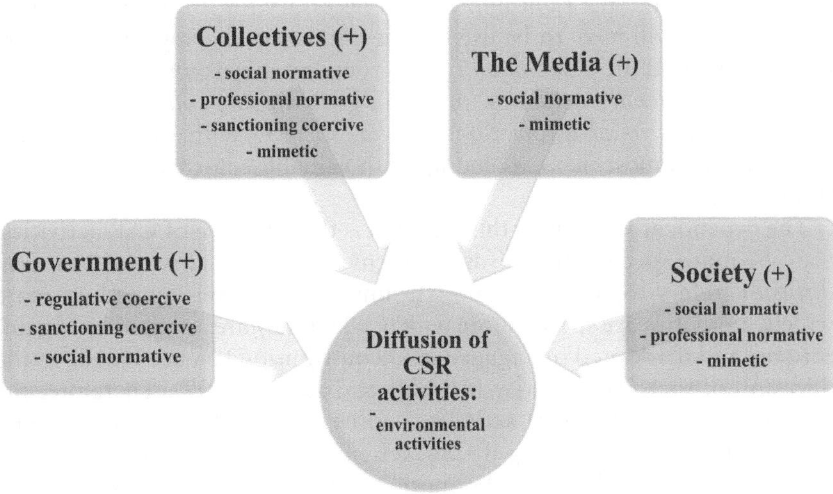

Previously described nonmarket institutions are all explained to have an positive influence on the diffusion of CSR activities via different types of pressures. This can be graphically depicted in a conceptual framework.

5. Methodology

The Central and Eastern European Online Library (C.E.E.O.L.) is an extensive and unique database based on online and offline sources of information. It is a database built by various (inter)national sources such as newspapers, magazines, and journals containing more than 36,000 articles. It is the largest provider of online news, company reports, and legal information. Because this database is possessing many sources, possibilities are offered to triangulate, which means that evidence is used from different sources to corroborate the same fact or finding (Rowley, 2002). Most database sources are stemming from newspapers. Therefore, the information that will be used for this research will largely stem from newspapers with different political opinions that present news from different angles: progressive newspapers with a social-democratic background, conservative newspapers, and liberal oriented. In addition to these national newspapers, regional newspapers will also be included within the analysis. Regional newspapers can contain important information about regional nonmarket pressures that may not be published in a national newspaper. By incorporating regional newspapers, a more complete view can be obtained of nonmarket pressures within Romania. These newspapers will be analyzed for containing information about nonmarket pressures aimed at organizations to engage in environmental activities. If this is the case, then an investigation will be made to discover which type of pressure is put on the organization and by which nonmarket institution. To find the right information necessary for this research, different keywords will have to be used in the database. The keywords that are going to be used are *sustainability*, *environment*, *environmental activities*, *environment-friendly activities*, *pressure*, *government*, *collectives*, *NGOs*, *activists*, *professional associations*, *media*, *society*. With the use of these keywords, it is most likely to end up with valuable information usable for this research.

The dependent variable in this research is the diffusion of CSR activities, or to be more specific, the diffusion of environmental activities. The term *diffusion* refers to the state of environmental activities spreading more widely. Activities are spread more widely when they are adopted by organizations, and if adopted or engaged in, a contribution has been made to the diffusion of that CSR activity (Antoldi & Todisco, 2007). Therefore, the diffusion of environmental activities can be measured through analyzing documents and investigating if CSR activities are adopted or when organizations engage in them. Furthermore, environmental activities remain as a broad concept. Different activities can be distinguished belonging to this category. First, improvements can be made in new technology and processes or procedures. This happens when an organization is for instance creating a self-sustaining energy source. Second, recycling and recovery can be classified as another type of environmental activities. Materials and resources within an organization can be reused or recovered. Third, modification or adjustments of existing processes can be made, which is the last classification of environmental activities. This classification includes minor or large modifications to existing processes and procedures. This last type of environmental activity captures organizations trying to diminish harmful activities, such as CO2 pollution. Lastly, a general overarching subcategory will be added for the environmental categories that are not very well defined. It is not expected that all articles that will be collected are defining environmental activities in great detail. For instance, articles may be found via C.E.E.O.L., which states that organizations are pressured to produce "in a more sustainable way" or adopt "activities that are more sustainable" or "better for the environment." Whether this means that there should be more attention toward recycling, modifications to existing activities, or inventing new clean activities is not clear. Therefore, this "general" category captures pressures by which it is not exactly clear which type of activity is pressured for diffusion.

The first independent variable is the government, and to be more specific, governmental pressures in relation to environmental activity diffusion. To find out which nonmarket institution is putting pressure on organizations, we need to know more precisely what a government is. The government can be recognized as those institutions that create and implement public policy (Lader, 2008). Governmental pressures can be measured by regulatory coercive, sanctioning coercive, and social normative pressures carried out on organizations. Regulatory coercive pressures imposed by the government can be measured by imposed laws and obligations. Sanctioning coercive pressures can be measured through imposed fines, lawsuits, or even closure of organizations. Furthermore, social normative pressures can be measured through incentives, covenants, recommendations, and speeches. The second independent variable influencing the diffusion of environmental activities is the pressure from collectives. These collectives can pressure organizations in various ways through sanctioning coercive, professional normative, social normative, and mimetic pressures. Sanctioning coercive pressures from collectives can be measured with lawsuits imposed on organizations. Furthermore, social and professional normative pressures can be investigated through different activities, from appealing actions directly to the corporations themselves, organizing demonstrations against them, pressuring local governments to force corporations to improve their behavior, and mobilizing media campaigns to bring public attention to certain alarming corporate or industrial practices (Campbell, 2007). Mimetic pressures imposed by collectives can be investigated by statements from organizations in which they indicate to adopt CSR activities because otherwise they would be brought under negative attention from collectives. The third independent variable is the media pressure, influencing the diffusion of environmental activities via social normative and mimetic pressures. Social normative pressures can be measured by sentences and quotes posed in media resources about inappropriate behavior of organizations regarding their environmental activities. This is negative media attention, in a social normative form, drawn on those organizations, which makes it more likely that they will alter their activities. Mimetic pressures are also measured by negative media attention, regarding an organizations' environmental activities, because this brings uncertainty toward those organizations. Furthermore, publications of organizational CSR activity performance can also lead to mimetic behavior when the bad-performing organizations try to imitate the good-performing organizations.

The fourth and final independent variable is the pressure stemming from society. These social normative and mimetic pressures can be measured as representing public opinion and public expectations regarding the firm's behavior with respect to environmental CSR activities. Furthermore, a negative public opinion will create mimetic pressures of organizations who are well positioned within society.

6. Results

First, in this paragraph, an overview of different types of environmental activities found during the analysis will be given. Then, the overall findings will be presented for each nonmarket institution. Each nonmarket institution will be discussed separately with respect to its degree of influence on the diffusion of environmental activities. A further distinction will be made regarding the type of pressure imposed by these nonmarket institutions. For each nonmarket institution, an overview will be given for the number of events found and the degree of influence of these events on the diffusion of environmental activities. This degree will be expressed as a positive influence or no influence at all.

Furthermore, different types of environmental activities can be performed by organizations. When analyzing the data, it was noticed that a lot of items found in the database did not describe the environmental activities in detail. Therefore, a lot of items were related to environmental activities, but a further distinction was not mentioned. Most events found were therefore put in the "general" subcategory. This can be seen in Table 2.1. To give a short example and explanation, one of the newspapers analyzed announced that a number of organizations engaged in environmental activities due to set up agreements or imposed laws. In this event, it is not clear in which type of activities they engage. However, this event is useful for this research since it contains pressures for environmental activities and is therefore incorporated in the analysis. Besides this "general" category, 30 items were found in which a modification of existing activity was pressured. It turned out that this type of activity was often related with CO2 or polluting reductive activities. A total of seven items were found were organizations were pressured for recycling activities. Lastly, nine items were found were organizations were pressured for implementing new and inventing clean activities.

6.1. *Government Results*

Table 2.2 summarizes data that have been found using content analysis. As can be seen, in the column "Label," this table refers to the government as a nonmarket institution. Furthermore, items are summarized according to the regulative coercive, sanctioning coercive, and social normative pressures that the governments used. As can be seen, most pressures from the government were imposed on organizations via regulative coercive means. Most of these pressures were influencing the diffusion of environmental activities positively. However, not all regulations were effective in spreading the environmental activities. Ten items were found to have no effect on the spreading these activities. This was for instance shown in another newspaper, which reported that the "green" energy at that time had existed for

Table 2.1 Frequencies of Environmental Activities

Modification of Existing Activities	*30*
Recycling/recovery	7
Implementation of new clean activities	9
General overarching category	81

Table 2.2 Results of Different Governmental Pressures

Label	*Type of Pressure*	*Number of Items Found*	*Degree of Influence on Diffusion of Environmental Activity*	
			+ *(positive influence)*	– *(no influence)*
Government	Regulative coercive	31	21	10
Government	Sanctioning coercive	12	11	1
Government	Social normative	11	9	2

10 years. However, it was argued that it was not a motive for celebration because energy companies and experts were complaining about the policy of the Romanian government. Independent experts were talking about a disastrous environmental policy and chaotic conditions. Furthermore, it was argued that the environmental policy of the government was not stable and that its regulations were confusing. Also, it was stated that Romania wants to become more sustainable but that the entrepreneurs miss a clear and stable investing climate. Moreover, some regulations even function as a barrier when trying to reduce the energy consumption. Other regulations are even superfluous. An article states that the government mandates that organizations must use sustainable wood and plastic. However, organizations are already meeting these conditions. Therefore, this regulation is superfluous. Furthermore, some organizations did not see the point in the imposed regulations and did not obey these rules.

Then, 12 items were found with sanctioning coercive pressures, initiated by the government. Most of these sanctioning pressures were positively influencing the diffusion of environmental activities. However, one item was found that showed no influence. This item announced that the multinational organizations are guilty of flagitious behavior such as environmental offenses. These organizations were punished by very high fines, but as it was stated in the article, "these can always be paid easily." Sanctioning coercive pressures can positively influence the diffusion of environmental activities, but it depends on the ability of paying a fine by an organization whether this pressure is successful.

Subsequently, 11 items were found with social normative pressures. Most of these items were showing a positive influence on the diffusion of environmental activities. For instance, an item showed governmental recommendations in which it stimulated an organization to engage in an activity that would be more environmentally friendly than they intended to perform beforehand. Only two items showed that the imposed social normative pressures did not influence organizations. For instance, the government insisted that a company lowers the CO2 emission, but it did not work out.

The results above show that the government positively influences the diffusion of CSR activities through, in most cases, sanctioning coercive and social normative pressures.

However, regulative coercive pressures were not always as successful since they show a reasonable number of items in which no influence occurred. Therefore, we can conclude that Hypothesis 1, which states that the government has a positive influence on the diffusion of CSR activities through social normative, regulatory coercive, and sanctioning coercive pressures can be partially accepted. It could have been fully accepted if the regulative coercive pressures were also having a positive influence. However, the data showed the opposite, so this hypothesis can, therefore, be regarded as partially accepted.

6.2. Results of Collectives

As Table 2.3 indicates, the frequency of items found for each type of pressure is about equal, except for social normative pressures. A total of 22 items were found for social normative pressures, imposed by collectives, which is a lot more than the other types of pressures. The other three types of pressures did occur less frequently ranging from four to five items per type of pressure. An explanation for this difference might be that social normative pressures are relatively easy to bring forward, such as demonstrations or lobbying. By these actions, the public can also be made aware, which can result in an even higher strength of the initiated pressure. Furthermore, being involved in a long-lasting lawsuit can be expensive and requires specific know-how which therefore might be avoided by collectives.

The data show that, in almost all items found, collectives have a positive influence on the diffusion of CSR activities. There was only one item in which the social normative pressure had no influence. An ecological

Table 2.3 Results of Different Collective Pressures

Label	*Type of Pressure*	*Number of Items Found*	*Frequency of Items in Relation With the Degree of Influence on the Diffusion of Environmental Activity*	
			+ (positive influence)	*– (no influence)*
Collectives	Sanctioning coercive	4	4	0
Collectives	Social normative	22	21	1
Collectives	Professional normative	4	4	0
Collectives	Mimetic	5	5	0

movement wanted Essent, a Romanian energy company, to stop building a new coal plant. They wanted to pressure them to engage in energy production that would cause less damage to the environment. However, Essent had already invested 2.6 billion Euros in this coal plant, which made it an unlikely success for the ecological movement.

Besides this single item in which the pressure of a collective did not have any influence, all other items found had a positive influence on the diffusion of environmental activities. An example of this positive influence, according to social normative pressure, can be given on the basis of an item which stated that collectives, which were standing up for the environment, started a campaign and demonstrations against Heineken. This was caused by the fact that Heineken started to make beer crates with very heavy metals such as cadmium, leaving a heavy footprint on the environment. In the end, Heineken promised to stop using cadmium in beer crates, and this substance was replaced by environmentally friendly dyes.

Overall, the data imply that collectives are successful in pressuring organizations to engage or adopt environmental activities. Of the total of 35 items found for collective pressures, 34 items were indicating a positive influence on the diffusion of environmental activities. Only one item indicated that the imposed pressure did not influence the performed activity of an organization. We can conclude that Hypothesis 2, which implied that collectives that have a positive influence on the diffusion of CSR activities through social normative, mimetic, sanctioning coercive, and professional normative pressures can be accepted.

6.3. Media Results

As Table 2.4 indicates, a total of 18 items have been found in which the media was putting social normative pressure on organizations. This type of pressure occurred three times more frequently than mimetic pressure (a total of six items). The data show that all these instances had a positive influence on the diffusion of environmental activities. There were no items found in which the pressure of the media did not have any influence on organizations. This implies that the media is a strong nonmarket institution when it comes to pressuring organizations for environmental activities.

Table 2.4 Results of Different Media Pressures

Label	*Type of Pressure*	*Number of Items Found*	*Degree of Influence on the Diffusion of Environmental Activity*	
			+ (positive influence)	*– (no influence)*
Media	Social normative	18	18	0
Media	Mimetic	6	6	0

Most social normative items found contained negative media attention, imposed on an organization. For instance, lately, Odfjell had some incidents leaking dangerous substances, which could have a damaging impact on the environment. The media reports about these incidents did increase the pressure on Odfjell. Some items showed that negative media attention triggered different collectives to start boycotting campaigns against organizations not engaging in the desired activities or behavior. In some cases, these pressures were bringing a mimetic pressure forward as well, through stimulating other organizations to engage in activities that would spare them, for instance, from media scrutiny. Several items were found in which organizations were ranked based on their degree of sustainable behavior or their sustainable activities, which is also a form of mimetic pressure.

The fact that the media had a lot of items in which a positive influence occurred might be a result of its power to influence and reach a lot of people. This was also stated in some of the collected items. Furthermore, organizations are inclined to engage in environmental activities when being pressured, to avoid negative appearances against them. Once an organization has the reputation of not being sustainable or not engaging in activities that are environment friendly, serious consequences may occur. Overall, the data imply that the media is successful in pressuring organizations to engage in or adopt environmental activities. The idea behind this strong influence is that organizations do not want to be placed within a pejorative context by the media. Subsequently, all items found indicated a positive influence on the diffusion of environmental activities. Therefore, we can conclude that Hypothesis 3, which implied that the media has a positive influence on the diffusion of CSR activities through social normative and mimetic pressures, can be accepted.

6.4. *Society Results*

Table 2.5 summarizes the collected data from the society as a nonmarket institution. It can be seen that a total of 36 items have been found in which the society pressured organizations to adopt or engage in environmental

Table 2.5 Results of Different Societal Pressures

Label	*Type of Pressure*	*Number of Items Found*	*Degree of Influence on the Diffusion of Environmental Activity*	
			+ (positive influence)	*– (no influence)*
Society	Social normative	24	23	1
Society	Professional normative	7	7	0
Society	Mimetic	5	5	0

activities. Most of these items mentioned social normative pressures, with a total of 24 items. In these items, it was often mentioned that society had certain expectations toward an organizations' environmental activities. Subsequently, professional normative pressures were found in seven items. In these items, the pressure occurs where the society expects an industry to engage in certain environmental activities. For instance, it was mentioned in one of the newspapers that society expects from textile manufacturers to produce cotton in a more sustainable way. Lastly, a total of five items was found for mimetic pressure. In these items, it was stated that organizations obeyed the societal expectations, which resulted in mimetic behavior and activities. Most of these societal pressures arose due to the fact that the organizations were carrying out environmentally unfriendly activities or behavior.

The data show that from all these pressures, one item was found where the social normative pressure did not have any influence. It was reported that the Romanian population wanted organizations to behave in a social way, that is, engaging in environmental activities. However, organizations did not follow this request by the society. All other items were found to have an influence on organizations.

Overall, it can be stated that society is successful in pressuring organizations to engage in or to let them adopt environmental activities. Almost all items found indicated a positive influence on the diffusion of environmental activity. Only one item indicated that there was no influence. We can conclude that Hypothesis 4, which implied that society has a positive influence on the diffusion of CSR activities through social normative, professional normative, and mimetic pressures, can be accepted.

7. Discussion

The results found in this study for the government as an nonmarket institution are partially supported by the existing literature (Campbell, 2006). First, the results showed that the government can positively influence the diffusion of environmental activities through sanctioning coercive and social normative pressures. This is in line with existing findings in the literature. Most of the negative sanctions found did indeed positively influence an organizations' environmental activities and behavior, which also has been previously argued in the literature by Campbell (2006). Only one item showed otherwise. This was due to the fact that most MNEs are capable of paying a fine since they have a large amount of liquidity. Influencing large organizations like MNEs is therefore less effective by imposing fines. Furthermore, a positive influence was found on the diffusion of environmental activities via social normative pressures. This result is supported by previous literature in which it was stated that the government can influence the diffusion of environmental activities via social normative pressures (Nidasio, 2004; Buhmann, 2006; Gond et al., 2011).

Second, the government had a less positive influence on the diffusion of environmental activities through regulative coercive pressures. This was shown in the results where it appeared that many regulative coercive pressures did not influence organizations. Organizations did not obey the rules in several investigated items. This was quite surprisingly due to the authorized regulative power which the government possesses.

This result did not match previous literature since it was stated that governmental regulations stimulate organizations to behave in an appropriate way (Steurer, 2010; Ayres & Braithewaite, 1992). Furthermore, it was argued by Campbell (2006) that regulations are necessary to force organizations to engage in the right and desired behavior. The results showed otherwise since organizations did not obey all the initiated governmental rules.

Different reasons may be found for why these pressures did not influence organizations. First, organizations often do not see the necessity of engaging in environmental activities imposed by governmental laws and obligations. This became evident since different items were found in which organizations did violate environmental regulations due to the fact that they were perceived as unnecessary. To counter this problem, it was mentioned in another item that the government could try harder to convince organizations with good arguments instead of forcing them via regulations. Second, it appeared that the Romanian government created a lot of confusion and that there was a lack of clarity in their regulations. This might also be a reason why organizations did not exactly know what the new standards and regulations were, which makes these regulations less meaningful.

Therefore, the results showed that collectives positively influence the diffusion of environmental activities through sanctioning coercive, social normative, professional normative, and mimetic pressures. This is in line with previous literature (Roberts, 1992; Lyon & Maxwell, 2008; Spar & Mure, 2003; Matten & Moon, 2004). Lyon and Maxwell (2008) stated that collectives can influence organizations by, for example, negative media campaigns, and this has been confirmed by several collected items. The positive influence of collectives may be the result of organizations fearing to get involved in a boycott or other reputation-damaging incident, initiated by collectives. Therefore, CSR activities may be diffused since "they can be used as a means to reduce or manage CSR-related risks such as the avoidance of negative press or customer/NGO boycotts" (Weber, 2008).

Subsequently, the results for the media, as a nonmarket institution, showed a positive influence on the diffusion of environmental activities through social normative and mimetic pressures. These results are in line with previous findings (Strang & Soule, 1998). It turned out that most items found during the content analysis contained negative media attention. In some of these items, the general awareness of the public did increase due to the attention drawn on these organizations with poor environmental activities which is in line with Buhr and Grafström (2006). Some of the items showed that the negative media attention motivated collectives to undertake action and scrutinize those organizations even more by boycotts, for example, which is in line with Nikolaeva and Bicho (2011). Furthermore, positive influence was achieved through different mimetic pressures occurred by the publication of "sustainability rating systems" and other published reports about sustainability and environment-friendly activities. This corresponds to the findings of Schultz and Wehmeier (2010) who argue that mimetic pressures occur by reports in which figures are announced about the sustainability and "greenness" of organizations.

Finally, the results for society, as a nonmarket institution, showed a positive influence on the diffusion of environmental activities through social normative, professional normative, and mimetic pressures. Most of these pressures were social normative pressures, and it was often mentioned in the collected items that society had certain expectations toward an organizations' environmental activities. These social normative pressures, caused by societal expectations, are in line with previous literature in which it was stated that expectations from society can pressure organizations to behave in a more social way (Carroll, 1979; Dahlsrud, 2006). It was shown that these societal expectations also pressured industries to alter their environmental activities. This shows that organizations try to get a good fit between societal expectations and their own performed activities, which was stated previously by Zenisek (1979). Organizations that met these societal expectations were also in some cases mimicked by other organizations to enhance their own legitimacy in society.

8. Conclusions

It can be stated that it is quite surprising that the government influenced the diffusion of environmental activities to a lesser extent than collectives, the media, and society. The government has legal authority which makes it plausible to expect that it can strongly influence organizations. However, in the case of the diffusion of CSR activities, it appeared that governmental regulations caused a lot of confusion and uncertainty. Some of these imposed regulations were even functioning as a barrier. That is why the government did not play a very large role in the diffusion of these activities. It could well be that different results were found if the government have had a different policy, implying that different environmental obligations were mandated in Romania. For the government to positively influence organizations, other regulations should be put in place or the existing rules that are functioning as a barrier should be removed or adapted.

In contrast to the government, collectives, the media, and society did influence the diffusion of CSR activities to a large extent. This can be explained by the fact that organizations fear negative publicity, campaigns, and lobbying forces against them, thereby risking a loss of their reputation and legitimacy. This is the overall essence of the influence initiated by these three nonmarket institutions. It is comprehensible that organizations engage in the type of activities that is expected from them since this can be beneficial in the end. Additional costs will have to be incurred to adopt certain CSR activities, but it is very likely that these costs do not outweigh the loss of reputation or brand image, for example.

8.1. Policy Implications

The implications for policy makers from nonmarket institutions or society itself are that we now know which pressures have a positive influence on the diffusion of CSR activities, specifically in Romania. This study shows that collectives can have a significant influence on organizations by letting them engage in CSR activities through different means like boycotts or demonstrations. This research can make collectives aware about their capacity to influence organizations, despite their lack of authoritarian power. Furthermore, the constant monitoring pressure of the media also influences organizations. This research showed that the media has the capability to influence the CSR activities by organizations, thereby stimulating the diffusion of these activities. Therefore, they should realize that they can play a role in the betterment of society through their own initiated pressures. The same applies to society itself since it was shown that societal influences can stimulate organizations to engage in CSR activities, which stimulates spreading of these CSR activities. Finally, this research showed that governmental pressures do not automatically influence the activities performed by organizations. This might be a wakeup call for the Romanian government because not all regulations turned out to be very effective. This is something that a government should realize, that despite its authoritarian and regulative power, this will not automatically result in the spread of CSR activities.

8.2. Implications for Literature

It was stated in the beginning of this research that relatively few studies have investigated how different types of institutions may influence the development and diffusion of CSR practices (Jackson & Apostelakau, 2009, in Jones, 1999; Stanwick & Stanwick, 1998). This study tried to add some insights and knowledge about this topic. The main implication for the scientific literature is that more research needs to be done, especially in one area. This additional research should be done in the area of governmental influence on the diffusion of CSR activities. This is because most literature argued that the government would have a large positive influence on the diffusion of CSR activities. The results of this research do not show a large positive influence from the government, and it can be regarded as a moderate degree of influence. Therefore, this finding does not correspond to previous findings in the literature, and more research needs to be drawn on this topic.

8.3. Limitations and Further Research

The first limitation to this research is the generalizability of this study. Generalizability can be defined as the degree to which the findings can be generalized from the study sample to the entire population (Polit & Hungler, 1991). The generalizability of a study is still an issue in all qualitative research (Myers, 2000). This is due to the fact that the results of case studies are always open to the charge of being random and non-verifiable (Bos & Tarnai, 1999). This is also the case in this research since conclusions have been drawn about all the Romanian nonmarket institutions, which are based on several items or "cases." In this research, we tried to cope with generalizability by incorporating enough cases for each nonmarket institution.

Second, the objectivity of the researcher may be questioned in qualitative research (Boeije, 2006). The researcher is a person with his or her own habits and thinking patterns, which makes it hard to analyze data neutrally since each person can interpret data differently. This can affect the data analysis. To analyze data as objective as possible, a coding scheme has been made. By analyzing data by means of a coding scheme, the possibility of overlooking important issues is reduced. Furthermore, it gives an insight to other scientists of how the content analysis has been executed.

Third, when investigating to what extent nonmarket institutions influence the diffusion of CSR activities, one must rely on news items published in newspapers. There is a possibility that certain events have happened that are not reported in the Romanian newspapers. This has earlier been addressed and is called selection bias which means that newspapers can be selective in what they present in their newspaper (McCarthy et al., 1996).

Subsequently, more research is necessary on this topic since only one single category of CSR activities has been analyzed. In this research, the diffusion of environmental activities has been investigated as a category of CSR activities. There are many other categories of CSR activities that can be mentioned, as was discussed in the theoretical chapter. It might be that different results will occur when studying the diffusion of another category of CSR activities.

Furthermore, the research setting was focused on Romania. Whether the results are generalizable for other countries can be questioned. Each country has its own culture, norms, and values, and therefore, the influence of nonmarket institutions may be different than the influence found in Romania. Investigating this kind of research in other countries may result in different outcomes, and it is therefore desirable. In particular, differences may occur in countries with a very different culture, norms, and values when compared to Romania.

Finally, more research should be drawn on the pressures initiated by the government as a nonmarket institution. As it was argued in theory, the government was expected to positively influence the diffusion of CSR activities.

However, it turned out that the government was not always successful in influencing organizations, which was not in line with the existing literature. Therefore, more in-depth research should be conducted on this relationship. This may help to clarify which actions the government should undertake to be more effective in influencing organizations, and why some of these actions are not successful, despite their regulative authorized power.

3 The Impact of Economic Policy on Environmental Responsibility

1. Introduction

The environment–economy relationship needs to be harmonized in time and space to allow the achievement of a net effect, even though the environmental protection would impose actions that limit the economic activity. This implies finding a balance between the negative effects of the economic activity and the positive ones of the environment protection. Pollution degree of the environment depends on the configuration of economic structures, on their developing level, and the performance degree of the utilized technologies.

The transition to Romania's market economy implied the reorganization of national economy taking into account the principles of lasting development. For a rational usability of resources, of raw materials, or to improve the quality of environment, it contributed to a large degree the reorganization of production and its new technologies as a branch in every production unit. These transformations led to a double economic and ecological efficiency, those performances that may express the decrease of consumption of raw materials and energy, the complex usability of waste, obtaining quality production by achieving special actions of environment protection.

By improving the degree of environment protection and respecting its quality parameters, it also depends on legislative and institutional adjustments to provide a set of regulations and a system of organization able to hold the responsibility of demands imposed by the necessity of long- lasting development.

Romania sets out a system of laws and normative acts concerning the environmental issues that include a series of acts approved, in the capacity as a European Union (EU) member when a newly born economic system was created.

In the Constitution, there are stipulated theses and general principles concerning environment protection, being guaranteed a human right to a favorable way of living. Moreover, the state warrants free access for every citizen to information about environment, labor, and living conditions and also the rational use of grounds in accordance with the national interests, environmental rehabilitation and protection, and maintaining an ecological balance.

The general legislative framework of environmental protection includes the Law on Environmental Protection; the Land Code, the Forest Code, and Romania's Water Code; Animal Protection Law, Ambience Protection Law, Civil Protection Law, and other normative acts in the field.

The Environmental Protection Law, being of an outstanding importance, needed to work out an additional series of documents to be practiced. Also, it was essential to implement new, non-traditional, economic methods specific to market economy: auctions for using resources, ecological certification of products and differential policy of prices, and ecological assurance. Simultaneously, it passed on to creating an ecological infrastructure, namely the ecological audit system of firms, to ecological consulting in estimating the impact on the environment, an entrepreneurship related to disparaging and recycling the waste.

As a EU member state, Romania lined up its legislation to international ecological standards. This was obtained in two ways: (1) by effecting the international expert appraisement of the new legislative documents by specialized international organizations and (2) by including the essential principles of the ecological legislation of Western countries elaborated in accordance with the EU and European Council directives.

International, ecological integration also provided Romania's adhering to a series of international conventions. As an acknowledgement of principles and documents adopted at the United Nations' Conference on Environment and Development in Rio de Janeiro, Romania signed a series of conventions.

The main part of solving the environmental matters is attributed to the Ministry of Environmental Protection. It holds a series of prior tasks: the state controls the using of natural resources and environment condition; the expertise and ecological survey; organizes and co-ordinates the environmental research; works on the biodiversity preservation programs; organizes ecosystems protection.

The current structure of environment supervision and its components gather the following government bodies in Romania: the Ministry of Environmental Protection, the Ministry of Health, the Ministry of Agriculture and Food, Romania's Geological Association, to which are added the NGOs and many other foundations. Abiding to the environmental protection law by economic agents and natural and legal people is provided by the Environment Guard.

After 1990, Romania joined a new philosophy, a new strategy of a long-lasting development, acceptable to the EU and spread worldwide. It is sensible to the fact that after an extended and traumatic transition to pluralist democracy and market economy, Romania still has fill out significant gaps considering other EU member states, simultaneously with the appropriation and transposition into practice of the principles and long-lasting development practices in the context of globalization. Despite of all progress achieved in the last years, it is a reality that Romania still has an economy depending on the intensive consumption of resources, a society and an administration, still looking for a unitary vision and a natural capital affected by the risk of damages that can be irreversible.

By the Strategy Elaborated for Long-Lasting Development, Romania established concrete objectives for passing, within a realistic and reasonable period of time, to a developing pattern, generating highly added value, impelled for knowledge and innovation directed toward continuous improvement of people' quality of life and their relationship in harmony with natural environment.

1.2. Environmental Policy and Lasting Development in Romania

1.2.1. European Directives in the Field

By transposition of European directives in the field, Romania adopted new laws and standards concerning the environment. Although they are costly and stressful, their implementation represented a radical change in national politics and the approach to environmental protection. The wide reorganization in industry and agriculture, the decrease of extraction activities of solid combustible, and using raw materials tended to improve the quality of environmental factors.

Beginning with 1995, Romania has adopted a series of norms and sector strategic documents, to consider the principles of lasting development. Regarding the development of Romania's less developed regions, taken into account by the EU cohesion policy, Romania still has to make essential investments in the environmental infrastructure, particularly in the water sectors, waste, and air quality. Romania also has to invest in developing efficient systems of environmental management, to improve the quality of services for people and to create a competitive business environment.

The new European dimension assigned Romania, as a EU member state, a better quality of the environment as the key condition. Some fields that required financial efforts to comply with and were implemented are the following: providing of drinking water, building of purifying stations for used water, closing improper depots, waste management, package management, as well as the control of industrial pollution.

ENVIRONMENTAL MANAGEMENT SYSTEMS: WATER PROTECTION

Romania is endowed with all types of fresh water resources: rivers, natural and artificial lakes, and subterranean waters. The most important resource of fresh water is the Danube River and other rivers. The volume of utilizable water is 2,660m^3/inhabitant/year, compared with an European average of 4,000m^3/inhabitant/year. This is mainly due to the contamination of resources in the past, to which economic activities are added.

Water pollution represents the biggest environmental issue in Romania. Water pollution proceeded from households or agricultural and industrial sources has a negative impact on fishing, irrigation, and fresh water supplying systems. The poor quality of water is mainly due to precarious surveillance of industrial unload, as well as the inadequately used water infrastructure. The collecting of used water is still limited in Romania. From the total volume of used waters that need to be filtered, almost 21% was filtered, while 79% got unfiltered or insufficiently filtered to natural receptors, especially into rivers. This is due to the lack of filtering facilities or to their inefficiency.

Improving the services of public utilities in the water sector is closely related to the efficient management of water resources, contributing to a lasting use of them. Nowadays, their objective is affected by the following aspects:

- Limited water resources and the transport of water resources to a long distance represent technical and economic difficulties; it cannot work out a national system of interconnection
- The available water resources from Romania are greatly affected by human activities.
- The capacity of stations for filtering waste water is insufficient.
- The distribution of fresh water in the providing water systems is insufficient.
- The number of installations for purging waste water is insufficient, and also there is a need to modernize the system.
- There is a lack of a systematic approach in establishing the investment projects.
- There are combined systems of sewerage.
- There is no Environmental Master Plan at the regional level.
- The management of sludge from the waste water cleaning stations is inadequate.

The main objectives concerning water protection in Romania, in accordance with the EU requests, include the following aspects: the improvement of water resources and aquatic ecosystems; protection of the drinking water; and the decrease of the adverse effects of floods and drought.

The water protection field requires significant investments. In the last years, the policy concerning this field aimed at improving the quality of water, more precisely by reducing the punctiform sources of pollution. Although the quality of rivers improved, the matter is still far from being satisfactory.

In Romania, there are over 263 urban waste water cleaning stations, and only 77% from the total flow is filtered, bailed out through public network drainage, and there are 47 urban locations that release the waste water without previous processing.

Although there was a progresses made regarding the building of stations for waste water cleaning, a significant part of them provide only biological and mechanical cleaning; therefore, the extension to advanced stages of purifying is necessary (removing nitrogen and phosphorus), taking into account the requests for sensible areas.

There were significant investments made for improving the water infrastructure and the waste water in the most important cities having over 100.000 inhabitants. These gained a lot of support by the EU co-financing programs. The essential issues still remain in the small and medium towns, where only limited investments have been accomplished so far were, and there is a reduced financial and institutional capacity as to develop ample projects.

From the above-mentioned, it can be concluded that the specific systems of domestic water use need to be developed and working. That on one hand implies the investment in suitable facilities for fresh and waste water, and on the other hand, establishing of efficient operational systems.

In the area of water resources management, there have been legislative measures taken regarding the correct transfer of European directives, and the national integrated system was reorganized for water monitoring, including the system for water quality control according to the Water Framework Directive. To implement the Water Framework Directive, internationally supported projects were initiated, among WATFRAME, Siret basin. The manual for modernizing and developing the Integrated System for Water Monitoring in Romania has been promoted that establishes the monitoring programs, inquiry sections, the requisites to equip the regional institutions, which will be making physical, chemical, and biological examinations of the Romanian waters.

In the meantime, many actions proceeded in the view of financing the necessary investments for rehabilitation and extension of supplying water and sewage systems and for water treatment stations. There were investment plans drew up for providing water requests to source the critical areas, to be financed by the World Bank and European Investment Bank. Projects with an international financial assistance have been initiated and are being unrolled. The reference material was prepared—supplying water, evacuation, waste water collecting, and treatment—where the state of the units issued by water administration is reported, or where the licenses of water managing were issued, it continued the controlling of how the legislative provisions are implemented, the themed controls disposed to economic agents, mainly the extraction activities of aggregates from the water flow, of piscicultural accumulation holders as the great pollutants.

SPECIFIC SYSTEM OF WASTE MANAGEMENT

In Romania, the waste management wasn't taken into consideration before 1990. Even though a progress has been made ever since, there are necessary important resources considering the improvement of waste infrastructure and to develop an efficient waste management. The waste management represents one of the most critical environmental issues in Romania. The statistics classify the waste into two categories: (1) assimilated municipal waste and (2) the industrial waste. The depositing constitutes the main method of municipal waste elimination. In the rural areas, there is no management of waste services, and that creates a large number of unauthorized deposits that seriously affect people and the environment. The quantity of generated waste has increased, while the selective collecting and recycling of waste points out to a slow progress.

Romanian and EU legislation on waste had a significant impact in the past years, but there are still necessary efforts to be made to be in compliance with the European standards.

Almost 350.000 ha were differently affected by these types of pollutants, of which 30.000 ha were seriously affected. The most important elements that lead to pollution/degrading of soil are the mining industry; decantation ponds, improper waste deposits; residue and inorganic waste; salty water from petroleum industry, oil pollution; the substances transported by air (hydrocarbon, ethylene, ammonia, dioxide of sulfur, chlorides, fluorine, oxide of nitrogen, lead compounds, etc.). Even though lately some industrial facilities were closed and others reduced their activity, the pollution of soil is still high in the affected areas.

The main issues in the sector referring to waste management and soil protection are the following:

- Storage, clearing out the waste, and a large quantity of improper waste
- A reduced proportion of revaluated and recycled waste
- Improper collecting infrastructure, transport, and waste removal

Until recently, in Romania, the public waste services were aimed at domestic waste. Before the current legislation was adopted, there were the public–private partnerships for building new deposits for solid waste or for its collecting and transport, but not for selective collection or for reaching the targets for recycling the waste, or even closing the deposits for improper waste.

For most of the counties, the existent infrastructure complies with only a small part of the foresights directives of the waste sector. The industrial safe waste, to which another valuable method as treatment or eliminating, is not feasible, are not deposited in suitable storages for safe waste beginning with 2009. Romania has to develop a new recycling and recovering equipment.

With a view to accomplish a realistic management of packaging waste, it is necessary do develop an adequate system for selective collecting of waste.

From the 42 districts, seven districts are currently implementing integrated projects of waste management, co-financed by ISPA Programme.

Another 11 districts have built new facilities, especially waste storages in the framework of some public–private type partnerships. The most acute problem is represented by the large number of old waste stores, both in the urban areas as in the rural, that affect the environment and human health and as consequence, they have to be closed because they are not in compliance the law. On the other hand, the contribution of capital in public services infrastructure aims to eliminate disparities in this sector between the regions.

Municipal waste is largely deposited, rather than selectively collected or recycled. Regarding recycling and capitalizing the waste, in the Waste Management Plan, certain objectives were established for different types of waste: material and energetic capitalization of biodegradable waste, energetic capitalization of sawdust, plastic, glass, and wood capitalization.

Only six municipalities developed selective waste collection and obliteration of biodegradable waste. The treatment of municipal biodegradable waste is a pilot program.

A special attention has to be given to reducing the production of waste packaging materials, to capitalize/recycle them, as also to diminish the risk determined by the presence of dangerous substances in the packaging material.

The management of dangerous waste became a global issue. This waste category has the strongest impact on human health and environment. An efficient management of waste represents a complex aspect, and it needs a coherent and methodically approach mostly to prevent them. To prevent production of dangerous waste, it has to be interdependent with the management of raw materials, of finite products and involved technologies.

Prevention of the waste production not only reduces the administrative costs for the involved firms, but it saves resources and energy, resulting in lower prices. It is necessary to take measures for protecting the environment within small and middle firms.

Also there is a small group of providers managing dangerous waste. They usually collect it, without transportation due to an inefficient capacity. The dangerous waste transportation is secured by waste producers. However more than 89% of dangerous waste is deposited nearby its source with minimal transportation fees. The medical waste represents an exception, as well as used oils, collected and transported with the purpose of treating/capitalization or final elimination.

Romania has to develop a dangerous waste management system to reach the following objectives:

- To lower the possibility of storage of dangerous waste in the same space with other industrial waste;
- To develop collecting and transporting waste to authorized treatment facilities, recycling, or/and final reducing in the interest of industry
- Regulation and activity control for collecting and transport to provide a safe transit of dangerous waste

Concerning the waste from demolition and constructions, nowadays in Romania, the total quantity of such waste is far less compared to other EU members. This type of waste is reused. Only a small percentage is separately collected and stored, which makes it clear why there are such reduced quantities in this category.

Simultaneously with the economic development, building new structures and restoring the existing ones and demolishing old buildings that no longer could be restored lead to a substantial quantity of waste from constructions and demolishing and will greatly change their quality. Thus, it is necessary to promote the investment in the reuse and recycling to properly recover/eliminate them, by a strict separation of construction waste and the waste that is a product of demolishing, and continuous improvement of the recycling and processing schemes.

Concerning the medical waste, the hospitals need to take measures to minimize the entire quantity of this dangerous waste. For the final elimination of dangerous medical waste, the private equipment has to be improved, the old incinerators will be closed, depending on the existing incinerators in the area, authorized for dangerous waste treatment. For preliminary treatment of medical dangerous waste, the mobile and stationary specific technology will be implemented.

Regarding the electric and electronic equipment waste, it is necessary to give a special attention to development of a selective collection system, as to give the most favorable solution for treating, storing, capitalizing, recycling, or eliminating and a rational ecologic management. Nowadays, in Romania there are no solutions for recycling/capitalizing of glass, plastics, and textiles coming from disassembling/treating electric or electronic equipment.

RECYCLING

Investments play a significant role in recycling of the municipal waste generated in people' households, commercial office units, and investments.

In different forms, paper makes between 35% and 41% of domestic garbage. There are three types of paper that can be directly recycled (the quality paper used for printers or copy machines, notebooks, magazines, envelopes, booklets), newspaper, and cardboard. Many types of paper, printed media, and packaging material have brought a good change to lifestyle. In this context, the lack of careful management and neglectful throwing of the waste lead to more intense forestry operations in Romania and other places.

With present technology, paper can be recycled not more than four times. The environmental benefits of recycling paper waste and reducing the quantity of wood are very important, decreasing the production costs: A ton of recycled paper equals 7,000 copies of national newspapers; a ton of recycled paper equals 17–24 of uncut trees and 27 kg of polluting substances delivered into atmosphere; a ton of recovered paper saves almost 2.5m^3 of space intended for waste disposal. To produce 700 shopping paper bags, a

20–23-year-old tree is required; to recycle 1 kg of paper instead of depositing it into the refuse pit prevents 900 g of CO_2 and methane from being delivered into the atmosphere; recycling only one half of the paper used worldwide nowadays could cover almost 75% of the new paper demands.

The reality proved that recycling reduces the clearing bill and the adverse effects (landslides, climate change, floods, destroying the habitats, the biodiversity, and recreational spaces); the wood import bill for cellulose; the air pollution up to 70%, and water pollution up to 35%. The residual water from processing the recycling substances contains three to four times less pollutants than the water used in cellulose processing); recycling also reduces the quantity deposited at the garbage platforms or incinerators.

PRESERVATION AND IMPROVEMENT OF NATURAL RESOURCES

In the last decades, national conditions and landscapes from Romania were influenced by the evolution of economic activities, as well as the economic growth in the last few years, that led to excessive exploitation. In these terms, many species of flora and fauna are endangered, and changing the scenery represents an important indicator of environment deterioration.

As a result of negotiations of Chapter 22 on Environment, Romania had to establish the Nature Network 2000 until the adhering day. After this date, Romania was involved in providing management and monitoring plans for all sites included in this network. This aspect refers to short- and long-term activities and first of all aims at preserving and efficient and balanced regenerated resources (water, flora, and fauna). A long-lasting development represents a necessity. The long-lasting criteria of natural resources take into consideration the permanent strategic objectives.

AIR QUALITY

Romania is accomplishing objectives as stipulated by the Kyoto Agreement, concerning the reduction of 8% of greenhouse gas emissions. Fossil combustible fuels are the main source of pollutants released into the atmosphere, which come from large burning facilities that generate heat and electricity, and they have a significant impact on the environment. There are over 170 large facilities, but only few of them are in compliance with the CE /80/2001 Directive; these facilities emit large concentrates of CO2, nitrogen oxides, and powders that create acid rains and endanger human health, especially in the industrial urban areas. In Romania, the main source of weak air quality in urban areas is the fuel of inferior quality. The energy sector relies on inefficient solid combustibles and crude oil containing high levels of sulfur, and low-income families rely on inferior coal for heating. Transportation represents an important factor in air pollution, considering that a large percentage of cars are old or badly maintained, using petrol with the largest content of lead from Eastern European countries. This last factor is decreasing due to legislative changes that aim to reach the European standards. The main issues in this field are the low air quality, especially in the industrial urban areas that frequently use unsuitable steam-generating stations.

Despite the major improvements brought to this area, efforts are still required to improve the air quality, mostly in urban areas, to reduce the level of energy consumed in the Romanian economy, and to replace the use of combustibles and pollutants, and increase the use of renewable energy resources, when possible.

In Romania, there are few economic agents that developed systems of auto-monitoring devices for atmospheric pollutants. Consequently, the awareness of economic agents is extremely important on the responsibilities they hold in the process of putting the environmental law into effect as also to implement the system of voluntary report and dissemination of information to interested public. Considering the fact that many areas are still greatly polluted by industrial sources, measures for improving the air quality have to be taken, especially for reducing the emission of sulfur oxides, nitrogen, and powders coming from large burning facilities. However, there will be promoted projects that aim to rehabilitate the centralized systems supplied with thermal energy. By implementing the 2001/80/CE concerning the restriction of emission of certain pollutants coming from large burning facilities into the atmosphere, environmental performances in conformity with the EU policy for improving the air quality are going to be reached.

As a general conclusion, Romania has to make significant efforts to comply with the internationally accepted environmental principles, maintaining at the same time historical traditions considering the socio-economical state of the country. An efficient management of the environmental issues in Romania represents the foundation of social acceptability and economic durability. Protection of the environment quality is a key element in providing the lasting means of living for modern generations as for the future. An investment program for improving environmental management systems will help Romania to become a more attractive business environment.

1.2.2. The Strategy for Protecting and Improving of the Environment Quality

The major priority in Romania includes a series of measures that will contribute to achieving the objectives for a long-lasting development. They promote a part of the activities presented at the UNO Summit on long-lasting development in Johannesburg, such as promoting cooperation between the research-development department and firms, producing clean energy, capitalizing regenerated resources of energy, and alternative technologies.

Romania intends to promote the introduction of innovation in firms, to realize the products/services or significant improvements with raised added value, on the ground of rational and efficient use of existing human and natural resources. A direct support is given to technological industrial production on environment, by supporting non-polluting technologies. Major investments in infrastructure are necessary in environment in less developed areas, to encourage the economic growth and convergence in the long term in member states. The existence of an efficient infrastructure represents one of the preliminary conditions for developing business environment and to create new places for work in the environmental sector.

The global objective is constituted by the protection and improvement of environmental quality, accordingly to Romania's economic and social needs, thus leading to a significant improvement in the quality of life by encouraging lasting development. Specific features are improving the standards of living by providing public utility services in the water and waste sector, at necessary quality and quantity; improving the quality of environment in compliance with European Union Directives; improving the water quality by adequate filtering of waste waters, providing an acceptable quality of fresh water, in accordance with the EU norms and by ecological measures for afferent areas simultaneously with gradual reduction of deposited waste; capitalizing recoverable waste, adequately separating and processing dangerous waste, and preventing the infiltration of surface water into the deposited waste; rehabilitating highly contaminated fields; air quality protection in the most exposed positions; improved management of natural resources concerning a lasting development.

Environment protection comply with national legislation and community acquis for equal chances. Lasting development represents a global concern. Romania intends to accomplish the three independent objectives of lasting development: environment protection, social development, and economic welfare.

The national or foreign environment investments represents an important contribution to solving economic and social matters in Romania: health care improving the quality of life and stimulating economic development.

The support of firms' investments will increase, especially in SMEs with a positive impact on the environment, including equipment, tools acquisition, and of new technologies, with law noxious impact on environment, and also the support for quality certification and environment. Stimulating measures imposed on research and technological transfer to be introduced in modern production technologies adapted to the European quality and environment standards will lead not only to improving economic competitiveness, but also to reducing the material and energy consumption, as well as the environmental pollution. Simultaneously the improvement of energetic efficiency on the entire chain is targeted: natural resources, production, transport distribution, and the use of electrical and thermal energy, by sustaining investments in the energy system, leading to a reduced pollution. Capitalization of renewable energy resources rely on using new technologies, with non-polluting impact on the environment.

The major projects involving the environment are financed by the Sectorial Operational Programme for Environment, a program that as an objective has lessening of the existent discrepancies between the EU and Romania, concerning the environmental infrastructure, both quantitative and even more qualitative, that needs to be materialized as efficient public services meant to protect to an extended state people's and environment's well-being. The specific objectives are determined and established depending on the following environmental factors: the water sector, waste management, soil protection, soil quality, air quality and climate change, nature protection and climate risks, etc.

2. Direct Foreign Investments Regarding the Environment and Their Role in Sustainable Development

What follows is an overview of foreign firms that invested in Romania to contribute not only to the economic development, but also to achieving a lasting economy.

Arcelor Mittal Galati invested in ecology through two technological projects estimated at 117 million dollars: reconstruction of a coking plant, total investment being 82.5 million dollars, and modernizing the chemical department of a coking–chemical factory, an investment of 34 million dollars.

Beyond technological advantages, as a double production capacity given the situation of the old coking plant, the new equipment will also help to protect the environment allowing air filtration at 99%. The equipment will capture dust when loading bunkers and will reintroduce it into the production process. The equipment will prevent dispersal of dust into air, recovering 800 tons of dust a year, which will be evacuated into the battery.

In addition, Arcelor Mittal Galati launched a forestation program that implies planting of a million of different trees inside and right next to the siderurgical platform. Also, Arcelor Mittal Galati began to implement 64 environmental projects estimated at 53 million dollars, included in the Compliance Plan signed with the Environment National Guard.

Sonae Sierra is a company specialized in projecting, building, and administrating of commercial centers that guarantee a high level of satisfaction to their clients. The environmental management system implemented by Sonae Sierra has mainly the following objectives: surveillance and reducing the use of electric energy, the quality of water and water consumption, air quality monitoring, and selective recuperation of waste and its recycling.

The initial funds are at disposal by the Contour–Global. Coca-Cola Hellenic offers the field surrounding their facilities production. This measure is part of the announced company's plan to emit less than 20% of CO2. The decision to build such centrals is a consequence of the results obtained by implementing this program at the production unit from Hungary, where in the first year, the CO2 emission was reduced to 43%. At the same time, the energy costs were reduced by 400,000 euros.

Greentech Buzau, Romania's plastic waste recycling pioneer, accomplished a series of recycling projects with an added value of 21.5 million euros. Greenoil is a project that aims to recycle used oil and fibers, in which 3.5 million euros were invested, and Green Tech, a raw material production line for alimentary packaging from the PET waste, was finalized with a total cost of 3 million euros. Greenfiber, a new line for polyester fibers from recycled PET, and Greenplast, a newly founded company for producing of euro pallets, dumping carts, from recycled plastic, are two other projects in which the company will invest a total of 7 million euros.

Iberdola Renovables and Eolica Dobrogea (Schweeiz) AG companies have contracted the biggest project on renewable energy worldwide. The value of investment ranges between 200 and 300 million euros, and the contract implies the development of a portfolio of 50 eolian projects located in Romania.

ENEL Distribution Dobrogea finalized the modernization of an electric station from Fetesti, a project estimated at 1.5 million euros. The modernization works were made by Siemens, and Fetesti station is in compliance with the European efficiency and safety standards.

Stena Metall, one of the biggest companies that offer complete recycling solutions, entered the Romanian market by its subsidiary, Stena Technoworld ab, which made an acquisition of 75% of stocks from a Bucharest company, DTM Waste Recycling. Stena hints at collecting and disassembling dangerous waste, a field not so much explored in our country.

DTM Waste Recycling began its activity in 2006 when they opened the first station for the processing of dangerous waste. The measure was intended for companies that generate low waste quantities and do not benefit from the services of big recycling companies. Taking into consideration the high-risk of dangerous waste, the company didn't set the quantity limits for clients. Nowadays, Stena DTM administrates three authorized working points for collecting, treatment, and the final elimination of electric and electronic waste and industrial waste.

ABN AMRO has a global politics concerning clients from sensitive sectors such as mining, processing metals, oil industry, and others. For a company with such a profile, which intends to access a loan, the bank needs more information on client's capacity to integrate the environmental, social, and ethical aspects in the management of the activity. Relying on this information, a score is determined and given by the bank on the international level, which influences the way that bank works with a particular client.

Concerning the available banking products, the bank mediates activities on the carbon market and transactions with certificates of conservatory gas effect emissions. On the international level, the bank has an entire platform of financial products related to a lasting development, including the climate change, called Eco-Markets.

German Energy Group RWE invests in the development of an energy company in Romania. Although they have been exploring the Romanian market since 2001, RWE has started off in 2009. The RWE officials expressed their interest in the building of Reactors 3 and 4 from Cernavoda Central.

RWE intends to own the first large functioning central following an integrated process to gasify coal. RWE plans to start working on dividing and storing CO2 produced during a technological process.

The main concern of Scholz Grup is recycling of the metal waste. The first commercial business started in Romania in 1998 involved only buying waste from the Romanian importers, and this wasn't a true investment in Romania. In 2003, Scholz made the first investment in our country, and it registered the first company, Remat Invest, in Cluj. The biggest accomplishment of the company in Romania so far is the stability of a network of almost 80 processing deposits per million square meters, fields that belong to the company, all over Romania.

In Romania, its main activity is recycling the metal waste (95%), and the rest is paper and plastic, these being fields that the company intends to develop in the future. More than 40% of Sholz investments are directly or indirectly dedicated to environmental protection measures. The company intends to bring all metal deposits from Romania to European standards by investing in concrete platforms, especially made to prevent oil to pollute the soil. Another 25% of investment is dedicated to buying modern equipment, called shredders, and to put five of them into function, all bought from Germany and intended for recycling automobiles. This program is essential to fulfill the obligation to recycle all cars so Romania could reach the quote assigned by the EU directives.

Smithfield Ferme is an American company and an agriculture promoter that relies on using an extended organic waste. The American company investments located in Banat in a non-polluting modern technology exceed 25 million euro. Smithfield Ferme is in compliance with the European and national regulations regarding the environment protection, contributing to the ecological involvement in the areas affected by the past polluting agricultural practices and intense use of chemical waste. By investing in the last-generation technology and conforming to environmental protection norms, Smithfield Ferme contribute to the mutual effort of authorities and professional associations from Romania to build a modern agricultural sector, in compliance with the best EU practices and standards.

Set in 1997, SC Romrecycling SRL, is a Romanian commercial company belonging to the Ecore group in Holland, which holds companies specialized in recycling in France, Hungary, Turkey, and China. SC Romrecycling SRL is today one of the most important commercial societies specialized in collecting, processing, recycling, and trading of ferrous and non-ferrous waste, electric, electronic, and electronic appliances, paper and plastic, wood, and also recovering the vehicles out of use.

Smithfield Foods is a leader in the meat processing and production regarding the research, environment, and social responsibility. The company invest its time and important resources in developing and implementing of new economic solutions, viable from an environmental point of view.

Smithfield Foods entered the Romanian market by the acquisition of local companies Comtim and Agrotorvis and setting up Smithfield Ferme and Smithfield Prod. The American company invested over 25 million euros in the equipment and eco-friendly technology. In the past years, to manage residues, Smithfield Ferme, invested over 21 million euros to build ultramodern tanks to deposit waste. The company is also preoccupied with monitoring and constant analysis of environmental variables, such as the soil chemical structure and subsoil and surface water quality. Every year, over 200,000 euros are invested by Smithfield Ferme in many studies that deal with soil analysis and water quality.

Scapa-Aiprom, the collecting system of pesticide packaging, is the most recent project by the Romanian Crop Protection Association: Aiprom. Aiprom focuses on promoting, transposing, and implementing the European legislation with regard to protecting plants in Romania. Aiprom includes both governmental organizations, such as ministries, agencies, research institutes, and laboratories, and nongovernmental organizations such agriculture associations, farmers' associations.

The concrete producer Holcim invested 3 million euros in an ecological concrete station. It is located in Bucharest, and it is supplied with filters that considerably reduce the noise and totally eliminate dust emissions. The ecological concrete station Bucuresti–Pantelimon is operational during the entire year due to air and water heating system that allows the production of concrete even when it is cold.

Direct foreign investments made in Romania in every area need to include the objectives of environment improvement and lasting development. The foreign investors support the development of non-polluting technologies in accordance with natural environment necessities to provide air quality products, of surfaced waters, and soil quality in accordance with the European and world standards. In this regard, we mention the activity of Lukoil company, which invested 51 million dollars in modernizing Petrotel Ploiesti Oil Distillery to comply with the EU norms regarding the product quality and medium protection. From this sum, the group will assign 15 million dollars to building of a production unit of bio-fuel at the oil distillery with an annual capacity of at least 50,000 tons.

In Romania, foreign companies invested in the energy sector, and they set up and increased the measures to prevent and reduce the air pollution. The energy sector is strategic for national economy. A lasting development strategy of the energy sector includes long-term objectives that reflect the national economy demands concerning the securing of resources, safety and energetic efficiency, using of renewable resources, and environment protection. Direct foreign investments in agriculture as an impact have increasing the number and developing of ecological products, and reduce the process of deserting and soil degrading.

Beginning in 2002, a perimeter of ecological reconstruction was made at the Danube Delta, with the massive investment and positive results.

The foreign companies that invest in Romania are interested in finding possibilities to reduce the effects of global warming and find the solutions to implement them. They also provide the services of non-polluting/non-contaminating industrial installations and dangerous waste removal.

By their activities, direct foreign investments effectively contribute to non-polluting equipment and contaminated places with dangerous waste, soil decontamination and transport, depositing, and eliminating dangerous waste.

This is only one fragment of the arguments that support the idea that foreign direct investments in economy are welcomed and necessary to straighten many activity sectors, but mainly for environment protection and securing a lasting development.

In the present context, companies need to prove social responsibility, both in terms of environment and economic development. For this reason, the company management needs to focus on finding all the methods for reaching the goals to protect and preserve the environment for future generations, simultaneously improving the quality of life.

4 CSR Disclosure in Emerging Economies*

1. Introduction

From an economic perspective, the main goal of a company is to create value through producing goods and offering services demanded by the society (International Chamber of Commerce, 2016). Companies thereby generate profit for its owners and shareholders, as well as social welfare. However, social and market pressures are gradually leading to a change in the scope of business activities. There is a growing understanding that a sustainable success and the shareholder value cannot be achieved entirely through maximizing short-term profits, but instead, companies should focus more on their market-oriented responsible behavior (European Commission, 2002). This responsible behavior is also known as corporate social responsibility (CSR). The concept of CSR refers to companies integrating social and environmental concerns in their business operations and in their interaction with their stakeholders (European Commission, 2002).

The increasing CSR awareness is also reflected in the increasing number of CSR reports, as well as the disclosure of CSR-related information (Gray et al., 2001; Kolk, 2005). Perrini et al. (2007) stated in their research that CSR and CSR disclosure merged together. This statement can be supported by the findings of Gamerschlag et al. (2011) who stated that, nowadays, large companies spend an increasing amount of money and effort on disclosing information on their social and environmental performance. In addition, they argue that due to firm-specific characteristics, such as visibility, profitability, and shareholder structure, companies have to deal with either more or less powerful stakeholders and thus face different levels of political and societal costs. By voluntarily disclosing information on their social and environmental performance, companies try to reduce these costs.

Matthews (1995) also elaborated on companies' motives to develop CSR disclosure initiatives. First, he argues that disclosing socially responsible information can positively affect the market performance of companies. Second, he argues that CSR disclosure can contribute to the establishment of legitimacy. Finally, he argues that CSR disclosure can ensure the establishment of a social contract between companies and the society in which they operate. In addition, Kolk (2005) argues that the reputation management is also an important motive for companies to disclose on their CSR activities.

The increasing global attention for CSR disclosure was the reason for various nongovernmental organizations (NGOs) to develop models or frameworks for reporting on CSR (Reverte, 2009). Before, there was no uniformity or standardization in terms of the items to be reported, or the way of reporting (Reverte, 2009).

Examples of models/frameworks are the Internationally Standards Organization (ISO) 14001, World Resource Institute (WRI), and the Global Reporting Initiative (GRI). The GRI reporting guidelines are widely acknowledged as the leader in the international standardization of sustainability reporting (Gray, 2010; Mahoney et al., 2013). GRI promotes the use of sustainability reporting as a way for organizations to become more sustainable and to contribute to sustainable development. GRI's mission is to make sustainability reporting a standard practice for all companies and organizations. The guidelines are being developed on a continuous basis with the latest version of the standard issue in 2013 (Global Reporting Initiative, 2016).

Several researchers (e.g., Dawkins & Lewis, 2003; Igalens & Gond, 2005; Welford et al., 2008) argue that the concept of CSR is constantly changing. In addition, they argue that CSR means different things to different stakeholders and companies in different countries. The concept of CSR has a relatively long history in Western countries, also known as developed markets (Carroll, 1999; Whetten et al., 2002). Developed markets are characterized by a high gross domestic product (GDP) per capita and low growth rates (Dögl & Behnam, 2015). Moreover, developed markets often have well-established norms and values of business standards, due to stable socio-economic and political conditions and a strong legal system (Peters et al., 2011). Although the topic is more established in developed markets, CSR has become increasingly important in emerging markets as well (Fetscherin et al., 2010). Contrary to developed markets, emerging markets are often characterized by a low GDP per capita and high growth rates (Dögl & Behnam, 2015).

CSR is believed to be useful in promoting social justice, equality, transparency, and accountability by holding organizations accountable for their actions (Belal, 2008). In contrast to the developed countries, emerging countries often have to deal with problems such as poverty, human rights violation, corruption, inequalities, and social exploitations. It is argued that organizations operating in emerging markets have a responsibility to address some of these issues. They may be held accountable in this way via disclosures addressing the issues as mentioned above. The growing awareness of CSR resulted in an increasing number of CSR reports, as well as disclosures of CSR-related information (Gray et al., 2001; Kolk, 2005). Research regarding CSR disclosure, and specifically determinants of CSR disclosure, has mainly focused on developed markets. There is little knowledge and research available yet on the determinants of CSR disclosure in emerging markets. The increasing importance of CSR in emerging markets can be found to be a reason to research this context as an extension of existing literature. The fast pace of development and the growing intensity of economic activities in emerging markets, the BRIC (Brazil, Russia, India, China) countries in particular, resulted in emerging markets being targeted as potential growth markets for Western companies. The growing importance of these emerging markets, as contributors to the world's economy, also indicates the importance of researching this context.

The main objective of this research is to define the determinants of CSR disclosure of multinational enterprises (MNEs) in emerging markets. As described in the literature, firm-specific characteristics, such as visibility, profitability, and shareholder structure, can act as proxies for the amount of information disclosed by companies (Gamerschlag et al., 2011). It is to be researched whether these firm-specific determinants, possibly resulting in different levels of stakeholder pressures, lead to variation in CSR disclosure for MNEs in emerging markets. The increasing importance of emerging markets in the world's economy combined with the lack of knowledge regarding the determinants of CSR disclosure in this particular research context indicate the necessity of this research being conducted.

1.1. Relevance

In recent studies (e.g., Campbell, 2007; Ioannou & Serafeim, 2010; Peloza, 2009), scholars have argued that the CSR research has mainly focused on the impact of CSR on corporate financial performance, whereas little attention was dedicated to characterizing determinants of CSR. This research will contribute to the latter. In addition, with the expansion of the global economy, CSR has also gone global (Fetscherin et al., 2010). However, research on the determinants of CSR disclosure is mostly conducted in developed markets. With a focus on the emerging markets, this study contributes to the literature by examining a relatively new research setting. Moreover, research in CSR still remains mostly on a local level (Lee, 2008). Giannarakis (2014) argues that further empirical research into CSR practices should examine CSR in more diverse institutional contexts. By examining CSR disclosure in emerging markets, this research covers a broader contextual level. Finally, this study contributes to a greater understanding of the determinants of CSR disclosure in emerging markets.

The managerial relevance of this study lies with the findings and results as provided by this study. Understanding why firms disclose information is useful to both the preparers and users of the disclosed information as well as to policy makers in an organization (Meek et al., 1995). Muller and Kolk (2009) argue that the obtained insight by managers, into CSR activities and in the firm-specific aspects most important in the local setting, will contribute to identifying the areas for mutual learning and further development.

Moreover, the findings of this study could be interesting for all actors considering setting up practices in emerging markets.

Concerns regarding CSR have grown significantly during the last two decades (Campbell, 2007). The identification of CSR disclosure determinants could lead to a better understanding of the CSR concept and it could lead to more transparency regarding the CSR activities undertaken by MNEs in emerging markets. Moreover, the increasing awareness of CSR activities amongst MNEs and their stakeholders could contribute to the macro-economic development of emerging markets, which could lead to sustainable benefits for the society.

2. CSR

In the literature, there are many different definitions of CSR. Broadly formulated, CSR implies specific attention to the ethical, social, and environmental implications of a company's actions (Kolk et al., 2010). Companies have economic responsibilities towards shareholders to undertake profitable activities. In addition, companies also have legal, ethical, environmental, and social responsibilities toward the society to comply with laws and regulations. In other words: to do no harm and to do good (Carroll, 1999; Crane & Matten, 2007; De Bakker et al., 2005; Whetten et al., 2002).

Historically, researchers have developed two competing views toward CSR. On the one hand, there is neo-classical economics or the shareholder approach. Researchers in line with this perspective (e.g., Friedman, 2007; Husted & Salzar, 2006) argue that a company's main objective is to maximize the shareholder value. Moreover, they argue that companies should only undertake actions that either increase profits or decrease costs, while following all legal principles and protecting integrity.

On the other hand, stakeholder approach comprises the theoretical foundation of most arguments supporting CSR (Freeman, 1984). Supporters of this view argue that CSR plays a considerable role in creating and maintaining a company's competitive advantage to meet its stakeholders' interests. This fulfillment of stakeholders' demands should in the long-term result in higher economic profits (Donaldson & Preston, 1995; Frooman, 1999).

A more recent and broader view of CSR is the societal approach. This view goes even beyond a company's stakeholders, and argues that companies are responsible to societies as a whole, of which they are an integral part. According to this approach, companies operate by a public "license to operate" to serve the needs of society to the satisfaction of society (Marrewijk, 2003).

2.1. Components of CSR

Throughout the development of the CSR concept, many researchers (e.g., Carroll, 1991; Dahlsrud, 2006; Garriga & Melé, 2004) have attempted to identify the components or dimensions of CSR. Carrolls' pyramid of CSR is one of those classifications, which is widely recognized (Carroll, 1991). In his research, he argues that a companies' CSR should be framed in such a way that it embraces the entire range of business responsibilities. This model, presented as a pyramid, suggests that four components of social responsibilities represent total CSR. These four components include economic, legal, ethical, and philanthropic responsibilities. Carroll (1991) argues that the components are not mutually exclusive and are not intended to position a company's economic responsibilities with its other responsibilities. In addition, he argues that considering the components separately helps managers to see that the different types of responsibilities are in a constant though-dynamic tension with each other and that the most critical tension is argued to be between the economic and the remaining components.

The first component of Carroll's pyramid represents a company's economic responsibilities (Carroll, 1991). This component indicates that a company should be profitable, which will function as the foundation upon which the other responsibilities rest. Carroll (1991) argues that historically companies were created with an economic purpose. Their main goal was to provide goods and services as demanded by society while in the meantime making an acceptable profit. Therefore, he argues that the profit motive was established as the primary incentive for companies and that all other business responsibilities are based upon the economic responsibility. This argument is in line with the shareholder approach, as discussed before. Examples of statements regarding economic responsibilities are "being as profitable as possible," "maintaining a strong competitive position," and "being consistently profitable" (Carroll, 1991).

The second component of the pyramid comprises a company's legal responsibilities (Carroll, 1991). This component indicates that, next to the profit motive, companies are also expected to comply with laws and regulations. As part of the "social contract" between business and societies, companies are expected to pursue their economic activities within the framework of law (Carroll, 1991). This responsibility has a mandatory nature as it is an obligation for firms to comply. Examples of statements regarding a company's legal responsibilities are "performing in a manner consistent with expectations of government and law," "being a law-abiding corporate citizen," and "it is important that a successful firm is defined as one that fulfills its legal obligations" (Carroll, 1991).

The ethical responsibilities represent the third component (Carroll, 1991). Carroll argues that companies are expected to be ethical, as they have the obligation to do what is right and to avoid harm. Ethical responsibilities reflect a concern for what is regarded as fair by different stakeholders (e.g., consumers, employees, shareholders, and society at large). Although the ethical responsibilities have a voluntary character, they are connected to activities and practices that are expected or prohibited by members of the society. However, these responsibilities are not obliged by the law. Examples of statements regarding a company's ethical responsibilities are "performing in a matter consistent with expectation of society and ethical norms" and "ethical behavior goes beyond the compliance with regulations and laws" (Carroll, 1991).

The fourth and last component comprises philanthropic responsibilities (Carroll, 1991). Carroll (1991) argues that companies have the responsibility to contribute resources to the quality of life of the society. This can also be described as "to be a good corporate citizen," which includes actively engaging in acts or programs to promote human welfare or goodwill. Similar to the ethical responsibilities, philanthropic responsibilities also have a voluntary nature. However, the main difference between the two responsibilities is that philanthropic responsibilities are not expected in an ethical or moral sense (Carroll, 1991). Examples of statements with regard to philanthropic responsibilities are "it is important to voluntary assist to projects that improve society's quality of life" and "performing in way that is consistent with the charitable and philanthropic expectations of society" (Carroll, 1991).

Dahlsrud (2006) also identified different dimensions of CSR, and he makes a distinction between economic, environmental, social, legal, and voluntary dimensions. Most of these dimensions are overlapping with the CSR components as proposed by Carroll (1991). Dahlsrud (2006) separately addresses an environmental dimension of CSR. This dimension stresses the importance of organizational awareness with regard to environmental concerns in business practices.

2.2. CSR in Emerging Economies

Emerging markets, in contrast to developed markets, are often characterized by a lack of norms and values of business standards due to unstable socio-economic and political conditions. Moreover, the legal system in emerging markets is often weak (Peters et al., 2011). Peters et al. (2011) argue that, due to these circumstances, companies in emerging markets have to deal with the challenge of showing that they are accountable and can be trusted.

In addition, CSR is believed to be useful in promoting social justice, equality, transparency, and accountability by holding organizations accountable for their actions (Belal, 2008). In contrast to the developed countries, emerging countries often have to deal with problems such as poverty, human rights violation, corruption, inequalities, and social exploitations. It is argued that organizations operating in emerging markets have an increasing responsibility to address some of these issues (Belal & Momin, 2009).

Further, Doh et al. (2015) argue that lower income levels, less awareness of environmental and social issues, lower levels of product variety, and greater emphasis on the basic value proposition of products are all reasons that could explain why emerging market companies are less sensitive to respond to pressures to engage in CSR practices. Studies (e.g., Welford, 2004) have found that companies from emerging markets tend to show weaker measures of CSR and therefore lag behind their Western equivalents with regard to CSR implementation and activities.

In addition to the above-mentioned characteristics, emerging markets are also characterized by rapid growth and large economies (Fetscherin et al., 2010). Moreover, the contribution of emerging markets to the world's economy is of growing importance (Doh et al., 2015). The internationalization process of emerging markets has resulted in an increased awareness of concerned stakeholders, such as governments, groups, and individuals about pollution, product quality and safety affecting the world around us (Fetscherin et al., 2010). Therefore, it can be concluded that the CSR of emerging market companies is a growing concern.

3. CSR Disclosure

In the last two decades, public awareness and interest in social and environmental issues as well as the increased attention of the media have resulted in more social disclosures (Kolk, 2003). Simply speaking, CSR disclosure can be defined as the external reporting of social, ethical, and environmental aspects of corporate activities (Belal, 2008). CSR disclosure has been defined by Gray, Owen and Maunders (1987) as

> the process of communicating the social [, ethical,] and environmental effects of organizations' economic actions to particular interest groups within society and to society at large. As such, it involves existing the accountability of organizations (particularly companies), beyond traditional role of providing a financial account to the owners of capital in particular, shareholders. Such an extension is predicated upon the assumption that companies do have wider responsibilities than simply make money for their stakeholders.

Given the increased importance of stakeholder engagement in CSR, Gray (2000, p. 250) refined the earlier definition as follows:

> the preparation and publication of an account about an organization's social, environmental, employee, community customer and other stakeholder interactions and activities and, where possible, the consequences of those interactions and activities. The social account may contain financial information but is more likely to be a combination of quantified non-financial information and descriptive, non-quantified information. The social account may serve a number of purposes but discharge of the organization's accountability to its stakeholders must be clearly dominant of those reasons and the basis upon which the social account is judged.

3.1. Classifications of CSR Disclosure

As described before, literature on CSR attempts to conceptualize CSR based on components and/or dimensions (e.g., economic, legal, ethical, and philanthropic components—Carroll's pyramid; Carroll, 1991). Literature on CSR disclosure uses a somewhat different classification.

First of all, a CSR disclosure can be broadly classified as mandatory or voluntary disclosure (Kavitha & Anita, 2011). Mandatory disclosure is the information that appears in the annual report in compliance with the requirements as stated by the law (Kavitha & Anita, 2011). Cowan and Gadenne (2005) in their study stated that the mandatory information in the annual report provides users of the annual report with factual information of the company's compliance with regulations over the reported period. Mandatory disclosures are mostly linked to the economic and legal components of CSR, as discussed in Chapter 2.1. A characteristic of voluntary disclosures is that they are considered in the decision-making process of several user groups (Kavitha & Anita, 2011). Cowan and Gadenne (2005) argue that companies do not only provide voluntary disclosure as a way to satisfy the stakeholder's rights to know, but also as a way to achieve legitimacy in society. Voluntary disclosures are mostly linked to the ethical and philanthropic responsibilities of a company's CSR, as discussed in Chapter 2.1.

Second, literature on CSR disclosure often uses another broad classification by distinguishing between social and environmental disclosures (Reverte, 2009; Kavitha & Anita, 2011). Prior studies have focused on either environmental or social disclosures or considered both categories simultaneously (e.g., Bewley & Li, 2000; Déjean & Martinez, 2009; Muller & Kolk, 2010).

Social CSR disclosure often comprises main subjects such as employment, health and safety, human rights, collective bargaining, labor, community, and corruption (Gamerschlag et al., 2011). Due to environmental issues being one of the major concerns companies are facing, the disclosure on environmental CSR is becoming more important. As industrial pollution is considered one of the main sources of global warming, companies are pressured to disclose about their environmental protection activities (Kavitha & Anita, 2011). Environmental CSR disclosure often comprises main subjects such as recycling, energy consumption, biodiversity, emissions, effluents, waste, spills, and environmental impacts (Gamerschlag et al., 2011).

The increasing global attention for CSR disclosure was the reason for various NGOs to develop models or frameworks for reporting on CSR (Reverte, 2009). Before, there was no uniformity or standardization in terms of the items to be reported, or the way of reporting (Reverte, 2009). The GRI guidelines are the most widely accepted guidelines for reporting on CSR (Gray, 2010; Mahoney et al., 2013). GRI's mission is to make sustainability reporting a standard practice for all companies and organizations (GRI, 2016).

3.2. Incentives of CSR Disclosure

In the literature, several theories attempt to explain the incentives for companies to disclose on their CSR activities (Jain et al., 2015). These incentives can be classified into two broad categories, which both consist of several theories.

First of all, incentives regarding strategic drivers are focused on the company and its environment (Jain et al., 2015). The two most well-known theories with regard to strategic drivers are stakeholder theory and legitimacy theory (Jain et al., 2015). Stakeholder theory suggests that firms accept that stakeholders have the power and capacity to influence the decision-making process. Companies will take into account the interests of stakeholders when making organizational decisions (Jain et al., 2015). The main incentive for companies is to disclose information to show that they are taking stakeholder views into consideration (Cotter et al., 2011).

Legitimacy theory emphasizes the link between the company and the rest of the society (Jain et al., 2015). Legitimacy theory argues that when public perceptions of the company differ from its actual performance, companies have an incentive to disclose on their socially responsible behavior to manage stakeholder expectations (Cotter et al., 2011).

Second, incentives with respect to economic drivers are related to issues of information asymmetry and costs (Jain et al., 2015). Two well-known theories with regard to economic drivers are agency theory and political cost theory (Jain et al., 2015). With regard to agency theory, it is argued that there is an incentive for firms to disclose information to encourage equity and debt holders to invest (Cotter et al.). In this context, the incentive stems from agency problems caused by the separation of managers from owners and investors, which is hindered by information asymmetry (Jain et al., 2015).

This specific research relies on political cost theory. This theory suggests that managers are concerned with reducing the costs associate with political actions (Healy & Palepu, 2001; Jain et al., 2015; Watts & Zimmerman, 1978). Gamerschlag et al. (2011) argue that the main incentive for companies to disclose information is "because it is in their economic interest." In addition, Jain et al. (2015) state that the incentive of disclosing information occurs when the benefits of doing so exceeds the risks of increased intervention by stakeholders if disclosure does not occur.

Besides politicians, nongovernmental interest groups and other stakeholders are also increasingly trying to influence companies' actions in favor of their own specific interest (Gamerschlag et al., 2011). With regard to political cost theory, Gamerschlag et al. (2011) explain that due to firm-specific characteristics companies have to deal with either more or less powerful stakeholders and thereby face different levels of political and societal costs. By disclosing information on their social and environmental performance, companies try to reduce these costs arising from the interaction between the company and its environment (Fields et al., 2001).

4. Determinants of CSR Disclosure

This study relies on the political cost theory for defining determinants of CSR disclosure. From a political cost theory perspective, Gamerschlag et al. (2011) argue that due to firm-specific characteristics, companies have to deal with either more or less powerful stakeholders and thereby face different levels of political and societal costs. This statement is supported by Agle et al. (1999), who also argue that companies face different intensities of external pressures due to their firm-specific characteristics. In addition, they argue that this intensity depends on the stakeholders' level of power, legitimacy, and urgency. Gamerschlag et al. (2011) argue that firm-specific characteristics determine whether CSR disclosure occurs or not. In an attempt to explain CSR disclosure, Cormier and Gordon (2001) and Meek et al. (1995) also suggested that firm characteristics are important determinants of CSR disclosure.

The relationship between firm-level characteristics and CSR disclosure has been well documented in the literature (Giannarakis, 2014). Prior studies (e.g., Gamerschlag et al., 2011; Ho & Taylor, 2007; Reverte, 2009; Tagesson et al., 2009; Khan, 2010) have used a wide range of measures for explaining CSR disclosure. Significant explanatory variables included the firm size, profitability, industry profile, ownership structure, media exposure, and the number of non-executive directors and foreign nationalities on the board. An extensive literature review indicates a lack of research on CSR determinants in emerging markets, the BRIC countries in particular, as most research has been conducted in developed markets or emerging markets other than the BRIC (Giannarakis, 2014).

This specific study focuses on visibility, shareholder structure, profitability, and board independence as possible determinants of CSR disclosure in emerging markets. These firm-specific characteristic are found to be significantly related to CSR disclosure in developed markets (Gamerschlag et al., 2011; Ho & Taylor, 2007; Reverte, 2009; Tagesson et al., 2009; Khan, 2010). Therefore, this study will test whether this is also true for a different research context, specified as emerging markets.

4.1. Visibility

Gamerschlag et al. (2011) argue that some companies are more visible to the public than others. This can mainly be explained by their degree of visibility due to the quantity of their press coverage (Gamerschlag et al., 2011). The media can play an important role in mobilizing social movements such as environmental interests groups (Reverte, 2009). Empirical studies have shown that the visibility of company due to media exposure has been influential on corporate environmental responses (Bansal & Roth, 2000; Bowen, 2000). Companies that are constantly in the spotlight will be more susceptible to political actions, as they attract more attention from stakeholders

(Deegan & Carroll, 1993). In addition, Branco and Rodriques (2006) argue that companies with the highest public profile are more willing to present a positive image than less visible companies to justify their existence to the society.

With regard to CSR disclosure, it is argued that companies with the highest degree of visibility will receive more attention from stakeholders (Brammer & Millington, 2006). These stakeholders, including pressure groups, are interested in the activities of the company and will try to influence these activities toward their own interests. As a result, visible companies are more affected by social restraints and pressures than companies that are less visible to society (Brammer & Millington, 2006). These highly visible companies will potentially experience higher political or societal costs as a result of their exposure to the public. Gamerschlag et al. (2011) argue that highly visible companies, in contrast to less visible companies, will disclose more CSR-related information to reduce these potential costs. Based on this reasoning, this study asserts that:

Hypothesis 1: Company visibility is positively associated with CSR disclosure of MNEs in emerging markets.

4.2. Shareholder Structure

The degree to which the ownership of company shares is distributed in the hands of a few large investors or distributed among many shareholders has been assumed to influence CSR disclosure (Roberts, 1992). The potential for conflicts between owners and managers is assumed to be stronger in companies where shares are widely dispersed among many shareholders rather than in a more concentrated setting. According to Gamerschlag (2011), this can be explained by two reasons: (1) in case of dispersed ownership, shareholders have little direct authority over managers and must therefore carefully monitor their activities; in addition, communication between relevant parties is hindered. (2) Companies with a few large shareholders, such as family-owned firms, have fewer motives to disclose on CSR-related topics, because the demand for public disclosure is relatively weak. Such family-owned companies are still common in emerging markets (Chau & Gray, 2002).

Voluntary disclosures are likely to be greater in companies where shares are widely distributed, allowing the owners to effectively monitor that their economic interests are optimized, while managers can exhibit that they act in the owners best interest (Chau & Gray, 2002). Companies with many owners are expected to disclose more CSR-related information than companies with more concentrated ownership (Prencipe, 2004). It is suggested that this is true, in order to reduce information asymmetries between the company and its owners (Prencipe, 2004). Thus, this study hypothesizes that:

> Hypothesis 2: A more dispersed shareholder structure is positively associated with CSR disclosure of MNEs in emerging markets.

4.3. Profitability

Previous studies have assumed that the profitability of a company influences the level of CSR disclosure (Roberts, 1992; Watson et al., 2002; Chandler & Ismail, 2005). Ng and Koh (1994) argue that highly profitable companies are more exposed to political pressure and public exposure and, therefore, use voluntary disclosure as a mechanism to avoid regulation. In addition, Inchausti (1997) argues that management in very profitable companies provide more CSR-related information to support their own position and compensation. According to Pirsch et al. (2007), another explanation might be that profitable companies have the necessary economic resources to make such information available. In companies with fewer economic means, management will probably focus on activities that have a more direct effect on the company's resources rather than focusing on disclosing CSR-related information (Roberts, 1992).

The results of Gamerschlag et al. (2011) indicate only a significant relationship between profitability and environmental CSR disclosure. They argue that environmental and social disclosures are driven by somewhat different stakeholder groups as reflected in different firm characteristics. Other studies (e.g., Haniffa & Cooke, 2005) have tended to find a positive relationship between profitability and CSR disclosure. Possible clarifications for this relationship included the level of political pressure, level of economic resources, and managers' continuance of their position and compensation. In addition, Haniffa and Cooke (2005) argue that profitable firms disclose CSR-related information to show their role to society's well-being, to validate their existence. Based on previous reasoning, this study proposes that:

> Hypothesis 3: Profitability is positively associated with CSR disclosure of MNEs in emerging markets.

4.4. Board Independence

Literature on governance suggests that the degree of board independence is related to the composition of the board (Gamerschlag et al., 2011). It is argued that independence will enhance the board's effectiveness (Said et al., 2009). Webb (2004) in her research found that socially responsible firms have a more independent board than non-socially responsible firms. It is argued that an independent board has the incentive to act in the shareholders interest (Said et al., 2009). In addition, Said et al. (2009) argued that independent (non-executive) board members are regarded to act as intermediaries for solving agency conflicts between managers and owners. The study of Webb (2004) also indicated that the independence of the board is important in enhancing a company's image and has a monitoring role in ensuring proper management. Moreover, it is argued that any consequences in not incorporating CSR will reflect a bad corporate image (Webb, 2004).

It is argued that the governance environment in emerging markets is weaker compared to the governance environment in developed markets (Dharwadkar et al., 2000; Mitton, 2002). This is explained by the absence and/or inefficiencies of formal laws and regulations such as accounting requirements and information disclosure (Young et al., 2008). The board's ability to effectively monitor managers has been indicated as important for corporate governance (Dharwadkar et al., 2000; Mitton, 2002).

Prior studies highlight the importance of independent board members in corporate disclosure behavior (Chen & Jaggi, 2001; Eng & Mak, 2003; Ho & Wong, 2001). It is argued that independent board members improve the transparency of the board and the voluntary disclosure of information (Chen & Jaggi, 2001). Eng and Mak (2003) argue that independent board members are less aligned to management and therefore have the power to force the management to disclose CSR-related information. Based on previous reasoning, this study proposes that:

Hypothesis 4: Board independence is positively associated with CSR disclosure of MNEs in emerging markets.

5. Methodology

5.1 Research Design and Sample Selection

To answer the research objective, a quantitative research is performed. Quantitative research is characterized by inferring evidence for a theory through measurement of variables that produce numeric outcomes (Field, 2009). This type of research is most suitable for this specific research, because all variables are measured by numeric outcomes. To analyze the data, we employ multiple regression analysis. Multiple regression is the appropriate method of analysis if a research includes one single metric dependent variable presumed to be related to two or more metric independent variables (Hair et al., 2014). This is true for this specific research, because it involves one dependent variable (CSR disclosure), and four independent variables (visibility, shareholder structure, profitability, and board independence).

The data for this research is obtained from Brazilian companies. As Brazil is one of the main emerging markets (BRIC), the country is suitable to represent emerging markets. The sample collected is based on 48 listed Brazilian MNEs addressed in the DataStream Asset 4 ESG database of Thomson Reuters. Due to missing data on the dependent variable, the final sample comprises 43 companies, which are all analyzed on their environmental and social responsibility profile. The companies in this study were tracked for 3 years (2010–2012) resulting in a total of 129 data points. Table 4.1 provides an overview of the sample distribution based on industry.

5.2 Measurement

Table 4.2 gives an overview of the operationalization of the variables.

Dependent Variable

The first concept to be operationalized is CSR disclosure. The amount of CSR disclosure is measured by taking into account both environmental and social CSR disclosure. The combined equation for total CSR disclosure is as follows:

$$CSRDTOT = CSRDENV + CSRDSOC$$

Data are collected through DataStream ASSET4 ESG (environmental, social, governance) scores. ASSET4 is an independent agency that has a reputation as one of the most diligent and trustworthy sources for CSR data, covering over 6,000 companies worldwide (Stellner et al., 2015; Ioannou & Serafeim, 2010). Following the ASSET4 classification of CSR disclosure, which is mainly based on the GRI guidelines, both environmental and social disclosure are divided into several main categories. In total, the environmental part comprises 46 data points a company can report on, for the social part 44 data points are included. Table 4.3 shows the main categories of disclosure.

Table 4.1 Sample distribution

Industry	N
Utilities	18
Industrials	12
Consumer non-cyclicals	21
Financials	27
Basic materials	27
Consumer cyclicals	6
Energy	9
Health care	3
Telecommunications services	6
Total	**129**

Table 4.2 Operationalization

	Abbreviation	*Explanation*	*Data Collection*	*Literature*
Total CSR disclosure	CSRDTOT	Total number of reported items, dependent	Datastream ASSET4	Cho et al., 2013; Gamerschlag et al., 2011; Khan et al., 2013
Environmental CSR disclosure	CSRDENV	Number of reported items (1/0), dependent	Datastream ASSET4	Cho et al., 2013; Gamerschlag et al., 2011
Social CSR disclosure	CSRDSOC	Number of reported items (1/0), dependent	Datastream ASSET4	Cho et al., 2013; Gamerschlag et al., 2011
Visibility	VISIBILITY	Hits when searching for company's name, independent	LexisNexis	Bowen, 2000; Gamerschlag et al., 2011; Reverte, 2009
Shareholder structure	FREEFLOAT	Free float in percentage of shares, independent	Annual and sustainability reports	Gamerschlag et al., 2011, Reverte, 2009; Roberts, 1992
Profitability	ROA	Return on assets, independent	Thomson one	Ho and Taylor, 2007; Khan, 2010; Ng and Koh, 1994
Board independence	BOARDIND	Percentage of independent board members, independent	Annual and sustainability reports	Chen and Jaggi, 2000; Eng and Mak, 2003; Said et al., 2009; Web, 2004
Control Variables				
Industry classification	IND	1/0, independent	Thomson Reuter (TRBC)	Brammer and Millington, 2006; Gamerschlag, 2011
Company's size	EMPL	Number of employees, independent	Annual and sustainability reports	Gamerschlag et al., 2011; Tagesson et al., 2009
	TA	Total assets, independent	Thomson one	Brammer and Pavelin, 2006; Gamerschlag et al., 2011; Khan, 2010

Table 4.3 Dimensions of disclosure

Total CSR disclosure (90 data points)	
Environmental Social	*Environmental Social*
Emissions reduction	Employment quality
Resource reduction	Training and development
Product innovation	Diversity
	Human rights
	Community
	Product responsibility

All data points are scored as a dummy; a score of (1) if a company reports on this data point, a score of (0) if the company does not report on this data point. Finally, these dummy scores combined give an overall score on total CSR disclosure. In addition, an overall score for environmental and social disclosure is calculated. By doing so, the dependent variable can be used as a metric variable, which is one of the criteria for regression analysis.

Independent Variables

Company visibility is closely related to the amount of media exposure the company receives. Gamerschlag et al. (2011) argue that the degree of visibility can be explained by the quantity of press coverage. Therefore, visibility is measured by the number of hits when searching for the company's name in the LexisNexis Academic database.

The free float, as percentage of common shares, is used as a measure for the company's dispersion of the shareholder structure. Roberts (1992) argued that the degree to which the ownership of company shares is distributed in the hands of a few large investors or distributed among many shareholders has been assumed to influence CSR disclosure. The data are gathered via annual reports, sustainability reports, or other corporate documents.[1]

Profitability is measured by the ratio "return on assets" (ROA). The ROA can be calculated by dividing the net income by total assets. These data will be collected via the Thomson one database. It is argued that highly profitable companies are more exposed to political pressure and public exposure and, therefore, disclose more CSR-related information (Ng & Koh, 1994).

Board independence is measured by the number of independent board members. Said et al. (2009) argue that the degree of board independence is related to the composition of the board. A board member is considered independent if they are form outside the company and are not socially tied to management (Hoitash, 2011). These data are collected via annual reports, sustainability reports, or other corporate documents.

Control Variables

The control variables for this research include company size, industry membership, and time. By including these control variables, this study controls for the effect of company size, industry membership, and time on the regression results.

Company size is the first control variable. Larger companies tend to be more visible to society and in addition often face greater political and other stakeholder pressures (Meek et al., 1995; Roberts, 1992; Watts & Zimmerman, 1978). To reduce possible political and societal costs, large companies tend to be more inclined to disclose more CSR-related information (Brammer & Pavelin, 2006). In line with research of Brammer and Pavelin (2006) and Gamerschlag et al. (2011), company size is measured by total assets (TA). This datum is collected via the Thomson one database. For an additional analysis, the number of employees (EMPL) is used as a proxy for company size. This datum is gathered via annual reports and sustainability reports.

The second control variable is industry membership. Brammer and Millington (2006) argue that the level of stakeholder pressures and the resulting political costs are related to the industry the company belongs to. With regard to environmental CSR, it is argued that companies with a high environmental impact will receive more attention and pressure from stakeholders, such as environmental interest groups (Gamerschlag et al., 2011). The classification of Thomson Reuters (TRBC) is used to classify the sample companies in nine industries. Dummy variables are used to distinguish between industries. The industry financials are used as benchmark. See Table 4.1 for the sample distribution based on industry.

The last control variable is time. Year dummies for 2010–2012 are included, whereby YR2010 is used as a benchmark.

6. Data Analysis and Results

6.1. Data Preparation

To determine whether these variables are useful in this study, the number of missing values per variable are evaluated (Hair et al., 2014). None of them is candidate for deletion, as all variables possess less than 15% of missing values (Hair et al., 2014). This is also true for the dependent variables and the metric control variables.

In addition, a univariate and bivariate analysis of the dataset is performed. Table 4.4 reports the descriptive statistics of the dependent, independent, and the metric control variables, including the transformed variables.

As indicated in the previous section, if a company would fully disclose about its CSR activities, the maximum score for CSRDTOT would be 90. The descriptive statistics for this specific sample indicate a maximum score of 67, which implies that no company in this sample fully discloses

Table 4.4 Descriptive Statistics

Variable	N	*Min.*	*Max.*	*Mean*	*Std. Dev*	*Skewness*		*Kurtosis*	
						Std. Statistic	*Error*	*Std. Statistic*	*Error*
Dependent Variables									
CSRDTOT	126	1.00	67.00	41.82	17.71	–0.418	0.216	–1.154	0.428
C SRDT O T_sqrt_rev	126	1.73	8.31	5.02	1.73	0.045	0.216	–1.230	0.428
CSRDSOC	126	1.00	38.00	24.60	8.55	–0.461	0.216	–0.843	0.428
CSRDENV	126	0.00	35.00	17.21	10.08	–0.217	0.216	–1.180	0.428
Independent Variables									
Visibility	126	3.00	1455.00	269.29	287.85	1.487	0.216	1.884	0.428
LnVisibility	126	1.10	7.28	4.95	1.25	– 0.314	0.216	–0.519	0.428
FreeFloat	126	1.80	100.00	46.57	21.19	0.813	0.216	0.597	0.428
ROA	126	0.76	50.82	10.06	9.65	2.054	0.216	4.592	0.428
LnROA	126	–0.27	3.93	1.94	0.87	0.072	0.216	–0.308	0.428
Board independence	126	0.00	77.00	30.65	18.58	0.750	0.216	0.144	0.428
Control Variables									
TA	126	445662.50	1149307548.00	69183348.26	173489510.20	4.076	0.216	18.866	0.428
LnTA	126	13.01	20.86	16.49	1.63	0.578	0.216	0.548	0.428
Empl	123	842.00	158509.00	34299.35	40880.96	1.400	0.218	0.674	0.433
LnEmpl	123	6.74	11.97	9.6637	1.36	–0.165	0.218	–0.663	0.433
Valid N (listwise)	123								

about its CSR activities or is involved in all aspects of CSR. Moreover, the results indicate a maximum score of 38 out of 44 for social CSR disclosure and 35 out of 46 for environmental CSR disclosure. In addition, when comparing the mean of social and environmental CSR disclosure, the results indicate that companies on average disclose more on their social CSR activities (μ = 55.9%) than on their environmental CSR activities (μ = 37.4%).

Table 4.5 presents the correlations of the dependent, independent, and metric control variables, whereas the year dummy and industry dummies are excluded from the table.

The correlation matrix indicates a significant negative correlation between CSRDTOT and LnVisibility and Board independence. In addition, the correlation coefficient of the independent variables is assessed. The results indicate no collinearity between the independent variables as the coefficients do not exceed the critical value of 0.9 (Hair et al., 2014). The correlation coefficients of the dependent variables report correlations close to and exceeding the critical value of 0.9 (Hair et al., 2014). However, this can be explained by CSRDSOC and CSRDENV being part of CSRDTOT. Finally, the correlation coefficient of the control variable total assets (TA) and independent variables Visibility and ROA are relatively high and significant. These correlations might need extra attention when analyzing the regression results.

Table 4.5 Correlation Matrix

		1.	*2.*	*3.*	*4.*	*5. 6. 7. 8. 9.*
1.	1. CSRDTOT	1				
2.	CSRDSOC	** **0.941**	1			
3.	CSRDENV	** **0.958**	**0.805****	1		
4.	LnVisibility	**−0.229**	***−0.182**	** **−0.247**	1	
5.	FreeFloat	−0.108	−0.054	−0.145	0.088	1
6.	LnROA	0.077	0.104	0.046	**−0.288****	−0.013 1
7.	Board independence	**−0.201****	−0.148	**−0.227***	−0.160	**0.254**** 0.049 1
8.	LnEmpl	**−0.258****	****−0.253**	**−0.239****	**−0.408****	**0.237**** **−0.428**** 0.028 1
9.	LnTA	−0.046	−0.051	−0.037	**0.528****	0.001 **−0.515**** −0.138 **0.683**** 1

**. Correlation is significant at the 0.01 level (2-tailed).
*. Correlation is significant at the 0.05 level (2-tailed).

6.2. Analysis

After adjusting the variables to get the best fit, the dataset is prepared to execute the regression analysis. Table 4.6 presents the results of the regression analysis, which is build up in three models. Model 1 comprises only the independent variables, Model 2 the control variables, and Model 3 is the full model which includes both the independent and control variables. For this model, Total Assets (LnTA) is used as the proxy for company size.

Visibility: natural logarithm of visibility, FreeFloat: free float in percentage of shares, ROA: natural logarithm of ROA; net income divided by total assets, Board independence: percentage of independent board members, Size: natural logarithm of total assets.

The *P* scores for CSRDTOT are reversed back to interpret them correctly.

Table 4.6 Regression Analysis

			Model 1	*Model 2*		*Model 3*	
N		*Prediction*	126	126		126	
R2			0.133	0.329		0.411	
Adj. R2 F value			0.104	0.264		0.331	
			4.645	5.084		5.120	
			(P = 0.002)	*(P = 0.000)*		*(P = 0.000)*	
			Sig.	*Sig*		*Sig*	
Visibility	H1	+	−0.298***			−0.248**	0.036
			0.001				
FreeFloat	H2	+	−0.031			−0.113	0.186
			0.729				
ROA	H3	+	−0.024			−0.009	0.915
			0.791				
Board Independence	H4	+	−0.255***			−0.180**	0.035
			0.005				
Size (TA)		−/+		0.147	0.137	0.246**	0.045
Utilities		−/+		0.471***	0.000	0.288**	0.011
Industrials		−/+		0.351***	0.000	0.189**	0.046
ConsNonCycl		−/+		0.335***	0.001	0.114	0.278
BasicMaterials		−/+		0.297***	0.004	−0.220*	0.062
ConsCycl		−/+		0.326***	0.000	0.158*	0.089
Energy		−/+		−0.008	0.929	−0.092	0.358
Health care		−/+		0.362***	0.000	0.241***	0.007
TelComServ		−/+		0.000	0.998	−0.139	0.119
2011		−/+		0.037	0.675	0.039	0.649
2012		−/+		0.114	0.197	0.102	0.232

Notes: *, **, and *** significant at *p*-value < 0.10, 0.05, 0.01 (two-tailed test).

Model 1

The multiple regression model statistically significantly predicts CSRDTOT ($F(4,121) = 4.465$, $P < 0.01$). R2 for the overall model is 13.3% with an adjusted R2 of 10.4%. This indicates that the variables entered explain 10.4% of the variance in CSRDTOT.

The regression results in Table 4.6 indicate that the coefficient for Visibility is a significant negative predictor of CSR disclosure ($\beta = -0.298$, $p < 0.01$). In addition, the coefficient of FreeFloat indicates a negative and non-significant relationship ($\beta = -0.031$, $p = 0.729$) toward total CSR disclosure. The same is true for ROA ($\beta = -0.024$, $p = 0.791$). Finally, board independence has a significant negative influence on total CSR disclosure ($\beta = -0.255$, $p < 0.01$).

Model 2

Model 2 comprises only the control variables. The regression results indicate that the model statistically significantly predicts CSRDTOT ($F(11,114) = 5.084$, $P < 0.01$). R2 for the overall model is 32.9% with an adjusted R2 of 26.4%. This indicates that the variables entered explain 26.4% of the variance in CSRDSOC.

For the control variables, industry membership significantly predicts total CSR disclosure. This is true because at least one of industry dummies is significant.

Model 3

Model 3 represents the full model, including both the independent and dependent variables. The multiple regression model statistically significantly predicts CSRDTOT ($F(15,110) = 5.120$, $P < 0.01$). R2 for the overall model is 41.1% with an adjusted R2 of 33.1%. This indicates that the variables entered explain 33.1% of the variance in CSRDTOT.

The regression results for the independent variables in Model 3 indicate similar results as described for Model 1. The coefficient for visibility is a significant negative predictor of total CSR disclosure ($\beta = -0.248$, $p < 0.05$). The coefficients for both freefloat ($\beta = -0.113$, $p = 0.168$) and ROA ($\beta = -0.009$, $p = 0.915$) indicate negative and non-significant relationships towards total CSR disclosure. Finally, board independence is a significant negative predictor of total CSR disclosure ($\beta = -0.180$, $p < 0.05$).

For Model 3, several control variables are found to be significantly related toward total CSR disclosure. The coefficient of total assets (TA) indicates a significant positive relationship ($\beta = 0.260$, $p < 0.05$). For industry to be significantly related to CSR disclosure, at least one of the industry dummies has to be significant. This is true, indicating that the industry membership of a company influences its CSR disclosure. Finally, the year dummies (YR2011/2012) do not report a significant effect.

6.3. Additional Analyses

In the first regression model, total assets (TA) is entered as a proxy for company size. The correlation matrix indicated relatively high correlations between total assets and the independent variables; visibility and ROA. Therefore, as an additional analysis, total assets is replaced by the number of employees (Empl) to check for changes in the effect of the control variable size. The regression results in Table 4.7 indicate that all models (4, 5, and 6) significantly predict the dependent variable. Model 4 reports $F(4,121) = 4.645$, $p < 0.01$, adjusted $R2 = 10.4\%$, Model 5 reports

Table 4.7

			Model 4		*Model 5*		*Model 6*	
N			123		123		123	
R2			0.133		0.327		0.392	
Adj. R2			0.104		0.260		0.307	
F value			4.645		4.903		4.599	
			(P = 0.002)		*(P = 0.000)*		*(P = 0.000)*	
	Prediction			*Sig.*		*Sig.*		*Sig.*
Visibility	H1	+	**−0.298** ***	0.001			−0.049	0.691
FreeFloat	H2	+	−0.031	0.729			−0.115	0.208
ROA	H3	+	−0.024	0.791			−0.100	0.275
Board independence	H4	+	**−0.255** ***	0.005			**−0.183** **	0.040
Size (Empl)		−/+			**−0.162** *	0.088	−0.149	0.229
Utilities		−/+			0.082	0.443	0.109	0.390
Industrials		−/+			0.043	0.641	0.100	0.273
ConsNonCycl		−/+			−0.012	0.904	0.044	0.661
BasicMaterials		−/+			**−0.372** ***	0.000	**−0.370** ***	0.001
ConsCycl		−/+			0.074	0.393	0.084	0.331
Energy		−/+			**−0.223** **	0.012	**−0.184** *	0.067
Healthcare		−/+			0.126	0.154	0.139	0.108
TelComServ		−/+			**−0.250** **	0.018	**−0.164** *	0.074
2011		−/+			0.042	0.637	0.051	0.557
2012		−/+			0.107	0.235	0.105	0.234

Notes: *, **, and *** significant at p-value < 0.10, 0.05, 0.01 (two-tailed test).

$F(11,111) = 4.903$, $p < 0.01$, adjusted R2 = 26.0% and Model 6 reports $F(15,107) = 4599$, $p < 0.01$, adjusted R2 = 30.7%.

The results for Model 4 are similar to the results as described for Model 1. In addition to industry membership as a significant predictor of total CSR disclosure, Model 5 also reports number of employees (as a proxy for size) ($\beta = -0.162$, $p < 0.1$) to be significantly predicting total CSR disclosure. It is to be noted that size is only significant at the lowest level ($p<0.01$). Moreover, the direction of this relationship is negative.

The regression results of Model 6 indicate that for all independent variables, only board independence ($\beta = -0.183$, $p < 0.05$) has a significant effect on CSR disclosure. However, different than expected, this effect has a negative direction. Other than in Model 3, visibility no longer indicates a significant relationship. This might be explained by the relatively strong correlation between total assets and visibility. Moreover, the results indicate that the control variable number of employees does not report a significant influence on CSR disclosure. Finally, industry membership indicates a significant effect on CSR disclosure.

See Table 4.6 for variable definitions. Size: natural logarithm of number of employees. The β scores for CSRDTOT are reversed back to interpret them correctly.

6.4. Hypotheses Testing

Based on the empirical results as presented in Table 4.6, the hypotheses of this study will be either accepted or rejected. Table 4.8 gives an overview of the hypotheses testing. Hypothesis 1 stated that company visibility is positively associated with the CSR disclosure of MNEs in emerging markets. The results indicate that visibility is significantly related to total CSR disclosure. However, different than hypothesized the direction of the relationship is negative. This indicates that the less visible a company

Table 4.8 Hypotheses Testing

Hypothesis		*Result*
H1	Visibility is positively associated with CSR disclosure.	Visibility is negatively associated with CSR disclosure.
H2	Shareholder structure is positively associated with CSR disclosure.	No significant relationship
H3	Profitability is positively associated with CSR disclosure.	No significant relationship
H4	Board independence is positively associated with CSR disclosure.	Board independence is negatively associated with CSR disclosure.

is, the higher the likelihood that the company will disclose on its CSR-related activities. As a positive relationship was expected, Hypothesis 1 is rejected.

Furthermore, Hypothesis 2 stressed that a more dispersed shareholder structure is positively associated with CSR disclosure of MNEs in an emerging market. In other words, the higher the percentage of freefloat of a company's shares, the more the company will disclose on its CSR-related activities. The results report no significant relationship between free float and CSR disclosure for MNEs in emerging markets. Consequently, Hypothesis 2 is rejected.

In addition, Hypothesis 3 stated that profitability is positively associated with CSR disclosure of MNEs in emerging markets. Profitability was measured by the return on assets (ROA). It was expected that the higher the ROA percentage, the more likely a company would disclose on its CSR-related activities. However, the results report no significant relationship, and therefore, Hypotheses 3 is rejected.

Finally, Hypothesis 4 stressed that board independence is positively associated with CSR disclosure of MNEs in emerging markets. The results indicate that board independence is significantly related to total CSR disclosure. However, different than hypothesized, the direction of this relationship is negative. This indicates that the less independent board members, the higher the likelihood that a company will close on its CSR-related activities. As a positive relationship was hypothesized, Hypothesis 4 is rejected.

Empirical investigations also show interesting results on the control variables. The first regression analysis (see Table 4.6) indicates that industry membership is a significant predictor for CSR disclosure. This remains true in the full model (Model 3) where the independent variables are added. Moreover, the adjusted R2 in Model 1 (independent variables) is 10.4%, whereas the adjusted R2 in Model 2 (control variables) is 26.4%. This indicates that the variables entered in Model 2 explain more of the variance in CSR disclosure than the variables entered in Model 1.

In the second regression analysis (see Table 4.7), total assets as a proxy for size is replaced by number of employees. Model 5 indicates that both size and industry membership are significant predictors for CSR disclosure; however, in the full model, only industry membership remains significant. The results again suggest that the control variable industry membership is a significant predictor for CSR disclosure. The adjusted R2 supports this argument as it reports 10.4% for Model 4 only comprising of the independent variables, and 26.0% for Model 5. This indicates that the control variables, as entered in the fifth model, explain more of the variance in the dependent variable CSR disclosure than the variables entered in Model 4.

7. Discussion and Conclusion

This study makes a contribution to the literature about CSR disclosure, while focusing on possible determinants of CSR disclosure. Other than most research conducted in this field, this study focuses on emerging markets as its research context. The research question underlying this study is, What are the determinants of CSR disclosure in emerging markets? Based on the political cost theory, four hypotheses are developed. Theory suggests that a company's visibility, shareholder structure, profitability, and board independence are positively associated with CSR disclosure. However, the empirical findings of the multiple regression analysis do not provide statistical proof for the hypotheses.

Contrary to previous research of Gamerschlag et al. (2011), for example, this study does not provide evidence that the more visible a company is, the more the company will disclose on its CSR-related activities. Different than hypothesized, the significant relationship reports a negative direction, which suggest that the less visible a company is, the more they will disclose on their CSR-related activities. A possible explanation could be related to companies' sensitivity toward pressures from stakeholders, as it was argued that a higher level of visibility would be related to more pressures from stakeholders. However, Doh et al. (2015) argued that emerging market companies tend to be less sensitive to pressures from stakeholders.

Furthermore, although prior studies (e.g., Chen & Jaggi, 2001; Eng & Mak, 2003) highlight the importance of independent board members for CSR disclosure, the empirical results do not support this argument. A significant relationship is found; however, the direction of the relationship is negative. This suggests that companies with less independent board members disclose more on their CSR-related activities. A possible explanation could be related to the governance environment in emerging markets, which tends to be weaker than in developed markets. This might influence CSR disclosure due to an absence and/or inefficiencies of formal laws and regulations on information disclosure.

In addition, no significant relationships are found for shareholder structure and profitability towards CSR disclosure. Finally, the regression results indicate that the proposed determinants do not have a strong predictive power with regard to the variation in the dependent variable total CSR disclosure.

Although not hypothesized, the results indicate that industry membership is a significant determinant of CSR disclosure in emerging markets. This suggests that the industry a company is part of will influence its disclosure on CSR-related activities. This is in line with previous research (e.g., Ho & Taylor, 2007; Khan, 2010; Haniffa & Cooke, 2005)

Possible explanations for the differences in empirical findings can be related to the context of this study. As described before, there are still major differences between emerging markets and developed markets. Unlike developed markets, emerging markets are often characterized by a lack of norms and values of business standards due to unstable socio-economic and political conditions (Peter et al., 2011). Without standardization, companies can decide for themselves how to deal with CSR-related activities and eventually the disclosure of these activities. An example of standardization with regard to CSR is the GRI guidelines. The GRI promotes the use of standard practices for CSR reporting for all companies and organizations. Contrary to Western companies, only a small amount of emerging market companies has adopted the framework (GRI, 2016). This suggests that there is still room for improvement for emerging market companies to keep up with their Western equivalents.

Moreover, several researchers argued that CSR means different things to different stakeholders and companies in different countries (Dawkins & Lewis, 2003; Igalens & Gond, 2005; Welford et al., 2008). This suggests that the determinants of CSR disclosure can be different for each country or each research context. As the proposed determinants were all related to company-specific characteristics, possible context-specific determinants have not been taken into account.

In addition, the proposed hypotheses are based on the political cost theory, which relates to the stakeholder approach. As described before, there are two competing views toward CSR: the shareholder approach (neoclassical economics) and the stakeholder approach. Followers of the shareholder approach argue that a company's main objective is to maximize the shareholder value and that they should only undertake actions which either increase profits or decrease costs (Friedman, 2007; Husted & Salzar, 2006). In addition, Doh et al. (2015) argue that emerging market companies are less sensitive to pressures from stakeholders to engage in CSR practices, among others because they put greater emphasis on the basic value proposition of their company and because they are less aware of the environmental and social issues. This suggests that a shareholder perspective, contrary to the stakeholder approach used as base for this study, might be relevant as well in defining determinants of CSR disclosure.

With regard to the content of the study, a possible explanation for the low predictive power of the independent variables could be that the proposed firm-specific determinants, which are based on previous research, are not completely relevant for the emerging market context. Other researchers (e.g., Ho & Taylor, 2007; Reverte, 2009) have approached the defining of determinants from an industry- and/or country-specific perspective (meso and macro level), which could be interesting in analyzing to better predict CSR disclosure in emerging markets.

Finally, a measurement-related explanation could be that CSR disclosure is measured based on a scale of 0–90 to determine whether a company discloses on a specific topic or not. In prior research, different methods, such as measuring the extent of CSR disclosure (e.g., Michelon et al., 2015) are used as well and could possibly lead to different results.

7.1. Theoretical and Managerial Implications

This study contributes to the existing literature on CSR disclosure by examining the relationship between possible determinants of CSR disclosure and

CSR disclosure. As most research concerning this topic has been conducted in developed markets (Fetscherin et al., 2010), this study touches upon a relatively new research setting: emerging markets. In addition, this study contributes to the existing literature by providing empirical data for CSR disclosure in emerging markets.

An attempt to define possible determinants of CSR in emerging markets has been made, while relying on political cost theory and taking a stakeholder perspective. A narrow focus has been chosen as firm-specific characteristics were introduced as the base of this study. The empirical significance of the theoretical framework, as presented in Chapter 2, is tested using four independent variables that could possibly act as determinants of CSR disclosure. The proposed determinants were found to be significant and positively related to CSR disclosure in a developed market context. However, in the emerging market context no statistical proof is found to support the relationship between the proposed firm-specific determinants and CSR disclosure, as none of the hypotheses is confirmed, although industry membership and size were found to be significant predictors of CSR disclosure in emerging markets.

As this research touched upon a small part of this relatively new research setting, it could possibly be the starting point in defining the determinants of CSR disclosure in emerging markets. Therefore, future research is necessary to extent knowledge and theories.

This study on CSR determinants of MNEs in emerging markets proposes some interesting insights for managers and policy makers. First of all, this study provides them with insights regarding this specific research context. A point of consideration could be that emerging market companies tend to be less sensitive to stakeholder pressures and in addition, tend to be less aware of CSR issues than developed market companies (Doh et al., 2015). Managers of developed market companies, intending to set up businesses in emerging markets, should take into consideration that the corporate motives for emerging market companies to engage in CSR disclosure might be different than the motives for developed market companies. As Meek et al. (1995) argued, understanding the underlying motives is useful to both the preparers and users of the disclosed information, as well as to policy makers.

Furthermore, emerging markets are often characterized by a lack of norms and values of business standards (Peter et al., 2011), and in addition, the CSR guidelines are often not yet adopted (GRI, 2016). This conception requires further development and mutual learning for emerging market companies to keep up with their Western equivalents.

7.2. Limitations and Suggestions for Future Research

This study has several limitations of which most can be transformed into suggestions for future research. First of all, the sample of this study was rather small considering the amount of MNEs in Brazil. The data for measuring the dependent variable CSR disclosure was gathered via the DataStream

Asset 4 ESG database, which only provided the data for 48 Brazilian MNEs. In addition, the industry membership classification is open to criticism, as some industries are represented by only a few companies. To overcome this limitation, future research could focus on extending the dataset, which could lead to different empirical results.

Second, the four determinants tested for this study are not exclusive. This study only takes into account firm-specific determinants, while leaving out possible industry- and country-specific determinants. Therefore, other determinants, as identified in previous research, could be included as well to identify the determinants of CSR disclosure. In addition, as the results indicate, the proposed model is not particularly applicable to the emerging market context. Future research should focus on identifying determinants specifically related to CSR disclosure in emerging markets. It would be interesting to take into account country- and context-specific aspects, as there are some important differences on these aspects between the developed- and emerging-market context (Belal, 2008; Belal, & Momin, 2009; Peter et al., 2011; Doh et al., 2015).

Third, as only one country has been researched, the cultural aspects can't be generalized. Future research could focus on analyzing data from other emerging markets, especially the (B)RIC (Russia, India, and China), to extend the empirical evidence for the emerging market context and make comparisons between these countries possible.

Finally, the increasing awareness of CSR in emerging markets demands more insights on CSR disclosure in this specific context (Fetscherin et al., 2010). Therefore, future research on this topic is necessary to fully understand the concepts of CSR disclosure and the determinants of CSR disclosure in emerging markets. As this study was fully based on quantitative data, future research could focus on gathering more qualitative data, for example, through interviews. These data could give more insight into the actual motives of emerging market companies to disclose on their CSR-related activities.

Notes

* This chapter was written in collaboration with Iris Braun.

1 Form 20-F, Reference form.

5 Social Responsibility and Its Involvement in the Economic Growth

1. The Endorsement of Internal Affairs and Economic Development

The attainment of a propitious business environment to carry on affairs constitutes a central element of Romania's economic politics, knowing the fact that providing auspicious terms is of a crucial importance for initiating and developing businesses on a free, competitive, and globalized market. The endorsement and development of the business environment is a field in which public intervention by elements of public politics can take the most various shapes and can have a significant impact on the economic growth. The public authority sets its objectives, the action lines, and also specific features within a complex process of strategic planning.

Creating an open and stimulating business environment for economic growth implies the following directions of action:

- An establishment of the dialogue structures between the government and business environment
- Providing a stable framework for settlement in accordance with international practices that consists of the uniform appliance of legislation and maintaining a climate for business, equitable for every investor; the active participation of the business environment in adopting the regulations; bureaucracy reduction; confronting the business environment experience with the expertise of public institutions having a regulating role
- Reducing the administrative barriers at the entrance/exit of the firms on the market
- The advantages of permanent monitoring of the public/private dialogue

The production and global competition increase the global economic efficiency because the global firms stimulate an international division of work so that the countries become more specialized in producing goods in which they own a competitive advantage. The firms constitute one of the most representative agents of contemporary economic progress. They are the vectors that promote the advanced technologies and wealth, contributing to the improvement of the living and business environment.

Romania's EU integration and its participation in the North Atlantic Treaty Organization, as in other agreements, treaties, and regional or bilateral conventions, made from it an equal partner in Europe and worldwide, offering advantageous terms to foreign investors and multinational companies.

Within an open and stimulating context of business environment for economy development stands out the necessity for a competitive culture. Among the most important factors that impose the knitting of a competitive culture, we mention the efficient application of competition by increasing the visibility of authority in the field, respecting the law, competition, and also receiving benefits from the state, transparency through permanent informing of the pubic; monitoring and influencing economic politics through consulting, selecting, assessing, and promoting criteria that are not making from benefits an element of distortion for competition. The role of firms in the economy is double: economic and social. *The economic role* is affected as follows: the companies attract and combine the production factors, and managers are permanently responsible for optimizing the combination of production factors; the purpose of companies is to provide goods and perform services, and the managers intend to produce at minimum costs; the companies deliver the incomes, meaning the remuneration of used production factors. *The social role* is contained in the fact that firms are economic agents whose activity cannot be studied but in the existent social context. The firms express a specific role: toward employees, the managers need to favor promoting of the staff and its participation in recycling, imposed by the streamline of techniques and technology to create conditions for cultural promoting; and toward consumers, the firm has to search the best arrangements of goods and services solicited by clients.

These are difficult to achieve, and that leads to a series of contradictions: between the employees' wages and owners' capital; between the interests of shareholders' incomes who want to earn as much as they can and consumers' who want to buy at the lowest price.

In the struggle for success, the companies deal with a great number of challenges. These are given by the national context, by history, and short experience in the business field, by the development degree of the country and its people. They can also be given by the context of globalization, by opening borders and eliminating barriers, by the competition between the companies and foreign products, by new technologies and the ways to produce and the market, and others being given by their internal capacity to manage in a competitive manner their own activities and resources. Romania's integration in the EU joined with the globalization phenomena of business, disparage the differences from technologies and the know-how field. The European market is also open for Romanian companies, the labor market has liberated, and the capital flows without restrictions. The globalization represented a catalyzer of redefining the corporations' universe. It opened the way to development of corporations as leaders, and the latter contributed to the globalization of the market. The globalization dictates the strategic decisions to corporations, including the internationalism, and these in return, next to state authorities, transpose it into practice and establish the degree to which these phenomena are accomplished.

An issue that Romania deals with is a delay in the globalization race. Because it experienced a communist environment, in a controlled state economy, Romania is among the countries that benefited last from the transportation revolution, communications, work productivity, and finally, information. Thus, the expensive products, inefficient economy, galloping inflation, and the crushing Western competition, put the Romanian economy in the corner.

A foreign capital is needed for development, because Romania cannot produce capital only from the internal sources. Because it is a country with various economic opportunities, tourism, agriculture, mineral oils, and metallurgic industry, Romania can become attractive to foreign capital, if it provides prosperous legislative and fiscal terms. Hence, the rapid mobilization of capital brought by globalization, in which companies lose their classical "national" identity, can become advantageous in terms of highly qualified labor, but cheap by comparison. On the other hand, some companies can gradually start to play a regional or international role in the future. It all depends on the speed with which the economic difficulties will be overstepped nowadays, developing the capacity of real partnerships. Even if there is a discrepancy between the CSR abroad and in Romania, the reality demonstrates that we are heading in the best direction, and in the following years, we will assist to a powerful development of this segment.

Romania needs to take measures for implementing corporate governance and to integrate corporative responsibility politics in the business strategy. The promoting of responsible products has to be outlined in addition to the charity acts. An important tendency will be the involvement of employees in social responsibility. In addition to voluntary programs, companies consult with its employees, who become an important factor in the decision making concerning CSR directions. Also, an even greater number of actions that endorse the social dialogues must be emphasized.

2. Corporate Involvement in the CSR Activities at the National Level

There are many companies that invest in the social development and in the community they belong to, wanting to be in a public spotlight with valuable initiatives. Every company has the areas of involvement, choosing to finance organizations with specific feature with a certain experience, projects that take place nationally, and not only in certain communities where the company operates.

We live in a world where temperatures are rising, water resources are diminished, energy is expensive, providing food is uncertain, and the gap between the rich and the poor is expanding. The sustainable and impartial development is the only acceptable model of activity.

By CSR politics, Orange Romania suggested to support, with the technologies they develop, the changes that take place in the society. However, the following priority actions have been established within the CSR strategy:

- To offer their employees the possibility to grow and develop
- To offer their clients transparent, safe, and quality services
- To adopt innovating solutions for environment protection
- To ease the access to technology for as many people as possible, especially for disadvantaged categories (people from the rural areas, disaster zones, and people with disabilities)

The main fields in which Orange Romania invests in considering the community development are education, technology access for people from the disadvantaged categories, and supporting people with communication disabilities.

The most important educational program of the company is the Orange Education Programme. Through the program, Orange offered students from the Polytechnic Economic Studies, the University of Bucharest, a chance to study thoroughly and to practice the accumulated knowledge during the studies through specialized courses.

Another initiative in the same field is represented by introducing on the market a new phone for older people. The phone is equipped with a large keyboard, loud volume, voice dial of the keys, and a button for emergency calls.

"You for Community" is a program through which the company stimulates its employees to actively participate in the communities they belong to, offering them a day off in exchange. The company is actively fulfilling its responsibility toward its employees and clients by initiating some inciting programs of involving employees into community. In a close cooperation with Green Revolution Association, Orange provides bicycles for employees to facilitate employees' shifting of professional interest. The program has started in 2010, and ever since more than 1,500 employees have borrowed bikes. The company follows the decision by the National Authority for Administration Regulation in Communications and publishes four times per year the quality indicators for provided services.

Orange Romania tries to decrease the carbon imprint in many ways. One of these is the reduction of energy consumption and resources. In the company's headquarters, there is a system of automatic computer shut-down after 8 PM and another one for collecting and recycling paper and printer cartridges. Moreover, the management announced that the company will be relocated into an efficient-energy-system building. That is the Green Court

Bucharest, a building project with a power-efficient facade, an environmental management policy, lighting system based on movement detection, and increasing number of charging stations for electric cars.

Unilever Romania, launched in 2010 a sustainable development strategy, called Unilever Project for a Sustainable Lifestyle. It includes the CSR objectives that the company strives to accomplish by 2020 in areas such as lowering the negative impact on environment, improving the lifestyle of consumers, employees, and providers, and ensuring a lifelong sustainability for their products.

The National Society of Natural Gas, Romgaz SA, is the biggest gas producer with a share market of almost 47%. They carried on a consultation process for interested parties, that allowed to identify, according to their expectations and concern, the strategic directions of social implication of the company. Consequently, the company decided to endorse initiatives in areas such as education, community development, health, environment, and promoting Romanian sports. They took initiatives in education such as school dropout prevention programs, a youth film project, and projects to stimulate education among young people.

In 2015, they signed a partnership with UNICEF Romania and committed financially to state the case for implementing prevention of absenteeism and dropping out of school in disadvantaged communities. "Cinema-edu" is a film education project initiated by Macondo Cultural Association. Within the project, film premieres, productions about social issues of young people, and animations and documentaries are presented in high schools. Together with Education for Europe Association from Cluj-Napoca, the company identified and awarded high school students who achieved outstanding results in 35 communities from Transylvania, where the company operates.

The company is involved in the development local communities through various events in the Natural Gas Romgaz Medias residence, for example, a gift to school library, and with voluntary support from the company employees, they granted financial support for art projects and contemporary culture. Supported by the local authority representatives, organizations, and educational institutions, the company hosts a series of events devoted to the community (book promotions, varnishing and plastic art, symposiums, communication sessions, and national or international celebrations). The company encourages the performance in Romanian sports by financing various activities such as chess, football, basketball, bowling, table tennis, lawn tennis, and model plane flying.

Danone Romania Company is a part of Danone Group, one of the top world leaders in food industry. Globally, Danone Group has undertaken to provide a sustainable food chain by activities displayed in four directions: fighting against climatic changes, protecting water resources, recycling of packages, and promoting sustainable agriculture.

The quality of products is one of company's priorities; thus in 2004, the company was authorized to export to EU states, and in 2006, it obtained the certificate ISO 14001:1996 for an environmental management system. In their laboratories, 20 experts perform between 1,600 and 1,800 analyses every day to provide the best quality of their products. The company has been constantly involved in the social value projects, ever since they entered the market: a program for sustaining small farmers, a project for improving the life of children with cancer, and a sport competition for children.

Among the environmental priorities are recycling of the used materials and using them as new resources, responsible waste management during the production flow, and responsible use of water.

Concerning waste recycling, the company acts in two directions: decreasing the quantity of packaging material on the market by using plastics with reduced density and recycling of packaging materials.

Auchan Romania, one of the biggest retailers from the local market, have celebrated 10 years since the opening of the first hypermarket, together with their consumers. They were invited to choose, for the city they lived in, one of the three community development projects that the company decided to support financially with 10,000 euros.

Auchan Retail Romania and New Horizons Foundation rearrange and supply a series of classrooms from many cities in Romania. For every city, they sponsored 10,000 euros. During sponsorship, a school benefited from new endowments, a non-formal learning laboratory, arranged in a creative manner from scratch, including the library area. Likewise, the teachers are trained in empirical knowledge, through games, stories, and projects.

Mobilizatron campaign called up clients from the eighteen cities where the retailer has 33 stores, inviting them to choose one of the three projects suggested by the campaign for local community development: education (creating alternative educational spaces), humanitarian aid (packages for children and old disadvantaged people), environment (ecological activities or forestation).

Germanos, an important company in Romania, started a CSR action called *Safe Drive*, with the following motto: “Take your life in your own hands!” This campaign implied to inform and educate both drivers as well as the future drivers using hands-free when they drive while are talking on the phone. This is the only safe legally allowed option. Considering some studies made in the United States and Canada, it has been ascertained that the drivers’ absentmindedness leads to 20% to 50% of car accidents. In the main cities such as Bucharest, Cluj, Iasi, and Timisoara, there were 74,960 flyers issued, 87,790 people were informed, 570 students from 20 schools as future drivers were informed on this campaign during the road legislation classes. As a consequence, the company became the signer of European Road Safety Charter.

Raiffeisen Bank spread out the Raiffeisen Communities granting program, which intends to finance small and medium projects in the communities where the bank operates. The bank has been running this online contest since 2011. The goal of the project is to financially support through direct involvement, such as volunteering and consulting, projects with an impact on local communities where the bank activates.

In 2014, Avon Romania presented a financing program for the projects that have as objective early breast cancer detection and intervention, as well as recovery. Within this project, the victims of domestic violence are also supported. This program addresses both the NGOs with an expert report in the two areas and public or private institutions that provide medical or social services that may solve these matters. The actions materialized into informing campaigns and fundraising, but also direct sponsorships toward the oncology institutions from our country. The company initiated the Respect Campaign through the agency of which various staff trainings at the shelter center for victims of domestic violence were organized, and also informing campaigns for the awareness on the matter. All six branches of Habitat for Humanity succeeded to offer a decent living for 16,000 people and other 2,000 Romanians who benefitted from the Disaster Prevention programs.

Rompetrol Group is committed to the environment protection through the Petromidia platform, the main asset of the Group. Among others, this commitment consists of increasing the degree of protection of the Black Sea and Siutghiol Lake, of the Danube Delta biosphere, and Midia Channel afferent ecosystem, as well as Navodari, Corbu, and Constanta. The investments of the Rompetrol Group from the past years in technology and environment on the Petromidia platform amount to over 600 million USD.

The social responsibility is important to Dacia Group Renault. The decrease of the negative impact on environment and preserving of the natural resources, professional development of employees and communities, especially by means of educational projects and investments in culture and diversity stimulation (gender, religion, ethnic, and social origin) are the main objectives of the CSR strategy. Their CSR policies closely reflect the international approach that Renault has on its markets. In 2013, Renault worked out a conduct code for company's acquisitions. That included employees' coerciveness to respect the laws, to treat the contractors equally, to ensure confidentiality, and to respect the CSR principles of the group. An important role in ensuring the gender equality at Renault Group is played by "Women@Renault." As a consequence, the percentage of women hired grew from 10% in 1999 to 17.6% in 2013. Women represent 32% from employees, and 30% among key positions are occupied by women. Furthermore, in engineering and production, women make 28%, which represent an accomplishment, if we consider the fact that this kind of jobs are less attractive to women.

Dacia and Renault have implemented Drive Your Future, a program through which students and master students benefit from apprenticeship practice for at least 3 months in various departments, working under tutors' supervision. The internships are paid. In the last 10 years, over 1,200 young people attended this program, and more than a third were hired by the company after graduation. In addition to that, the company co-finances with the Embassy of France a scholarship program for training professional automobiles building. Furthermore, they provide to the selected candidates with an opportunity to be hired by the company after graduation. In addition to the investments for developing less pollutant products, Dacia made even a more efficient production process. Starting in 2000 on the Mioveni platform, an investment of over 28 million euros has been made for preserving the natural resources, treatment of waste waters, soil, air, and waste resulting from a manufacturing process. In addition, it conducted a successive modernization of automobile manufacturing equipment. All these led to a significant decrease in the negative impact on the environment. In Romania, Dacia supports local communities from Mioveni and Pitesti, financing their projects, even if is through the equipment supply or public education institutions, or organizing cultural-art events. Therefore, a CSR campaign plays an active role forming a constant interaction with the community, and employees of the company are also being proud of participating in such events.

3. Providing Voluntary Activities

Volunteering is a form of learning by practice that helps improving the knowledge and abilities. Volunteering is an important factor that helps in creating a competitive labor on the European market, and at the same time in developing education and professional formation as for the social solidarity growth. The Romanian state acknowledges the social value of volunteering acts as an expression of active citizenship, of solidarity and social responsibility, also being a professional value as expression of personal, professional, intercultural, and linguistic development of the people that participate in these activities.

Finding a place to work after graduating is a touchstone for every new graduate from different points of view especially from the perspective that the majority of the employees prefer to select people with certain working experience. Young people don't have a well-established system to achieve the necessary experience to be hired, so it comes to everyone to research, to imply, and to choose proper voluntary acts to obtain the required experience which will complete the theoretical knowledge from studying.

Volunteering is of a great importance beyond a doubt, and its rightful recognition in the Romanian society is just a matter of time, especially in the European context, where it is considerably more appreciated. All interested factors from Romania concerned with volunteering have to take upon themselves the responsibility of acknowledging its value and to support a quality act, particularly in their field of activity and competence. The main responsibility belongs to the organizers of voluntary activities, who have to offer the experience in quality volunteering, to efficiently coordinate, and to involve the volunteers in a complex impact assessment of voluntary activities.

Petrom and Red Cross spread out a national campaign for training people in case of disasters such as drought-affected Dolj county, educating 600 students concerning the protection standards in case of earthquakes, and the project "Volunteer for a Day." The social cause of the campaign took into consideration the natural calamities that had begun to increasingly trouble conspicuous Romanian lives, in addition to those being mentioned, drought, earthquakes, and floods. To fight the effects of drought in Dolj, three significantly deep wells were drilled, and over 9,000 people benefitted from the fresh water from those wells as a result. Another essential part of the campaign was educating young people from six schools in Bucharest about the proper behavior in case of an earthquake. The organizers chose the capital city because it is an earthquake-prone area. The result of "Volunteer for a Day" materialized in 38 employees from Petrom completing the First Aid course, 80 employees donated blood, and 1,500 people participated in the campaign "Donate Blood! Donate Life!"

An important campaign carried out by Petrom was "Andrei's School." The project consisted of an ample national contest on the environment and civic duties. The project appealed to pupils in the primary schools. There were almost 6,000 pupils and 361 teachers from 320 schools involved.

Orange implements social, cultural-educational, or environmental causes through the agency of social responsibility programs, and the employees are consistently involved as volunteers in activities intended for supporting these causes. To stimulate their employees to participate in voluntary activities, the company offered them a chance to be involved in various activities chosen by them, by organizing a marathon of activities in the interest of community.

The campaign suggested to bring to employees' attention the causes they can sustain, stimulating in this way their participation in the voluntary activities regardless of the city they work in. In this regard, September is the month for corporate volunteering. The activities that the Orange employees were involved in during the "Volunteering Month" were education and environment protection. Among the most important activities that took place are mentorship for high school students; assisting hearing-impaired children in education-recreational activities; assisting children with mental deficiencies; renewing and rearranging educational, social, or medical centers, assisting children with autism during dancing and painting classes, ecological activities within Let's Do It, Romania!

Rompetrol celebrated the Environment Day through an ecological action at Corbu beach. The initiative was a part of the CSR platform of the campaign "Energy Comes From the Heart," and it represented a way for employees to support the communities they work in.

In Romania, the development of volunteering on the local, national, and international level is sustained by respecting its diversity and independence to fulfill the artistic and cultural, sports and recreational activities, scientifically and research, environment, health, social, solidarity, communitarian development, humanitarian aid, civically or philanthropic, and so on. The Romanian state sustains the development of volunteering through all its institutions that operate in the areas in which the voluntary activities are carried out according to the law.

4. The Sponsorship of Local Events

The firms are encouraged by the law to provide consistent sponsorship because it is possible to make deductions from the profit tax, which the firm would otherwise have to pay to the state. A local development can be defined as a process of growth and structural change, which offers welfare for the inhabitants of the locality or region, being a result of the transfer of resources from traditional to modern activities, by economic commitment, introduction, and transmitting innovation. The development of local economy and improving competitiveness are crucial, because the success of communities depends on the level of changes that take place in the external environment. The sponsorship implies supporting the projects carried out by legal people without patrimonial purpose, having as objective educational activities regarding the environment in schools and universities, ecological activities, removing garbage from the environment and recycling it, the activities and measures promoting a healthy lifestyle, sport, and nutrition, without limitations.

5. Labor Force Employment

Romania's EU integration implied that human resources specialists reflect on their role due to the fact they need to contribute to increase the organizational efficiency level. In the business environment, a frequently encountered situation is the current reputation of the HR department, which proves its importance in the firms' sustainability context in Romania. Managers and HR experts need to leave their offices to understand the employees' world they represent. For a fair position of the department, HR specialists need to be open to public relations activities with their employees. Companies find themselves in a perpetual organizational changing to follow the changes in the market, and to survive under these circumstances, they hire motivated people, with a clear vision of the future, who show initiative, team spirit, and the sense of responsibility. The companies need to understand that HR represents the expectations for the future of a firm. It is difficult to set up a firm with such a culture, because the process is long term and expensive, but at the same time, it is crucial for a successful outcome.

The National Agency for Employment oversees the Bucharest agency, 41 county agencies, 8 county centers for professional training of the unemployed, and 8 regional centers for adult professional training.

The main objectives of the National Agency for Employment are

- to institutionalize the social dialogue in employment and professional training area;
- to apply strategies in employment and professional training area; and
- to apply measures of social protection for the unemployed people.

To accomplish their objectives, the National Agency for Employment has the following competences:

- organizes, carries out, and finances, in compliance with the law, professional training services for unemployed people;
- guides the unemployed people and mediates between them and the employers concerning the balance between supply and demand on the internal labor market; and
- implements programs granted from the European Social Fund.

An increase in the interest of large and very large companies is distinguished to externalize the fundamental functions (wage, legal statements, payment obligations, vacation administration) and an increasingly intense cooperation with the recruiting companies to attract specialists. In the last years, a series of promoted reforms was meant to put on a solid base on the pliancy of the labor market, to increase the attendance, and to create stable jobs. That includes revising the Labor Code, emphasizing active politics on the labor market, and improving business environment to reduce companies' costs transactions, including a simplification of companies' registration. The effects were an advantage and led to an increase in the employment rates.

On the other hand, time management, efficiency reckoning, the need for training, career development, and other fundamental issues such as loyalty and an increased employees' profitability, are completely ignored by the HR departments. Regarding the use of the information technology, it is needed only for establishing of a staff strategy. For now, the demand for IT solutions in the HR management comes only for few multinational companies who brought with them the management culture of the groups they belong to.

With regard to the business environment, Romania is concerned with sustaining private companies and stimulating free initiatives. The actions intend to support a more sustainable business environment, to clear away the unjustified economic state monopoly, to consolidate free competition, to increase transparency in the business environment and governmental politics, introduce monetary policies, deregulate the labor market, and disperse the CSR principles into economy.

6 Motives Underlying CSR Practices of Western MNEs in Emerging Economies*

1. Introduction

Although corporate social responsibility (CSR) is a recent term, business ethics, social dimensions, and the general idea of corporate statesmanship have been around for decades (e.g., Carroll, 1999; Blowfield & Frynas, 2005). Ideas on business practices based on moral principles or serving the community instead of a lucky few have a long history. A clear definition of CSR was advanced by Davis as the "firm's consideration of, and response to, issues beyond the narrow economic, technical, and legal requirements of the firm . . . [to] accomplish social benefits along with the traditional economic gains which the firm seeks" (1973, pp. 312–313). The modern era of CSR really started with global deregulation and the shift away from state intervention in business policies within developed countries, freeing up the possibility for organizations to act opportunistically and giving rise to questions around why and how organizations would intrinsically act in socially responsible ways, without real external pressures from the government.

As a result of this governance shift and the regulatory vacuum that arose from it, an increased scientific interest in CSR within developed countries became apparent in the early 1990s.

CSR entails a variety of practices that expand beyond economic (profit maximization) goals and are meant to solve social problems, increase social benefits, or support constituency external to the firm's corpus (Marquis et al., 2007). CSR practices address various issues and can take a wide range of forms, amongst which the most popular include cash contributions, investments in social initiatives or programs, employee volunteer efforts and in-kind donations of products or services, leading to a specific level of resource commitment. After redefining CSR and placing it in a broader context as an umbrella term for a variety of theories (Blowfield & Frynas, 2005), a lot of empirical research on the topic has been conducted in developed countries. A vast body of literature discusses CSR and its possible implications to organizational performance (Kolk et al., 2010). If firms are not obliged to do so, that is, do not have the compulsory liability toward social constituencies

(Dentchev et al., 2015), then why would companies engage in CSR practices? What motives underlie CSR practices?

Research has indicated that, if managed effectively, CSR practices could assist companies in retaining and even increasing their customers (Levy & Kaplan, 2008), fostering a sense of commitment from employees (Zappala, 2004), and strengthening their corporate reputation as a caring business (Brammer & Pavelin, 2006). As a result, CSR practices have come to be perceived more as strategic activities rather than voluntary (Beddewela & Fairbrass, 2015). Other studies maintain that companies undertake CSR practices as a result of stakeholder and institutional pressures and interactions between various stakeholder groups. Firms are motivated to undertake CSR practices to avoid certain stakeholder influences or to use these influences to their own economic benefit. Additionally, through CSR practices, firms can use the media's influence to craft their image or to build civic legitimacy among stakeholders at large in the host society (Wartick, 1992). Scholars also propose that CSR practices are motivated by the economic and social roles of companies in the media, or by various other stakeholders (Capriotti, 2009; Hillman & Hitt, 1999). Finally, some studies argue that an opportunity to establish, maintain, and increase legitimacy in the environment lies within CSR practices (Campbell, 2012).

In contrast to this vast body of literature on CSR in developed economies, there is little or insufficient knowledge and empirical evidence originating from emerging economies in the field of CSR. Muller and Kolk (2010) argue that, although in recent years, the attention on CSR in emerging economies has increased, the majority of research done in this field still focuses on developed countries. Rapid economic development in emerging economies is accompanied by an increase in environmental pollution and waste output. It should therefore be important to ensure that organizations act in socially responsible ways, to minimize the damage to the environment. Research into CSR practices within these countries is, on this basis alone, a sufficient reason to argue for their necessity. Moreover, the noticeable differences between the types of CSR in developed and emerging economies are a driving force for the interest in emerging contexts.

It is thus interesting to explore the underlying motives behind CSR practices of Western multinational enterprises (MNEs) in China. Such an exploration would provide insight into CSR practices, as it is an important topic in the emerging economy context, while also more generally adding to the understanding of CSR as a concept. As China moves toward a more liberal economic model, observing CSR practices and their underlying motives may give an indication as to whether firms in China are in the process of adopting the stakeholder model of the firm. This further contributes to understanding the involvement of the government in economic activity and its role in price controls, since looking at CSR practices might suggest what role the private business sector will play in the social well-being of citizens. Our study may also reveal how the Chinese context is in the process of adjusting to another significant pressure, globalization. Since reduced barriers have allowed Western firms to compete for business against Chinese firms, our study would also provide insight into the extent to which Western firms voluntarily allocate slack resources to CSR activities that are not business related and for which there are no clear expectations as to how firms should perform (Wartick & Wood, 1998).

Despite the increasing globalization that the world is facing today, most studies of CSR practices mainly refer to Western countries, institutions, ethics, and norms. However, considering the fact that CSR practices vary along societal and ethical norms/cultures, different CSR dynamics are likely to exist in different parts of the world. Xu and Yang (2010) suggest that Chinese and Western views on CSR, even though slightly overlapping in certain areas, have a very different underlying quality, due to historical and cultural differences, as well as due to institutional differences.

There are two key differences between CSR with Chinese characteristics and the Western ideas on CSR. First, CSR in China has largely been approached through a mandatory governmental imposition. The mandatory approach to CSR, through laws and regulations, has kept many corporations from embracing the primary ideas of CSR as good for their company and at the same time good for their people and the environment. For many, there is a prevailing belief that the government is imposing a trade barrier that hampers economic growth. Because the principles behind CSR are lost in its implementation, the goals of CSR as dictated by the West cannot be achieved.

Second, there is the concept of social harmony, which is different in the East from what it is in the West. The Chinese view of social harmony has its roots in the Chinese traditional teachings of the Confucian virtue of righteousness, which means behaving in a way that is appropriate for approval, protection, and favor upon inferiors. The hierarchical idea of righteousness hinders the interpretation of the multi-stakeholder dialogue, a key element in Western CSR. While CSR in China is still at its infancy and continues to develop, 35% of Chinese managers regard the undertaking of social responsibility as a financial burden on their companies. For this reason, this research might help diminish the gap regarding what CSR practices might entail and the motives behind the CSR practices.

The structure of the study is as follows. Section 2 discusses the main literature perspectives on the motives behind CSR practices in general, and in particular, for MNEs. Section 3 presents a description of the sample, the data collection, and the method of data analysis. The empirical results are presented in Section 4, while Section 5 discusses the research findings, the conclusions, the contribution of our work, and the implications for practice.

2. Literature Framework

The motives underlying CSR practices fall along two main categories: strategic motives (Husted, 2001; Husted & Allen, 2007; Husted & Salazar,

2006) and moral (sustainability) motives (Carroll, 1979; Wartick & Mahon, 1994). The roots of this debate can be traced back to an early definition of CSR (Carroll, 1979, p. 500), where the phenomenon is deemed to comprise of economic, legal, ethical, and discretionary responsibilities.

Strategic motives include two types: instrumental or profitability motives (Story & Neves, 2015) and institutional or legitimacy motives (Dentchev et al., 2015). Instrumental motives stem from the belief that engaging in CSR practices will enhance profitability, either by protecting current profit levels or by improving them. Under this umbrella, firms strategically engage in CSR practices for profit-maximizing reasons. Studies show that high-profile CSR activities (e.g., voluntary efforts to reduce pollution or to improve working conditions for employees) are more likely to be undertaken when such activities can be more easily integrated into a firm's differentiation strategy and that different types of CSR actions can actually contribute to profit maximization (Manescu, 2011; Belu & Manescu, 2013).

Institutional motives are related to adjustment toward institutional pressures, that is, targeting organizational legitimacy. By conforming to such external institutional pressures, organizations can build support and gain legitimacy for their activities in specific institutional environments (DiMaggio & Powell, 1983). Broadly defined as institutional isomorphism, these consist of mimetic, normative, and coercive isomorphic pressures.

Coercive isomorphism is said to occur when organizations are required to adopt different practices, due to imposition by a more powerful authority, such as a national government. Normative isomorphism is deemed to exist when appropriate organizational practices are promoted by professional groups with which the organizations need to comply. Not adjusting to such normative pressures could lead to consumer intolerance, public scrutiny, and sanctions on companies who misconduct (Brønn & Cohen, 2009). Finally, mimetic isomorphism takes place when organizations respond to practical uncertainties, by imitating those practices that have been adopted by other successful organizations in the same industry or in different industries. Specific legitimacy motives include improving the corporate image, serving the long-term interest of the firm, fulfilling stakeholders' expectations, and being recognized for moral leadership (Greenwood et al., 2005).

Moral motives for engaging in CSR practices are based on the assumption that organizations have to give something back to society, that is, it has to do with altruistic motivation, concern for society's future, personal satisfaction, strengthening of global networks, learning from social agencies, and sharing resources with society (Brønn & Cohen, 2009). Theories such as stakeholder management (Freeman, 1984) advise companies to actively engage in CSR and manage external social issues effectively. From this perspective, companies cannot simply comply with institutional pressures to gain legitimacy: they also need to proactively develop CSR activities specifically targeted toward legitimacy-building. Suchman (1995) argues that organizations need to strategically (and instrumentally) manage their institutional environment by "adopting managerial perspectives instrumentally to manipulate and deploy evocative symbols in order to garner societal support" (Suchman, 1995, p. 572).

Moral legitimacy is described as resulting from "a positive normative evaluation of the organization and its activities" (Suchman, 1995). According to Suchman, a morally legitimate company is judged through its accomplishments (consequential legitimacy), its work in accordance with socially accepted procedures (procedural legitimacy), its capacity to perform well (structural legitimacy), and by having a charismatic leader (personal legitimacy). Palazzo and Scherer (2006) take this idea a step further by arguing that moral legitimacy results from a conscious moral judgment on the organization's output, procedures, structures, and leaders. They suggest that moral legitimacy is socially constructed through a deliberation of reasons that are used and that are considered to justify a company's actions, practices, structures, and results. Koppell (2008) refers to moral legitimacy as the "true meaning of the word legitimacy," because cognitive and pragmatic legitimacy imply only that an authority is acknowledged and submitted to.

The moral reasoning underlying CSR practices is that such actions help build a good public image, further attracting customers and better employees (Jamali et al., 2015). The viability of the business argument is also closely related to institutional theory: Companies should adhere to social norms and values in order to protect their survivability (Dentchev et al., 2015).

Other arguments in favor of CSR practices are less based on reason, but more on emotion. Many argue that institutions, local and global, have failed to protect society and the environment sufficiently, so maybe it is time for business to take up its share in terms of social activities. Davis (1973) makes the argument that businesses should not be doing less than what other institutions/organizations, as they have resources available, such as management talent and expertise, which could prove more beneficial when it comes to the outcome of social involvement than if it comes from other stakeholders. Through CSR practices, some problems could be converted into possibilities, if companies make use of their innovation capabilities. Finally, Davis (1973) argues that it might be wiser to deal with social problems earlier, rather than waiting until issues escalate and hinder operations.

When looking specifically at MNEs, generally CSR practices are responsive and have adapted to the context, pointing out the benefits in terms of legitimacy (Weigelt & Camerer, 1988). Jamali (2010) argues that local CSR practices should be tailored according to national differences and preferences. The ability to meet local legitimacy demands, across national institutional environments, can be a form of differentiation. So, rather than viewing CSR practices as behavior that brings additional costs, the legitimacy which can be the result of such behavior can be seen as an intangible asset and source of competitive advantage and thus profitability (Gardberg & Fombrun, 2006).

On the other hand, there is also room to argue that MNEs are inclined not to adjust to CSR practices due to efficiency reasons, such as standardized and globally integrated CSR policies. Standardized policies and procedures facilitate headquarters to monitor and control subsidiaries on their actions, decreasing the direct costs of engaging in CSR practices. Arguably, a more local, decentralized approach hinders effective control (Jamali, 2010). These arguments highlight the financial and cost-saving benefits of a global CSR approach for MNEs. Such an approach could also serve a different and important objective: upward standard setting. Jamali (2010) argues that countries have different CSR standards, and if MNEs pursue a global CSR approach, they will have to rise up to the standards of the most demanding country and apply these standards to all countries. This could lead to substantial benefits for countries with lower CSR expectations. This motive differs substantially from arguing about the economic gains of a global CSR policy, and it is likely to eventually lead to even higher costs when compared to a local strategy. A MNE dedicates itself to high standards, which might lie far above the local host norms, implying higher costs than if local structures were simply applied (Dahan, 2005). Initially seen as an approach implying lower costs, the global CSR approach, due to upward standard setting, can thus imply higher costs when compared to a local approach. If the MNE adopts and implements global CSR practices, as a manner for upward standard setting, then such reasoning comes closer to arguments around legitimacy and should thus be considered as a legitimacy motive, rather than a company following a global strategy for efficiency reasons.

However, it is important to notice that profitability and legitimacy motives apply to both local and global ways of approaching CSR practices, depending on the context and interpretation (Kostova & Zaheer, 1999). With legitimacy motives seeming most important for companies in engaging with CSR practices in non-foreign environments, the importance of this motive is expected to increase when companies go abroad. While the financial gains from global CSR practices might appeal to many companies, the costs of legitimacy issues can outweigh these. Therefore, we assume that MNEs engage in CSR practices mainly due to legitimacy motives, emphasizing profitability motives less.

3. Methodology

3.1. Sample Description and Data Collection

The sample population for this study is represented by Western MNEs operating in China, and particularly in the Beijing area, with the international headquarters located in Western countries. According to Xu and Yang (2010), Western CSR dimensions are applicable to firms from Europe, North America, and Australia, but these dimensions differ across the Chinese approach. While CSR in China is still in its infancy and continues to develop, 35% of Chinese managers regard the undertaking of social responsibility as a financial burden on their companies.

Table 6.1 presents an overview of the characteristics of the study's group of participants. The average year of founding among the Western MNEs

Table 6.1 Overview of the Characteristics of the Respondent Group of the Study

Respondent	*Years of MNE in China*	*Nr. of Employees in China*	*Home Country*	*Establishment Year of MNE*	*Subsidiaries Globally*	*Industry*	*Function*	*Experience of the Respondent in Years on the job*	*Category*
1	8	250	England	1975	6	Manufacturing	Employee at Chamber of Commerce	8	Expert
2	10	80	Germany	1993	8	Chemical	General manager	10	Business
3	10	160	Germany	1995	10	Chemical	Employee at Chamber of Commerce	5	Expert
4	19	200	Belgium	1967	17	Manufacturing	Ambassador	10	Business
5	21	180	Germany	1925	28	Chemical	Founder; Journalist	6	Expert
6	14	600	England	1994	15	Chemical	Consultant	8	Expert
7	22	290	Belgium	1976	9	Chemical	Owner	12	Business
8	16	340	Sweden	1959	12	Manufacturing	Director	15	Expert
9	25	170	Germany	1979	22	Manufacturing	Director Safety, Health and Environment	20	Business
10	15	550	France	1980	30	Chemical	Director	10	Expert
11	19	80	France	1972	60	Manufacturing	Financial controller	5	Business

12	30	500	France	1950	52	Manufacturing	General manager	12	Business
13	12	150	Belgium	1965	4	Chemical	Several	11	Expert
14	11	400	Netherlands	1873	17	Manufacturing	General manager	28	Business
15	20	60	Netherlands	1992	12	Manufacturing	Project manager	20	Expert
16	11	3000	Netherlands	1933	200	Transportation	Assistant general manager	14	Business
17	42	600	Netherlands	1920	60	Chemical	Project manager	32	Business
18	7	32	Netherlands	1977	34	Manufacturing	Director Health and Environment	3	Business
19	62	600	France	1998	63	Chemical	Director Safety, Health and Environment	11	Business
20	8	600	Netherlands	1969	7	Manufacturing	Director Health and Environment	5	Business
Ave	19.1	442		1965	33			12	
Min	7	32		1873	4			3	
Max	62	3000		1998	200			32	

in our sample was 1965; the oldest company was founded in 1873, and the youngest company was established in 1998. The home countries represented in the sample were the United Kingdom, Germany, the Netherlands, Belgium, Sweden, and France. On average, these MNEs had 33 subsidiaries, with a maximum of more than 200 subsidiaries and a minimum of four subsidiaries. The Western MNEs had operated in China for an average of 19.1 years, with a minimum of 7 years and a maximum of 62 years. These companies mainly operated in the manufacturing industry and chemical industry, with another company in the transportation industry. The average number of employees among the MNEs was 442, with a minimum of 32 and a maximum of 3,000 employees.

In-depth interviews were conducted with the respondents, who were mostly general managers/directors, all of whom were involved in the design, implementation or execution of CSR policies within their companies. Thus, they were all deemed able to provide the most insight into the CSR practices of their subsidiary. To select respondents, we applied the snowball sampling method (Baarda et al., 2005). The positions occupied by the respondents included owners (1 respondent), general managers (10 respondents), directors of safety, professionals in health and environment (6 respondents), financial controllers (1 respondent), ambassadors (1 respondent), and assistant general managers (1 respondent). The average experience of the interviewees in the field was 12 years, with a minimum of 3 years and a maximum of 32 years. On average, the managers had been working for the firms for 12 years, with a maximum of 32 years' working experience and a minimum of 3 years of experience.

Alongside the managers of the Western MNEs, we spoke to 8 informants-experts. According to Baarda et al. (2005), an informant is an interviewee who does not necessarily answer questions from his or her own perspective, but who can share information on the subject. While these informants formed no part of the research unit, they can be seen as very helpful in the data collection that this research unit conducted. The 8 informants were experts in corporate social responsibility (CSR) in China, all of them professionals working in the CSR sector in Beijing. Among these experts, 2 were journalists at a CSR magazine, 2 were employees at the Dutch Chambers of Commerce in Beijing, and 4 were consultants at different agencies. These experts were strikingly valuable for the research, because they were very knowledgeable about the field of CSR and could provide information on various CSR practices and strategies applied by many other Western MNEs.

When conducting exploratory research, it is important to maintain an open vision and to remain flexible to new ideas, insights, and clarifications (Stevens et al., 2006). For this reason, we chose to conduct in-depth face-to-face open interviews with the Western MNEs in China in the summer of 2012, to get a deeper understanding of the dynamics involved and the motivation behind CSR practices. Face-to-face conversations are more flexible than written mediums and could also capture non-verbal language and aspects such as tone of voice. Interviewing the managers, through open questions, was a good opportunity to get a thorough understanding of the choice for particular CSR practices, about their particular approach, and about the areas of adaptation.

Before collecting the data, an interview protocol was created, which included the main topics and the guiding questions. During some interviews, new concepts were introduced, including a variety of motives for CSR practices, which were not mentioned in the literature. It also became clear that some motives were not relevant at all for the interviewees. Considering the fact that several new motives were addressed by the interviewees and others were considered irrelevant, the choice for an open interviewing technique seems very suitable in retrospect. The audio fragments of the interviews were then transcribed literally into written text documents; the method with which they were analyzed is described in the next section.

3.2. Data Analysis Technique

The data collected through the interviews was analyzed through content analysis, which generally uses four entities of analysis: analysis on words, sentences, fragments, or themes (Baarda et al., 2005; Weber, 1990). Because the characteristics of the topic and the specific contents of the statements matter in this research, the unit of analysis is in fragments. This leaves room for the researcher to combine sentences that belong together into one fragment, to honor the initial content of the statements. Thus, the data retrieved from the interviews were separated into fragments, which were used as a starting point for the actual analysis of the qualitative data, which involved the creation of labels. Table 6.2 provides a clear overview of the labeling scheme used in the study.

4. Empirical Findings

Our empirical findings can further explain and detail the collection of motives that were described as plausible reasoning underlying CSR practices, discussed in the literature section. Table 6.3 represents the number of people who mentioned each motive, sequenced by the interviewees' attention and by the importance assigned to each motive.

4.1. Improving Government Relations

Improving government relations was indicated by 81% of the respondents as an important motive when engaging in CSR practices. Several interviewees even sustained that cultivating government relations is a widespread phenomenon among MNEs and that it could actually even represent the number 1 motive in engaging with CSR practices in China. Other indirect objectives also were mentioned, beyond improving the relationship with the

Table 6.2 Labeling Scheme

Coding Sheet				
Code	*Name*	*Subcode*	*Subcategory*	*Explanation*
GLOBAL VS. LOCAL CSR APPROACHES				
1.1	Global stakeholders	1.1a	Government	Does the CSR strategy focus on international governments?
		1.1b	Media/Civil society	Does the CSR strategy focus on global media, customers, NGOs, society?
		1.1c	Shareholders/ investors	Does the CSR strategy focus on global shareholders or investors?
1.2	Global CSR fields	1.2a	Charity	Does the CSR strategy have a global approach on charity?
		1.2b	Supply Chain	Does the CSR strategy have a global approach on supply chain?
		1.2c	Environment	Does the CSR strategy have a global approach on environment?
1.3	Global norms and values			Is the CSR strategy based on global/European norms and values?
1.4	Following corporate guidelines	1.4a	Positive	Does the MNE follow corporate guidelines for better CSR?
		1.4b	Negative	Does the following of headlines decrease the CSR efforts?
1.5	Local stakeholders	1.6a	Government	Does the CSR strategy focus on Chinese government?
		1.6b	Media/Civil society	Does the CSR strategy focus on Chinese media, customers, NGOs, society?
		1.6c	Shareholders/ investors	Does the CSR strategy focus on Chinese shareholders or investors?
1.6	Local norms and values			Is the CSR strategy based on global/European norms and values?
1.7	Development local strategies			Indicating a shift from a global to a local strategy

(*Continued*)

Table 6.2 Labeling Scheme (Continued)

Coding Sheet			
MOTIVES			
2.1	Improving government relations	2.1a	Affirmative comment
		2.1p	Privative comment
2.2	Improving image	2.2a	Affirmative comment
		2.2p	Privative comment
2.3	Attracting and maintaining employees	2.3a	Affirmative comment
		2.3p	Privative comment
2.4	Cost efficiencies	2.4a	Affirmative comment
		2.4p	Privative comment
2.5	Fulfilling stakeholder expectations	2.5a	Affirmative comment
		2.5p	Privative comment
2.6	Solving social problems	2.6a	Affirmative comment
		2.6p	Privative comment
2.7	Meeting shareholder demands	2.7a	Affirmative comment
		2.7p	Privative comment
2.8	Serving long-term interest	2.8a	Affirmative comment
		2.8p	Privative comment
2.9	Upward standard setting	2.9a	Affirmative comment
		2.9p	Privative comment
2.10	Risk management	2.10a	Affirmative comment
		2.10p	Privative comment
2.11	Being recognized for moral leadership	2.11a	Affirmative comment
		2.11p	Privative comment
2.12	New business opportunities	2.12a	Affirmative comment
		2.12p	Privative comment
AREAS OF ADJUSTMENT			
3.1	Social stability	3.1a	Affirmative comment
		3.1p	Privative comment
3.2	Guanxi	3.2a	Affirmative comment
		3.2p	Privative comment
3.3	Employment	3.3a	Affirmative comment
		3.3p	Privative comment
3.4	Environment	3.4a	Affirmative comment
		3.4p	Privative comment
3.5	Employees	3.5a	Affirmative comment
		3.5p	Privative comment

Table 6.3 Overview of Motives to Engage in CSR Practices

Motives to Engage in CSR		*Mentioned by # People*	*Mentioned # Times*
Improving government relations	Affirmative	13	28
	Privative	4	7
Attracting and maintaining employees	Affirmative	12	30
	Privative	0	0
Improving image	Affirmative	11	16
	Privative	0	0
Risk management	Affirmative	5	7
	Privative	0	0
Cost efficiencies	Affirmative	4	10
	Privative	0	0
Fulfilling stakeholder expectations	Affirmative	3	6
	Privative	3	6
Meeting shareholder demands	Affirmative	3	4
	Privative	2	2
Upward standard setting	Affirmative	7	20
	Privative	0	0
Being recognized for moral leadership	Affirmative	3	3
	Privative	1	1
Solving social problems	Affirmative	2	3
	Privative	3	3
Serving long-term interest	Affirmative	3	6
	Privative	0	0
New business opportunities	Affirmative	1	1
	Privative	0	0

government, that is achieving the provision of adequate operational space as well as achieving less control from the authorities over the company's overall activities.

> If new entrant MNEs would ask themselves who should we pay to do our government relations, then the answer would be: you won't need to hire/pay, if you give money to the government by CSR projects directly, then you're set. That is your consultancy money right there.
>
> (Respondent 16)

Other respondents highlighted the high survivability risk a company runs when the government holds an unfavorable attitude toward it. This again appears as a strong motivator toward CSR practices, oriented at building and maintaining relations with the government.

> If we can reach out to the government through CSR practices, we will certainly do so, because you know you can expect something back. Let me put it this way: the good relations between [our country] and China and the good relations of our company with the air authorities have made it possible that our company can fly to five different airports. There are other companies who cannot get this approved by the Chinese government. How did we succeed? Because we have excellent government relations.
>
> (Respondent 16)

Good government relations also help in gaining more information on the business environment and in avoiding missing out on opportunities, as well as in becoming aware of potential threats. Similarly, other interviewees mentioned the emergence of new business opportunities after establishing favorable government relations.

> Before expanding their operations to a new area, foreign MNEs will first go to the government and say: "I would like to build a factory here, but what does the community need? How can we contribute?" [Anonymous] MNEs did this with a certain bid. The government replied that they could offer lessons on how to use the computer to the locals. The company won the bid and it is now the leader in computer manufacturing.
>
> (Respondent 17)

4.2. Attracting and Maintaining Employees

CSR practices are considered an important tool in attracting and retaining a good workforce. Many interviewees discussed the difficulties that Western MNEs experience in keeping their staff. Building loyalty through CSR practices was seen by 75% of the MNEs as an effective tool to keep employees. Chinese workers are much more driven by salary level and promotion opportunities than Western employees, making it more difficult to retain staff. Empirical exploration suggests that CSR practices can work to increase employees' loyalty; however, it is crucial to get the right balance between CSR practices, salary, and status.

> We want our employees to balance their professional-personal life well. Our motivation is to build more loyalty and to have more people staying. This is a good output for the company, an output that can be reached through CSR practices.
>
> (Respondent 20)

As a tool in making staff more loyal, CSR practices cover a variety of actions. Some MNEs organize special daily coach transfer for employees to their homes, to make commuting less inconvenient. One MNE has created a green garden/oasis next to their production facility for the employees to enjoy their lunch time in a cleaner, pollution free, and more relaxing environment. Other MNEs offer various facilities, aimed at attracting staff or improving work–life balance, such as providing proper housing for employees who do not live in Beijing or through offering a variety of training programs. Some companies encourage their employees to participate in volunteerism, which is said to increase loyalty.

Besides the CSR practices as efforts to maintain staff, some companies engage in specific CSR projects, aiming to recruit new staff. Many Western MNEs combine CSR practices and recruitment activities, by sponsoring students to study in the home country of the MNE, hoping to recruit the "cream" of the Chinese students for a future job within their organization.

4.3. Improving Image

Improving corporate image was indicated by 69% of the MNEs as a motive in engaging in CSR practices; however, less striking comments were made here.

> Companies working in China for a long time have been thinking about how they can use such CSR programs to build their brand image.
>
> (Respondent 20)

The improvement of image is mentioned by some respondents as the second most important motive after government relations. Our empirical findings highlighted the greater acceptance in China of explicitly exposing CSR efforts; foreign MNEs experienced this kind of behavior as less accepted in other parts of the world. In this context, Western MNEs take advantage of the local features and use their CSR practices to build their reputation and image.

> Sometimes you can operate on more ideological grounds, but in China you must ensure that it generates publicity. You want people to think that your company is a social organization, which does not only focus on making money. Of course, I would say, we do mostly focus on making money: we are in China. But you have to create the right image, work on the perception.
>
> (Respondent 16)

A very important conclusion, shared by some respondents, was that CSR focused on generating publicity, which in turn could improve the company's image; this view seemed to be much more common in China than in the

United States or Europe. It also seems to be more socially acceptable in China to exhibit CSR efforts overtly to the Chinese audience, via various mass media. As a respondent from the chamber of commerce said: "That is the way to build your brand here."

4.4. *Risk Management*

A smaller number of respondents (31%) seemed to consider CSR practices as a way to manage risk within the firm. CSR was thus seen as a way to diminish or counter-balance possible risks that can arise within a firm. Some interviewees mentioned the negative publicity that occurred when there were accidents within factories or when faulty products entered the market. This was closely linked to the motive of improving the image, but instead of promoting the company, it seemed to be more focused on the protection of the company or on buffering the effects of a negative occurrence. It was understood that if the MNE was publicly known as a strong CSR undertaker, when a certain negative event took place (i.e., an accident or faulty product), then society at large would be expected to be less inclined to assign a negative image to the company; thus, the event would rather be seen as an unpleasant incident, an exception from an otherwise socially involved organization.

> Additionally to certificates and licenses, we need to make the effort to do CSR, in order to show this not only to our clients but to all our stakeholders.
>
> (Respondent 7)

In a similar reasoning line, the companies from the chemical industry tend to use CSR practices to diffuse or distract attention from the negative outcome of their activities (pollution and other environmental damage).

> It is about damage limitation during the shareholder meeting. Everybody knows that the strategy of NGOs at the moment is to buy some share of the company, so they have access at the shareholder meeting. They you can stand up in front of 800 people . . . and say: "I'm here for Greenpeace and I'd like to tell all of you that." But if you are covered by, first and foremost, good deeds, then the right license and certificates, it makes things a bit easier.
>
> (Respondent14)

4.5. *Cost Efficiencies*

Cost efficiency, as a motivation underlying CSR practices, derives from the aim to have fewer accidents, less time needed for production, or to make savings on insurance costs. While many companies might consider cost saving an extra benefit of CSR practices, some companies explicitly focus their CSR efforts on cost efficiency, appreciating the combined benefits of protecting employees and improving the company's reputation, as well as the financial situation of the company.

> For many small MNEs, it is much more cost orientated; if there are any CSR practices, then they have to provide direct returns on investment.
> (Respondent from the Chamber of Commerce)

4.6. Upward Standard Setting

Many companies explicitly engage in CSR practices in China, because of specifically aiming to increase current CSR standards within the country. They consider Western norms and values regarding CSR to be at a higher level than in China. The chamber of commerce considers that it is not difficult to improve standards and that many improvements can be made by Western MNEs that operate in this setting. Furthermore, the respondents mentioned the spillover effect they hoped to reach with their CSR campaigns, achieving more than just good labor or improved environmental conditions within the company, but educating the workforce, their families, and the community. The interviewees made rather bold statements regarding this motive, indicating that upward standard setting was taken seriously by Western MNEs.

> If every company teaches the coming generations that CSR is an integral part of their organizational life, this would become normal and implicit.
> (Respondent from the Chamber of Commerce)

> At the time when local labor regulations were not clear yet, Western ethical standards did not prevail in our Chinese production sites, and we didn't make sure they were. But this was not nearly sufficient. Nowadays, the Chinese government has emphasized business ethics more; but MNEs themselves have the ability and responsibility to change the playing field.
> (Respondent 8)

4.7. Being Recognized for Moral Leadership

Only three interviewees mention this motive as important in engaging in CSR practices; however, this is mentioned on the basis of contradictory perspectives, leading us to the conclusion that empirical results provide no insightful indication of moral leadership as a motive for CSR involvement. While one MNE was said to explicitly target the Dow Jones Sustainability Index, to see how sustainable their operations are (Respondent 17), another

MNE claimed that moral leadership is too farfetched and that the goal of the company is to make a profit, not to be a moral hero (Respondent 9).

4.8. Solving Social Problems

Due to the opposing and puzzling views provided by respondents, the motive involving the resolution of social problems was disregarded and wasn't seen as something that underlies CSR practices.

> How can we call ourselves successful in a failing world? As a company you cannot just say "This is where we make money and I do not care about the rest of the world." We are a large global corporation, and we are partially responsible for what goes around in the rest of the world.
> (Respondent 17)

> It depends on which scale you want to tackle social problems. If there are social problems within the company, this is obviously very important. But if it means we have to do something within society, it becomes a much bigger issue and frankly, less important.
> (Respondent 16)

4.9. Serving Long-Term Interest

Serving long-term interest is in some ways related to solving social problems; the MNEs which consider solving social problems important for corporations also tend to regard long-term interest as vital for their survival. It was argued by some respondents that the long-term survival of the company would be endangered if society does not function properly.

> We must keep in mind how we can prepare ourselves for the future, to operate within society, so that operations can continue in the long run.
> (Respondent 12)

However, this view was taken by a small number of respondents, and for this reason it cannot be regarded as a highlight among the motives for CSR practices.

Additionally, some other motives in engaging with CSR practices, such as fulfilling stakeholders' expectations, meeting shareholder demands, and solving social problems, even though mentioned in the literature, were not considered very important by the MNEs.

> When you prioritize motives in engaging with CSR practices, government relations go first, corporate image is second . . . I wouldn't even consider shareholders' intentions on that list.
> (Respondent 13)

5. Discussion

The objective of this study was to explore the underlying motives for engaging in CSR practices among Western MNEs in China. The case of China, with regards to CSR practices, is extremely interesting for many reasons. Until not long ago, the sole focus of the Chinese economy was profitability, with almost no concern for social issues both on the part of businesses and on the part of the government. China is known for its strict state-controlled economy; bureaucratic planning and allocation, quotas and discipline have been key to the communist approach (Oi, 1995). However, the Chinese government has switched toward a market-oriented economic approach. Attracting foreign investors has been an active policy of the contemporary Chinese government to foster economic growth and attract innovative technology within its borders (Weldon & Vanhonacker, 1999; Wu, 2001). This transformation not only attracted foreign investors, but also led to continuous changing perspectives in terms of the ways that business was done in China. Amongst these changes, the role of business organizations as economic and social entities started to develop. However, the government still plays an important role in shaping these ideologies. More recently, the government started to direct attention to a more responsible, social, and ethical way of doing business.

Improving government relations appears to be a strong motive related to the more localized facet of CSR practices, that is, local stakeholders. Through solid government relations, Western MNEs also gain information and maintain operational space. The fact that MNEs use a CSR approach to improve government relations underlines the importance of this stakeholder. These findings support the results of Tan and Litschert (1994), who stress the Chinese government's important role in business operations. Alternatively, the comments of participants who worked at smaller companies, ones who wished to remain under the radar, illustrated, in line with Peng and Heath (1996), the volatility and unpredictability of the Chinese government. Despite the Chinese government's fearsome reputation, it is nowadays more accessible to MNEs, since it has placed CSR more prominently on the agenda. The finding referring to the idea that building government relations through CSR seems a widespread phenomenon was quite surprising. Previous research regarding motives for CSR mention avoiding regulation (Brønn & Cohen, 2009) or delaying regulation (Davis, 1973; Lynes & Andrachuk, 2008); but these motives can be viewed as submotives of the aim to improve government relations, especially in those cases when non-transparent Chinese government policies could potentially be tackled by CSR initiatives (as indicated by managers). The diversified range of underlying motives for the improvement of government relations indicates that companies benefit from solid government relations through multiple channels. Thus, the discriminatory treatment of the government as well as the knowledge liability regarding the host setting can be decreased through CSR projects. Improving government relations can be categorized as a motive concerning legitimacy, because it aims to enhance the government's and other stakeholders' acceptance of the MNEs' presence in the host environment.

Improving image is another underlying motive for CSR activities, targeted at Chinese civil society, the media, and other stakeholders. Our empirical findings indicate that improving image appears to be second in importance for implementing CSR. However, improving image is not a motive specifically applicable to China, as many researchers also mention image when investigating reasons for CSR practices (Lynes & Andrachuk, 2008; Sohn, 1982). Brønn and Cohen (2009) even mention this as a top motive underlying CSR initiatives. We support the arguments of Brønn and Cohen (2009), regarding the importance of image for engaging in CSR; however, our results place this motive in second place, following after the improvement of government relations. While many MNEs indicate that CSR is often a way for image building, the importance and position of this motive seems to differ in China compared to the Western world. Thus, different priorities and dynamics are valid in China, when compared to the Western business environment. In China, CSR practices are much more targeted on generating publicity than they are in the West.

> It is much more socially acceptable to display CSR efforts explicitly and overtly here; this is the way to build your brand image.
>
> (Respondent 20)

However, in 2008, Gefei et al. predicted that this situation would continuously change, towards less emphasis on the public display of charity and more attention to the actual content of CSR projects (Gefei et al., 2008). This prediction does not hold for our research setting, because in China the improvement of image through CSR practices is mainly focused on generating publicity and targets the national media, society, and the local stakeholder; thus, it is closely associated with localized and "in the public eye" CSR practices.

Our results make the argument that building a positive image is necessary in reaching local stakeholders and in winning more market share. This is in line with Gefei et al. (2008), who state that favorable brand recognition in the Chinese market is needed, if MNEs want to increase their market shares. Even though image improvement can generally be regarded as a motive having to do with legitimacy, nonetheless, the link to profitability is very clear. If MNEs fail to attract Chinese customers with their corporate image, it is unlikely that they will gain a solid position in the Chinese market, which is a further link to profitability.

Specific to the Chinese context is the fact that Western MNEs have a costly staff turnover. The necessary training given to employees is essentially an investment; in China, there is a quick turnover of employees at the work place, not allowing companies to achieve a return on the investment put into training employees. Multiple interviewees pointed out that Western MNEs in China are not used to the low level of employee loyalty. For many of these MNEs, CSR projects have proven to be a valuable strategy in decreasing employee turnover, through rather simple CSR practices that can increase loyalty. Even though some skepticism remained, the majority of the interviewees agreed that CSR practices can help retain staff and could lead to an overall decrease in employee turnover.

Apart from retention of employees, MNEs also use CSR activities to attract talented and skilled employees. Weldon and Vanhonacker (1999) outline that Chinese people receive a different education, with less of an emphasis on creativity and on "thinking outside the box." "Chinese people tend to learn what to learn, not how to learn" (Weldon & Vanhonacker, 1999, p. 95). This makes it difficult for Western MNEs to find suitable employees prone to creativity and proactive ideology. Often, CSR projects target education programs, hoping to find suitable and talented employees. Attracting and maintaining employees through CSR practices clearly falls under the category of profitability, whereas MNEs try to limit employee turnover, which is costly, cleverly combining CSR initiatives with recruitment processes. This motive was only mentioned by Davis (1973) as important in attracting better employees. More recent studies have not incorporated this motive in their endeavors (Stoian & Zaharia, 2012). This indicates that this phenomenon is probably specific to the Chinese situation, whereas Western MNEs use CSR practices to tackle high employee turnover and recruitment issues.

Another interesting finding is represented by the upward standard setting as a motive for CSR practices, which was not mentioned in the literature but arose during the interviews. Many MNEs consider it their duty to bring higher standards to their Chinese operations, because they want to honor their reputation. Western businesses are generally regarded as more socially involved and responsible than Chinese businesses, not only by Western companies, but also by the Chinese public and stakeholders at large.

Risk management, as part of CSR practices, is closely aligned with image improvement. While image improvement tempts to establish a favorable attitude on the part of the public towards the company, risk management is more focused on prevention and on the buffering effects that could damage the corporate brand. This motive leans more toward profitability, while image improvement can be clearly seen as a legitimacy motive.

In conclusion, the main motives for CSR activities are categorized as having to do with legitimacy, that is, improving government relations and image improvement through CSR, the maintenance of a conducive attitude on the part of the government, as well as on the part of civil society. Attracting and maintaining employees is a profitability motive, whereas the return on investment in employees is key, along with the existence of a smooth recruitment process.

Taking into consideration the overall motives which were found to be important in this study, we can make up a more nuanced balance. Among profitability motives, we can range them as follows: attracting and maintaining employees (75%), risk management (32%), and cost efficiencies (25%). The main legitimacy motives are improvement of government relations (81%), image improvement (69%), and upward standard setting (44%). Legitimacy motives outweigh the profitability motives underlying CSR practices, which seem to be employed by MNEs in China in tackling issues specific to the country; for example, the non-transparent government policies and the high employee turnover. Our initial assumption seems supported: Legitimacy motives seem to have a more prominent place when compared to profitability motives in engaging in CSR practices. However, perhaps more striking than the actual balance between legitimacy and profitability motives is the fact that two out of the three motives are not mentioned in the mainstream CSR literature. This indicates that Western dominated CSR research cannot cover the range of motives for CSR practices in China (Li et al., 2013).

6. Conclusions

Liability of foreignness burdens the foreign companies with costs that local companies do not face, and one way to cope with this unfamiliarity is to focus more on establishing legitimacy within the environment. Legitimacy can be seen as social conformity (Suchman, 1995). There is strong evidence that the greater the institutional distance, the higher the need to adapt organizational practices to meet host country legitimacy requirements (Kostova & Zaheer, 1999), this is highly evident for the Western MNEs in China. Additionally, while the wish for stronger government relations often arises from the non-transparent government policies in China, the quest for a better image originates from the rising public awareness and empowerment of the Chinese people. These two stakeholder groups take a central place in the CSR PRACTICES approaches of Western MNEs in China. While the government is a firmly rooted stakeholder for MNEs, the importance of the Chinese civil society is growing. Furthermore, MNEs employ CSR projects to create a good workforce, a well-known challenge in China. The focus on these three main motives leads to a mix in global and local approach to CSR. MNEs tend to stick vastly to their global norms and values, which is appreciated by the Chinese government and by their employees. The focus on local stakeholders enables the MNEs to target Chinese audiences, rather than the global audience. Concluding, we can see that MNEs try to enhance their legitimacy in China by focusing on local stakeholders, while attempting to remain somehow bounded in their Western norms and values, and to further appeal to the local Chinese stakeholders through these Western norms. The institutional differences between Western countries and China manifested in governmental policies and work ethics shape the CSR practices of Western MNEs operating in China.

Normative differences also suggest that Western companies operating in China should adjust their approach to CSR practices toward the more Chinese norms and values, thus legitimacy motives seem justified by various theoretical perspectives.

The inference that the reasons behind CSR practices are separated into two distinct categories, economic and noneconomic, legitimacy and profitability, is perhaps too simplistic. Even though much research has been conducted, no conclusive results appear in close sight. Maybe there is a good reason for this: Time has come to actually interpret them/see these results not as contradictory, but as complementary and as a trait of reality. The reality is that we cannot delimitate the social motivation for CSR PRACTICES from the financial motivation behind the same actions. The fact that there is no clear delimitation between the economic and noneconomic motivation should make us conclude that companies implement CSR for both social and financial benefits, as complementing stimuli. Thus, the legitimacy and profitability motives as intrinsic organizational CSR practices stimuli are neither dichotomous categories, nor mutually exclusive. While studies put a lot of emphasis on delimitating these two categories, we argue that they should be regarded as complementary and that the delimitation between legitimacy and profitability motives behind CSR practices is perhaps a false dichotomy.

Furthermore, even though CSR is growing as a management issue, China still represents a novel environment for social performance (Moon & Shen, 2010). The recent rise of CSR in China can be ascribed to internal and external factors (Zu & Song, 2009) with the national government enforcing social performance by law (companies need to report their social and environmental impacts) (Zhang, 2006). Externally, the rise in trade and relationships between Chinese and Western companies also caused tension between business practices based on profit maximization and the Western values concerning social performance. This development is often labeled the import of global social norms (Zhang, 2006).

Future research can continue to tackle some of these interesting issues, and more confirmatory research should be done in the field to re-affirm the results. Overall, the case of China regarding CSR practices seems particularly interesting, because as respondents indicate, the country- specific barriers could be eliminated by effective CSR practices. Also, the effectiveness of a global and local approach to CSR practices elicited substantial comments from the interviewees which indicates that there might be significant differences between the two. Another interesting research direction entails the dynamics of the legitimacy and profitability motives as complementary dynamics. An indexed approach and sustainable balance is quite hard to investigate at this point, but nonetheless fascinating and useful for many stakeholders: business, scholars, government, society, media, etc.

The world is facing a complex sustainability challenge, manifested in many interdependent crises, from climate change, biodiversity loss, hunger and poverty, drinking water scarcity, public health problems, to political conflicts, decreasing social trust and institutional failure. The way companies' leaders manage these challenges will not only matter in the bottom line for their organizations but might well change the course of life on the planet. Several scholars (e.g., Scharmer, 2009; Waddock & McIntosh, 2009) agree that such times call for new leaders' capabilities to meet challenges in a more effective way. Thus, a valuable research direction is the instructive role of MNEs in the field of CSR. MNEs (un)intentionally enhance the knowledge on CSR among their workforce, but also communities, stakeholders, and even the entire country. The knowledge level of CSR differs greatly between Western countries and emerging economies, where the societal awareness of CSR is still low (Gefei, 2008).

Note

* *This research was conducted in collaboration with Sabine Kester.*

7 Business Ethics and Social Responsibility

1. Corporate Role and Responsibilities

With their operations spread all over the world, achieving the maximization of their profits, the corporations took upon themselves an extraordinary power, often overcoming the one of the government. Thereby, they are operating on the international market developing fabrics where the labor force is cheap and where the resources are at a lessened price.

The importance of corporations for the technological innovation process is considerable. The biggest part of the expenses for the development research, which represent the base for the nowadays technological development, is focused on the interior of the transnational society's complexes. This weight factor is estimated to 75%–80% of the total development research expenses from the civil sector worldwide. Regarding the international commerce with technology, the corporations centralize 90% of the total. Many corporations have learned that they have limits concerning what they can carry on and that there are also responsibilities they have to bear.

The social responsibility is entirely known as being essential for the establishment of an attractive investment climate, characterized by the existence of some competitive companies and some efficient financial markets. The promotion of social responsibility principles, as well of the efficient measures of corporative administration, became a main problem of the reforms and of the economies for the countries with developed economies, but also for the developing ones.

The quick evolution in the structure of the corporations is reflected likewise in the operations unfolded in the developing world, where the level of direct foreign investments has increased rapidly. In the developing countries, the corporations have diversified their production, overcoming the primary production and extraction industry phase and developing the manufacture, assembly lines, contributed to the increase of the markets and autochthonous services.

The nature, the goal, and the speed of the economic changes have brought new strategic challenges for the enterprises and their capital owners. The corporations have the opportunity to implement the best practical policies for sustainable development, which aim to ensure the coherence between the social, economic, and environmental objectives. The ability of the corporations to promote a sustainable development is implicit, mainly when the commerce and the investments are made on open, competitive, and adequately regulated markets.

Many corporations have proven that the respect toward the conservation of high standards in the management of businesses can improve the economic growth. The current competition is sharp. Given the circumstances, some companies might be tempted to neglect the proper conduct standards and principles, trying to gain inappropriate advantages.

The corporations must take into account the established polices in the operating countries, and to acknowledge the opinions of the shareholders. In this regard, the companies have the following obligations: to contribute to economic, social, and environment progress in order to accomplish a sustainable development; to respect the human rights in relation to trained people in their activity, according to the obligations and international commitments of the host government; to encourage the growth of local potential through a healthy commercial activity; to support the forming of human capital, especially by creating new workplaces and facilitating the specialization conditions for the employees; not to search of to accept exceptions from the statutory or normative framework regarding the environment, health, security, work conditions, taxing, financial incentives; to support and maintain the social responsibility principles, to develop and apply a well practice of the social responsibility; to encourage, when possible, the business partners, including the suppliers and the sub-contractual parties, applying therefore the corporative conduct principles which are in accordance to the OECD advices.

Presently, the corporatist identity of a company, as well as its image became of absolute importance. The transparency and the rightness of an organizations are an essential element in its development, as the manufacturing of a good product is not enough, but it has to prove to be a good corporative citizen. Lately, the companies are being evaluated from the point of view of their contribution of the social life they belong to and not according to the quality of their products or their economic results.

The corporate social responsibility (CSR), in Romania and in all the countries where it's practiced, means fulfilling a duty towards a society which is more and more sensitive to the social and ethical problems. The managers need to take into account the rising request for having an active purpose in the society. The social involvement of the corporations became a frequent subject because of the entirety of factor such as the tendency to exhaust the resources, the economic globalization, the diminishing of the public sector's role, and the pronounced increased of pollution.

Business ethics is a field of applied, systematic study concerning the determination of moral principles, conduct, and behavior codes, which regulates the relations between business partners.

The ethical responsibility covers all those standards or norms that reflects the concern for what community considers as being right, fair, or in connection with respect or protection of participants at the business process. From a certain perspective, ethical changes or values go before to lay down as a rule some legal principles, because they become the creative force of laws and regulations.

The evolution of business ethics clearly determined ethical responsibility as part of social responsibility. This category of social responsibility must be considered in a dynamic interaction with legal responsibility. Thus, legal responsibility unceasingly amplifies assigning vast expectations regarding the methods and standards of corporations' actions. The programs of social responsibility require efforts from the entire corporation. The following activities can be distinguished: overseeing promotional actions of the company, exposing of important data for designing of the products, studying consumers' satisfaction and processing their complaints, solving customers' questions, elaborating guarantees, supervising product packing and labeling, selecting contractors, improving the quality control, conducting a study concerning the growth of products' safety, elaborating the educational programs for clients.

Romanian companies perceive CSR mostly as a marketing tool, that may bring them profit, and not as an assembly of strategies of economic, social, and environment involvement. The processes and standards applied in a corporation refer to politics of social responsibility, the reference concerning social involvement, social entrepreneurial, new organizational forms, and conduct codes. The financial reports are sporadically and often inconsistent, because in Romania, only few societies (often multinational societies) publish, more than financial results, enforced by economic law, other type of reports—social and environmental. Romanian companies avoid to elaborate social and environmental reports, preferring to publish aleatory data.

In Romania, the reference concerning social involvement is shallow, more quantitative than qualitative, and the debate on this subject rather refers to the dimensions of involvement, to the catalyzer of the phenomena and to the barriers against it, and also spreading out on a large scale of this type of behavior, especially among the autochthonous organizations. However, many years have passed since the change of communist regime, and Romania still faces difficulties regarding the manifestation of responsible social behavior of organizations, which even though diminished, haven't vanished.

2. Stakeholder Involvement

As institutions based on ethics, the companies are fully engaged to ensure the observance of the specific legislation, the avoidance and elimination of interests conflict, keeping the confidentiality of clients data, and including the regulations for fighting corruption. For that purpose, the operating ethical practices contribute significantly to the constant improvement of the performance, competitiveness of the companies, and their acknowledgement.

A social responsible company means not only to fulfill its legal obligations applicable in its own activity field, but to go further on, investing more in the human capital, in the environment, and in the relationships with the interested groups: suppliers, partners, and clients. The experiences with the investments made in responsible technologies and management and business practices that went beyond the simple abidance by the law, showed that they lead to an increased competitiveness and have a direct impact on the company's productivity.

In regard to the survival and development of any company, an important role is represented by the loyalty of the consumers. This is not easy at all now that we can notice how the competition has become even stronger. The key for a company to keep its consumers close throughout the life of its products and services is to give them constant quality updates, as well as regarding the innovation, the prices, the accessibility, but also the safety, finding therefore a way to stand out for the targeted audience.

To win the trust of its customers, a company needs to keep its promises. The trust is built while the expectations of the consumer are fulfilled regarding the product, and most of the companies that fail do so because they break this bond of trust with the consumer. This is because currently, the consumers are better informed than before, skeptical and thorough. Generally, the product and service offers are among the most generous, and the obvious answer for any disappointed client is to focus their attention on the offers by the competition.

The corporations must take the responsibility to inform periodically its partners and the public regarding the strategic objectives, the activities, and orientations toward the business ethic.

Any corporation must prove to the customer that it cares if it wants to win and to bear the customer's respect. The corporation that keeps its public promises, which constantly update its products, which gives transparency, visibility, which simplifies the way of use is the one that gets to have the respect of consumers.

Between corporations and their consumers, the bonds of loyalty and respect are built, and their duration is ensured by emphasizing the emotional bond. At the same time, the created bond is a win–win situation because the consumer feels respected and valued by having his wishes taken into account, while for the companies, the loyal customers represent the most important, believable, and non-costly source of advertising.

The corporate responsibility is a concept that mirrors the obligation of corporations to consider employees', shareholders', and customers' concern, but also other ecological aspects and the influence towards the unfolded economic operations of the environment. CSR is a profitable management strategy, which generates the long-term credibility and trust, which helps the companies to strengthen their relations with the shareholders, business partners, or customers.

The corporations can form within their applicable legal framework their own governance system to ensure the customer confidence and satisfaction, the share value growth, and the social responsibility.

Corporations aim to create a working environment where the individual differences are accepted and appreciated. Positive or negative discrimination of any kind based on actual or supposed attributes of the given person, including but not limited to the skin color, nationality, ideological conviction, ethnic, disability, political views or of any other nature, civil status, and so forth, is forbidden.

Corporations need to refrain from any behavior that could lead to the restriction of the competition on the market or to the abuse of their dominant economic position. Such behavior can include, among others, entering into an unfair economic competition (in a manner that violates or jeopardizes the legitimate interests of the customers, competitors, and/or partners); making or accepting proposals to agree on prices; and the exchange of marketing information that affects the competition or divides the market and the customers.

One of the essential requirements for the confidential relationship between corporations and their clients is the strict protection of the business secrets and the customer information.

The corporations must be responsible by imposing fundamental values, such as trust, engagement, and development. They need to be involved in improving the purchasing power and the quality of life of as many customers as possible, along with responsible, professional, passionate, and valued collaborators. The key concern is to reduce the ecological footprint, to promote healthy eating, meet the safety and quality requirements, to engage in social solidarity activities, meet the customer's needs, contribute to the local economic development, but to give everyone a chance to succeed at the same time.

3. Business Ethics in Marketing

Advertising is very important both for the companies who advertise and for the consumer. In the case of fair publicity, the latter has the possibility to know better from numerous points of view about the existing products on the market and thus choose the most advantageous product. Companies should not confine themselves to offering quality goods or services. They must inform the consumers about their advantages to create a degree of gratitude and acceptability in each one's consciousness. To do this, businesses need to use properly the mass promotion tools of advertising, sales promotion, and public relations.

Advertising is a good way to inform and persuade to create preferences for a particular product or to motivate the consumers to consume a certain product.

As a result of the profound social and economic changes that the current Romanian society is aware of, as well as the spectacular evolution of an increasingly dynamic environment, companies are looking to find new solutions to gain a privileged position within a reference market.

At the same time, consumers are becoming more demanding and anxious to have quality products and services that would offer them maximum satisfaction. Consumers are better informed and benefit from the communication techniques used by advertisers and their advantages.

Commercial advertising must comply with certain principles, limits, and obligations. To ensure their fulfillment, certain control procedures have been established. In Romania, the Romanian Advertising Council was set up in 1992, a self-regulatory body in the advertising field, which represents the interests of the advertising industry in relation to the Romanian authorities. The Code of Practice in Advertising has been developed, which addresses all those involved in the advertising field, establishing ethical rules of professional conduct.

Referring to the legal framework and the areas of commercial advertising in Romania, we find that the advertising agencies, sales offices, and owners of publishing places must consider a series of normative papers: the 2000 law on advertising; the 2004 law on advertising and sponsorship for tobacco products; the 2008 law on misleading and comparative advertising; the 2007 law on consumer protection; and the Code of practice in advertising.

In Romania, the main control body is the National Audiovisual Council. It issues audiovisual licenses for the radio and television stations while ensuring that all broadcasters comply with the relevant legislative provisions in the field, in particular those relating to advertising. The control over the object, content, and the ways of programming the shows is made while they are broadcasting and not before. Other institutions that can claim a certain control over the adherence to the advertising rules are the National Authority for Consumer Protection and the Ministry of Public Health.

The Romanian legislation aims at protecting the consumers of products and services, protecting the general public interest against misleading advertising, protecting from the negative consequences of advertising, and setting out the conditions under which comparative advertising is allowed.

Advertising must be decent, accurate, and developed in a spirit of responsibility. The advertising that is delusive; prejudiced in respect to human dignity and public morality; includes discrimination based on race, language, social origin, and ethnic or national identity; attacks religious or political beliefs; damages the image, honor, dignity, and private lives of individuals; takes advantage of the superstitions, unwariness, or fear of individuals; compromises people's security or incite to violence; and encourages behaviors that damage the environment is prohibited.

Misleading advertising is any advertising that is likely to deceive the consumer and influence his economic behavior, either through presentation or by a misguided or ambiguous content, or by cutting out the essential information.

Misleading advertising can refer to any element that is likely to alter the consumer's behavior:

- Incorrect or cut information may refer to the economic operator, identity, and qualification.
- The characteristics of the products or services: by their availability, nature, geographical or commercial origin, the method by which they were manufactured.
- The price, the product or the service to which the price refers, the possible conditions to be respected, and so on.

Manipulation, along with persuasion, propaganda, and advertising, is part of the large family of communication forms, used in the sphere of social influence.

Manipulation is a widespread phenomenon, present in almost every dimension of our social life: politics, art, education, advertising, or even in interpersonal relationships.

The impact of the audiovisual message is very high, because it has one major asset: the image. Many times, after broadcasting an advertisement on TV, it happens that Romanians buy the products they would not normally consume.

The purpose of advertising should not be to trick one's emotions. Ads combining the visual with the auditory effects have the greatest impact. Good advertisements are those that work strictly on human motivation. We get into contact with so much information that the most important aspect for consumers is the critical spirit, the ability to discern.

Organic advertising developed under conditions where the environmental protection has become a subject that can no longer be avoided by the economic operators. Organic advertising is growing increasingly important in product labels and media. This refers to a product or service and the effect it has on the environment, including the production methods, used materials, packaging, and even the way the product will be used, for example, recycling.

Organic advertising faces a series of issues. The ads involved in this type of advertising are not always true. Economic operators often rely on the punctual easing of a single attribute of their product or service to show that it respects the environment, but a general statement can only be based on an overview examination of the product's life cycle and the assembly of its characteristics. It is possible for consumers to check if the ads are true. Verifying the effectiveness of a product at the moment of usage is relatively easy, but checking whether a product or service is as environment friendly and not polluting as the ads claim requires more knowledge than most consumers have. The trust in the green and clean labeling is a fundamental requirement for any design of a labeling scheme. By falsely indicating that a product or service is environmentally friendly and non-polluting traders do not encourage the responsible consumption. When the false indications are revealed, the consumers lose their trust in the green and environmentally friendly labeling, and the companies have to lose.

8 Ownership and Sustainability Practices in Emerging Economies*

1. Introduction

From the late twentieth century until present, the world has been changing rapidly due to forces such as globalization and information dissemination. This new age of globalization and information has reshaped entire industries across the globe resulting in falling entry barriers, less tight governmental legislations and control, and even boundaries across nations have eroded due to increased telecommunications and the internet. All these forces contribute to an ever-globalizing world in which many multinationals arise and economic traffic between organizations from numerous countries across the globe are becoming more standard than exception. These shifts give rise to the development of new theories, to better cope with the changed environment, and to trends that emerge in the field of management literature. One of these trends that have gained substantial scholar interest in the last couple of decades is corporate social responsibility (CSR). Although corporate social responsibility is a recent term, business ethics, social dimensions, and the general idea of corporate statesmanship have been around for a very long time (e.g., Carroll, 1999; Blowfield & Frynas, 2005).

Recordings of particular ideas on business practices based on moral principles that should serve the community as a whole instead of a lucky few date way back. But as time changes, so does our perception of what CSR entails, so as Carroll (1999) state, the modern era of CSR begins in the 1950s with the upcoming of social responsibility, or as Jenkins (2005) argues, the current definition of CSR really started with global deregulation and the shift away from state intervention in business policies took place within the developed countries in the 1980s, freeing up organizations possibilities to act opportunistically, and giving rise to the question of *who*, *how*, and *if* these organizations are willing and able to act socially responsible intrinsically, without real external pressures from the government.

As a result of this deregulation and the regulatory vacuum that arose, an increased scientific interest in CSR, within developed countries, became apparent in the early 1990s. After redefining the CSR definition and putting it in a broader context as more of an umbrella term for a variety of theories

(Blowfield & Frynas, 2005), a lot of empirical research has been acted out on CSR in developed countries. A vast body of literature has investigated CSR and its possible link toward organizational performance and financial performance in particular, for companies within developed countries, such as the United Stated, the United Kingdom, Western Europe, and Japan. The findings of different studies on the influence of CSR on organizational performance are contradictory and inconclusive. Studies that suppose a long-term beneficial influence on organizational (financial) performance are contradicted by research showing the opposite, and vice versa (Blowfield & Frynas, 2005; Kolk et al., 2010).

In contrast to this vast body of literature on CSR in developed countries, there is little or insufficient knowledge and research done, in emerging countries, in the field of CSR. Firm development in emerging markets is intertwined with sustainability and the need for sustainable world development. The economic dimension of sustainability focuses on an increased return on investment (ROI), revenue and market share increases, lower costs, reduced risks, etc. The environmental dimension encompasses activities to preserve, protect, conserve, and restore ecosystems and natural resources (e.g., climate change policies, preservation of natural resources, and minimization and prevention of toxic waste). The social dimension addresses conditions and actions that specifically affect humanity (e.g., poverty, unemployment, education, health, human rights, etc.). Sustainability is critical for the developing world to ensure long-term business success, while significantly contributing toward sustainable world development through a healthy environment and a stable society. Institutions, both formal and informal, facilitate or hinder sustainable business practices.

As Muller and Kolk (2010) state that although in recent years the attention for corporate social responsibility in emerging countries has increased, the majority of research done in this field still focusses on developed countries. As the emerging countries, and the BRIC (Brazil, Russia, India, China) in particular, contribute, by their rapid growth, substantially to the world's economy on the one hand and are potential growth markets for Western firms on the other hand, it is necessary and useful to investigate them more thoroughly. Rapid economic development goes accompanied by an increase in environmental pollution and waste output, and it should therefore be important to ensure that organizations act socially responsible to minimize the damage to the environment. Research into CSR practices within these countries is on this ground alone a sufficient reason to argue necessity.

Additionally, there are noticeable differences between the types of governments when comparing developed countries and the governments of the emerging countries. These differences form a driver for the interest in emerging countries according to Muller and Kolk (2010) for there has been the idea that CSR, as a Western concept, is not by definition applicable elsewhere, and therefore needs further investigation. This means that CSR may be interpreted differently across countries and regions, which implies that judging local companies on "Western" standards will yield few useable results (Muller & Kolk, 2007). While the governmental structures and influences differ between developed countries and emerging countries, and therefore the pressure that governments put on organizations to act socially responsible differ, this gives need to study what drives CSR within emerging countries.

There are a lot of potential factors that drive CSR practices acted out or implemented by organizations within the emerging countries. One particular interesting driver is partially linked to the governmental structures and regulations that an emerging market's government enforces. As stated above, as privatizing and deregulation became apparent for developed countries in the 1980s, it becomes more and more apparent in developing countries nowadays. In China for example, it just became easily possible to enter the Chinese market without needing to start up an equity joint venture with a Chinese based, mostly state-owned organization. China in particular would be a feasible setting in which to conduct research on CSR. Although most emerging countries still have a substantial public domain, with much state-owned companies, they are starting to privatize rapidly. But does this privatization, this freeing up the market by allowing more ownership structures, have any influence on the way organizations see CSR or how, or which type of practices they implement or act out? Does it matter if an organization is state owned or privately owned when it comes to CSR practices?

This research contributes to the literature by providing an enhanced insight in the contradictory debate between scholars on the effects and influence of ownership structures on CSR initiatives (e.g., Baskin, 2006; Jenkins, 2005). The current literature is contradicting in its findings whether ownership structure has any effects on CSR practices. Various studies, mostly done in developed countries are contradicting and inconclusive. Our research shifts this debate from developed countries to emerging countries, but also by testing these contradicting outcomes in a specific and totally new setting to provide a more complete view on CSR in emerging countries and an enhanced insight in the ongoing CSR debate.

The results of this study into CSR initiatives in emerging countries and their relationship with ownership structure allow the public to formulate a well-substantiated opinion on the way that particular organizations, namely those investigated in this study, carry out their businesses. It will increase public awareness on which organizations really contribute to their community and which do not. This effect will be the most plausible for the public within the explored emerging market for that CSR practices reflect culture and are partially country specific (Pietro-Carron et al., 2006). This means that the types of CSR practices organizations indulge in possibly differ between countries, while the cultural views on what is important of even what CSR is possibly differ. So, the CSR practices implemented in an emerging market may not always reflect the societal views, on what is thought to be important, of the public in developed countries. Furthermore, as Muller and Kolk (2010) state, the obtained insight by managers, in CSR activity and the aspects most important in China, contributes to identifying the areas for mutual learning or further development and interest, which are key for managers in order to create and act upon risen opportunities and possibilities.

2. Theoretical Framework

2.1. CSR Practices

The formulation and definition of CSR has changed over time. As Windsor (2001) states that there are significant difficulties in distinguishing whether business behavior is truly a moral conduct or instrumental adoption of an appearance of moral conduct as useful reputational strategy, every definition of what CSR implies and ought to entail is therefore open for debate. In the period from the 1990s until present, the focus has shifted partially from defining what CSR is, to conducting empirical research to assess the CSR practices in the field. One of the most generally used contemporary definitions of CSR today is that which Prieto-Carron et al. (2006) have adopted from the commission of the European Communities (2001), which states that CSR is "a concept whereby companies integrate social and environmental concerns in their business operations and in their interactions with their stakeholders on a voluntary basis." This definition is therefore the definition applied in this research. As the introduction clearly states, most studies done on CSR empirical as well as conceptual or literature reviews have focused on developed countries, and there has been a lack of knowledge on CSR practices within emerging countries. For these countries are becoming increasingly important and dominant players within the world's economy, it is relevant and necessary to investigate these countries. CSR has been interpreted and viewed in a variety of ways throughout time as the construct developed. Throughout the development of CSR, certain dimensions became visible; although scholars named them differently, a clear distinction was made. According to Dahlsrud (2006), these dimensions are Economic, Environmental, Social, Legal, and Voluntary. He also described CSR practices as "a set of management practices that ensure that companies maximize the positive impact of their operation on society or operating in a manner that meets and even exceeds the legal, ethical, commercial and public expectations that society have of a business." Different dimensions consists of different practices or actions that organizations can or must implement to satisfy society.

Economic practices of CSR are practices that organizations use in relation to financial aspects. So practices can relate to profit maximization, economic development, and business operations. This means that this normally is an organization's primary goal to ensure business continuity and to stay in business (Dahlsrud, 2006).

Environmental practices of CSR are practices that have to do with the natural environment. Particular practices are restricted or have to be implemented for governmental legislation demands it. An example is the restriction on the total amount of toxic waste production factories are allowed to produce. But environmental practices within CSR stress the organizations awareness of environmental concerns for they implement them in business operations. Examples of CSR practices are waste reduction and recycling (Dahlsrud, 2006).

Legal practices of CSR are those practices that are forced upon organizations by governmental legislation. This legislation can be seen in various dimensions of an organization's environment. Examples are legislation on work or labor aspects, imposing taxes, etc. This legislation set boundaries for organizations to operate within (Carrol, 1991).

Social/voluntary practices of CSR are those practices not prescribed by law, but based upon ethical values. They are voluntary by nature and are based upon the relationship between the organization and its social environment (society). Examples of social/voluntary practices of CSR are donating and community work (Carrol, 1991; Dahlrud, 2006).

2.2. CSR in China

The introductory chapter stated that a sizeable body of literature has been built up on the concept of CSR within developed (Western) countries. More recently, attention to CSR has grown in emerging countries, but it remains under researched, especially in empirical sense, in comparison to the body of literature on developed countries. Although there are a number of countries that are named as emerging markets, research tends to focus on the BRIC (Brazil, Russia, India and China) countries in particular. From these countries, the notion of CSR seems to hardly have been studied in China as Kolk et al. (2010) state in their article. They provide a decent overview of academic research done with regard to CSR initiatives and practices in China up until 2008. What becomes apparent from the literature on CSR in China is that most of the Chinese managers have "mistaken ideas about CSR," and they tend to view it as similar to charity, and as a concern for the government and large companies, not the smaller ones (Kolk et al., 2010). They tend to see CSR as a burden that delineates them from their core task of generating profits.

The main drivers to act socially responsible and to implement CSR practices were to generate wealth for the society, promote the nations development, and brand building. Also a cultural context possibly contributes to the Chinese reluctance to CSR, for they might see CSR as a Western scheme to price China out of the cheap labor market, as stated by Chen (2005). The Chinese government plays a leading role in the development of CSR practices in China, for they formed regulation, which imposes restrictions on, for example, environmental pollution and improved working conditions.

Thus, CSR as a practice has first been "enforced" upon organizations by the government as an external regulatory institution. It should be noted that ensuring compliance to these regulations is rather problematic within China for as Dyer (2007) state that in the environmental sector, we see Chinese legislation that is even stricter than European law, yet implementation is sometimes non-existent. Although government pressure on companies in China to publish environmental information has increased, environmental reporting was still uncommon (Kolk et al., 2010; Welford, 2005). This notion is recurrent in the CSR literature on China, the environmental dimension of CSR seems to be most discussed and problematic throughout the CSR literature available on China, and generally, it tends to be seen as a cost for companies at this stage of development. Although reporting on CSR by Chinese companies is still very limited, a trend toward more openness and publishing of reports is visible in China. This gives rise to the argument that CSR practices are becoming more accepted and implemented by Chinese organizations.

The construct of CSR in China is becoming increasingly popular among researchers to investigate, with most studies focusing on the dilemma how to combine economic growth, environmental protection, and the improvement of labor standards. The next step is to empirically test CSR in the field across a variety of Chinese industries to analyze to what extent Chinese organizations implement CSR practices and which practices they implement.

2.3. *Ownership Structure*

The ownership structure represents the distribution of equity with regard to votes and capital, but also to the identity of the equity owners. These structures are of major importance in corporate governance because they determine the incentives of managers and thereby the economic efficiency of the corporations they manage. So, it distinguished between the ownership of the organization and the control of the organizations. This means that for listed organizations, the shareholders are the owners, but the appointed management is responsible for the control of the organization. There are numerous different types of ownership structures possible, which all differ in ownership and control forms.

When looking at differences between markets and countries, it becomes apparent that there are substantial differences between them. When looking at the developed markets, the state has low stakes in particular profit organizations, while the government believes in a free-market policy without much governmental interference. Ownership structure in emerging countries such as China is formed differently. Emerging countries and China in particular tend to have a vast public sector, which means that a lot of companies and institutions are state owned. Although most of the emerging countries move toward a more free-market principle, the role that the central and local governments play is still substantial.

Generally, there are five dominant ownership structures: individual ownership, shared ownership, government ownership, outside ownership, and managerial ownership. When looking at China, three of these ownership structures are also dominant (Xu & Wang, 1999; Bai et al., 2000): *individual ownership* meaning that all the decision-making power lies concentrated within one person or family; *shared ownership*: the decision-making power lies with the different groups of shareholders; and *government ownership*: all of the decision-making power lies with the government who is the sole or main owner of the organization.

Furthermore, China has also adopted a strategy of reforming the state-owned enterprises (government ownership), by privatizing particular sectors to make them more competitive and cost efficient from the 1990s (Bai et al., 2000). A trend is visible of a growing private sector of listed stock companies (shared ownership), listed on the Chinese stock markets and stock markets abroad. These companies, called stock companies in this research, are included in this study. This is truly a substantial part of Chinese organizations still owned and controlled by the state and is therefore going to be included in this research. The second type of companies is called state-owned enterprises or SOE's in this research. Next to these two ownership types, stock companies and SOE's, is a third dominant structure, namely private companies (individual ownership), which is investigated to compare the three different domains of public, semi-private, and private firms in China. A discussion and a definition of these specific ownership structures will be stated in the following subsections.

2.3.1. State-Owned Enterprises

SOEs are, in this study, defined as organizations owned, controlled, and governed by a government (Xu & Wang, 1999; Bai et al., 2000). SOEs have particular characteristics from which they can be distinguished from other organizations and from which ownership structure can be derived. SOEs are in general vast organizations, which means that they are substantial in size. Their large size is not only reflected in the number of employees, but also in available resources and turnover. Although it is plausible to argue that a SOE from the Netherlands is relatively small in size when compared to a SOE from a large country such as China, when compared to the size of an average stock or private organization from the Netherlands, it can still be described as substantial. The size of SOEs also has its drawbacks because they are mostly very bureaucratic organizations with multiple layers of management (decision makers), which slows the decision-making process substantially and decreases its capability to change, thus promoting inertia. (Bai et al., 2000). SOEs in China differ from SOEs that were visible or are still visible within developed countries. Within developed countries, SOEs were mostly organizations and regulatory agencies that were owned and controlled by the government, while they had a public function. Examples of this are utility services, such as electric companies, water facilities, and public transportation. Governments argued that these functions and services were or are directly linked to the public's well-being, and arranging them to function properly was a task and the responsibility of the government (Bai et al., 2000). Where most developed countries tend to have a substantial private domain, this is not the case for the emerging countries and China in particular (Xu & Wang, 1999). In contrast to the developed countries in which there are just a few SOEs that arrange public services, there are numerous SOEs within China and throughout all types of industries. In addition, the fact that SOEs are regulating and arranging public services, and the stated difference between developed countries and emerging countries considering, not only the number of SOEs, but also the usage of these SOEs by the state, differs between developed countries and China, according to Xu and Wang 1999.

2.3.2. Stock Companies

Stock companies are defined as a listed company with a mixed ownership structure with three dominant groups of shareholders, namely the state, legal persons (institutions), and individuals (Xu & Wang, 1999). Stock companies are a common form of ownership structure, which means that these particular companies are listed on stock exchanges, and entities, persons, and other organizations are able to buy shares of a particular company. Stock companies are visible throughout Europe from as early as the thirteenth century, but in those days there were no exchanges in which people traded their shares. There were only collaborations by different merchants to gain advantages and produce more efficiently (Tu Kha Tran, 2008). As Tu Kha Tran (2008) states, the initial emergence of joint stock companies was parlayed through brotherhood for the advancement of mutually beneficial transactions. The Merchant Adventures of England was one of the first organizations that were "officially acknowledged, though indirectly recognized by act of parliament" (Lingelback, XXII) in the late sixteenth century. Stock exchanges also arose in the sixteenth century in Europe, with the Dutch stock exchange being the first in 1611 (Tu Kha Tran, 2008).

Stock companies and stock markets did not exist in China until the late 1980s. In the beginning of the Chinese reformation of SOEs into stock companies, companies in which outsiders were able to acquire stakes, stock trading was still prohibited in most industries, and low liquidity of stocks made it difficult for the companies to market their initial offerings (Xu & Wang, 1999). Consequently, black market trading emerged in several large cities across China. To end the chaotic black market trading, the State Council decided in 1989 to establish two national stock exchanges. The Shanghai Stock Exchange (SHSE) and the Shenzhen Stock Exchange (SZSE) opened in 1990 and 1991, respectively. The number of listed companies, trading volume, and total market capitalization has increased drastically since the opening of the two exchanges. The total number of firms listed increased from 183 in 1993 to 323 in 1995, and over 500 in 1996 (Xu & Wang, 1999).

Although the Chinese government had started a reform strategy, for some SOE's incurred substantial losses, the stock companies that were privatized in the early stages did not go without governmental supervision and control. (Tsui et al., 2004) The Chinese government merged free-standing SOE's into "holdings that were allowed to select a subsidiary from its larger group of organizations in which shares could be sold to individual and institutional investors on both domestic and international stock markets" (Tsui et al., 2004). This shows that Chinese stock companies differ from traditionally Western type stock companies, in which the government does not have any control, governance structures, or stake in (Tsui et al., 2004; Demsetz & Lehn, 1985). For as Xu and Wang (1999) state, the government is still one of the dominant groups of shareholders within Chinese stock companies, something that is uncommon for Western stock companies, the influence of the Chinese state is still visible within these companies.

When looking at the trend visible during these last decades, governmental influence or the importance of the Chinese government as a shareholder in newly erected stock companies is declining according to Xu and Wang (1999). Rules and regulations have loosened to the extent that it is allowed to form a stock company without direct influence, through shares, from the government. So, new organizations that have been founded during this last decade, and are listed on the stock exchanges, do not necessarily have the state as dominant shareholder to deal with when executing their business. While this is true, still the largest group of stock companies on the stock exchanges deals with the state as one of the dominant groups of shareholders.

2.3.3. Private Companies

Private companies are companies or corporations whose ownership is private. Private companies issue stocks and have shareholders, but their shares do not trade on public exchanges and are not issued to the general public. A private company is treated as a single legal entity with rights and liabilities separate from its owners. Owners and other private investors are shareholders in the private company. Private companies or private limited companies, as they are referred to in the United Kingdom and the United States, are characterized by a number of distinct characteristics. Private companies are usually owned by family members. These companies are formed by at least minimum two shareholders to maximum 50 shareholders. A private limited company is considered as one of the most easily managed and cost-effective business structures (Goktan & Ucar, 2012). Private companies are the most common form of business structure and therefore ownership structure within the Western developed countries. (Goktan & Ucar, 2012) This is because they are easy to start up, have no size restrictions, and have no strict filing requirements for their annual reports as public or stock companies do. When looking at private companies within China, it becomes apparent according to Bai et al. (2000), that these companies are usually relatively small family-owned businesses, passed on from father to son. Although there is no restriction to the type of industry in which private companies are founded, they are usually started in less capital intensive markets. This means that there are more private companies found in retail than in manufacturing. In China, there is also a substantial informal circuit of small local companies that operate but that are not listed officially as private companies (Xu & Wang, 1999). While this study is investigating the possible relationship between ownership structure and CSR practices, these informal businesses will be excluded, for ownership structure cannot be determined confidently.

2.4. Hypotheses

By linking the different types of ownership structures with different types of CSR practices, this section elaborates on the possible relationships between them.

SOEs and CSR Practices

As Bai et al. (2000) state that SOEs in general are charged not only with the task of efficient production and generating economic gains, but have also the obligation and task to provide and increase social welfare for the society as a whole. SOE's are not able to achieve this desired and expected improvement of societal welfare by acting irresponsible and chasing pure economic gains without looking at the consequences. By implementing numerous CSR practices, SOEs are able to achieve better labor standards, environmental output reduction, and serve society as a whole. Also true for Chinese SOE's for Zu and Song (2009) state that "Chinese enterprises, especially in the State sector, always had a tradition of taking social responsibility for their employees by providing safety nets and social protection through its work-unit system known as Danwei." Economic gain becomes more important even for SOEs, the managers are still appointed by the Communist Party, and they would "naturally share their ideology with the state in favor of the communist tradition. For them, the external fashion defined as CSR might just match the remnants of their socialistic beliefs." Therefore, we formulate the following hypothesis:

> Hypothesis 1: State-owned enterprises in China implement more CSR practices than stock or private companies on all different types of CSR practices.

Stock Companies and CSR Practices

Stock companies as stated by Xu and Wang (1999) are of mixed ownership and subjected to various stakeholder pressures. Whilst for stock companies in developed countries the state or government is not a dominant stakeholder, CSR practices are implemented by pressures from shareholders and public opinion. Although certain legislation on environmental and labor standards is imposed by the government, these standards are "easily" met and are not a measure for CSR practices driven by the companies themselves. Stock companies in general are thus "free" to initiate CSR practices on all fronts discussed earlier. For China, this is not entirely true given the fact that the Chinese government is one of the dominant shareholders within stock companies, they are likely to put pressure on these companies to act socially responsible. As Xu and Wang (1999) state, in close to 50% of the stock companies, the board of directors is dominated by state officials, which allows them to put severe pressure on the other board members to achieve their objectives. But another pressure coming from outside the organization is believed to be a stronger and greater incentive to act socially responsible for this type of companies. This pressure is formed by the fact that most stock companies in China are multinationals (MNCs) and they sell their products across the globe. Western society (governments) and other regulatory agencies (EU, US) put pressure on these companies to implement CSR practices as this is a perquisite to be allowed onto the European and US markets. As Western society emphasizes the importance of adequate labor standards (child labor, sweat-shops, etc.) the following hypothesis is stated by this research.

> Hypothesis 2: Chinese stock companies will implement more CSR practices related to labor standards rather than to other types of CSR practices.

Private Companies and CSR Practices

Private organizations are entirely free to seek maximum economic gain whilst respecting the governmental legislation and restrictions for the specific industry they operate in. As Lin-Hi (2010) states, private organizations are mostly smaller organizations that in general do not see implementing CSR initiatives as very beneficial. Owners reason that the costs to implement CSR initiatives are too great to bear. Within the Chinese context, private companies are argued to be organizations without state interference that are free to pursue purely economic gains. For this type of organizations do not arise from privatization initiatives and state reform as the stock companies do and, therefore, have to be built from the ground up, they tend to be seen as smaller, locally based organizations with less resources. For they are free to pursue economic gains as sole entrepreneurial goal, their potential for growth is theoretically enormous. Private companies have less pressures put on them to implement CSR practices for they, mostly, do not sell abroad, but operate and sell locally and have less governmental pressure placed upon them. But as Xu and Wang (1999) state, a pressure from the local society is to be distinguished for these type of companies, for they are mostly dependent on the local community to sell their products. The local community serves as their local market, and without them, they will not be able to stay in business. So, this pressure coming from the local society is argued to be a pressure toward implementing CSR practices that are beneficiary for the local community. Therefore, we formulate the following hypotheses:

Hypothesis 3: Private companies in China will implement less CSR initiatives than Chinese SOEs and Chinese stock companies in general.

Hypothesis 4: Private companies in China will implement more social-related CSR practices rather than other types of CSR practices.

3. Methodology

3.1. Data Collection Procedure and Sample Selection

The data collection procedure started with the formation of the questionnaire based on the earlier studies as mentioned before. This first English version was reviewed internally, and the content and order of the questions were adapted. After this first adaptation, the questionnaire was put online via questionpro.com. We have chosen this website for this is one of the only online survey websites that support the Chinese language. The English version was posted online, and we asked some managers to test it. Meetings were scheduled in which feedback was received. These meetings led to slight adaptation of the questions and the layout. To address the unit of analyses, namely top managers within Chinese organizations, a database, called INFOT BUSINESS DATABASE CHINA, consisting of more than 9,000 Chinese companies and accompanying e-mail addresses was acquired. After filtering, we obtained possible 4,500 respondents, which we consider a good population size sufficient to obtain a useful sample size. After 4 months, our English questionnaire had 134 views, 31 starts, and 14 completed the survey. Our Chinese questionnaire was used far more often and had 789 views, 409 starts, and 265 finished surveys. The effective response rate was 279 out of 4,500 which is about 6%. But as the table below shows the usable surveys dropped to 111 for a lot of respondents did not fill in all the questions. Table 8.1 shows the complete overview of response statistics.

In this study, there were three groups that all needed to consist of a sufficient number of respondents. A rule of thumb is that the sample size needs to be at least 20 respondents per group to ensure an adequate analysis and

Table 8.1 Response Statistics

Language	Views	Starts	Completed	Usable
Chinese questionnaire	789	409	265	98
English questionnaire	134	31	14	13
Total	**923**	**440**	**279**	**111***

Table 8.2 Division of Respondents

Group	*Respondents*
State-owned company	35
Mixed state/private institutions	34
Private company	37
Total	**106***

* The difference between the 111 useable respondents (Table 8.2), and the 106 respondents stated in this table are the missing values. These missing values are below the 10% cut-off point and show no particular pattern, so this is not problematic.

that group sizes are approximately equal (Hair et al. 2014). The division of respondents over the three groups is shown in Table 8.2.

3.2. *Operationalization*

The operationalization of the different variables is shown below in Table 8.3.

Control variables: Because size and industry have been suggested in previous articles as factors that affect both firm performance and CSR, both of these characteristics are used as control variables (Brammer & Millington, 2006). Size is an important control variable, since larger firms seem to adopt the CSR principles more often. Therefore, in this study, we control for the possible effects of size.

Furthermore, according to Brammer and Millington (2006) some industries are more visible to the public than other industries, and therefore, stakeholder pressure will be greater for firms operating in these industries. Organizations in those particular highly visible industries may be legally forced to uphold a higher CSR standard than other organizations. This effect is also applicable to emerging markets, and therefore, we control for the effects of industry in this study.

3.3. *Measurement and Technique*

Ownership structure has been measured through a single nominal item offering a choice between the three groups (SOEs, stock, and private companies).

Table 8.3 Operationalization

Concepts	*Variables*	*Indicators*	*Source*
CSR	Social responsibilities (Philltotal)	— The amount of money donated to charity per year — Philanthropic contributions in different fields — Community projects in different fields	Muller and Kolk (2009)
	Environmental responsibilities (ENVtotal)	— Renewable energy in percentage of the total energy — Recycling in percentage of total waste produced — Days of environmental training for non-management	Muller and Kolk (2009)
	Labor responsibilities (LABOURtotal)	— Women in management in percentage of the total management — Days of vocational training per employee per year — Days lost per employee per year	Muller and Kolk (2009)
Ownership structure (OS)	State-owned enterprises (SOE)	— State owned	Bai et al. (2000)
	Stock companies (mix)	— State/ institutions/ individuals	Xu and Wang (1999)
	Privately owned companies	— Public limited companies	EF Fama and MC Jensen (1983)

For there are no other ownership structures, a possible fourth option which consists of other has not been presented in the questionnaire.

The variable industry was measured in the questionnaire as a multiple-choice item which consists of ten industries: mining and ore processing, machine building, textiles and apparel, chemicals, consumer products, food processing, transportation, communications, services, and other. When assessing the data that the respondents provided, it became clear that there were a lot of different industries present in the sample. Although this normally is a positive finding when wanting to control for industry, the division between these industries was not equally distributed and, as stated earlier, some industries have a higher visibility than other industries. For this is

Table 8.4 Recoded Industry Variable

CSR Visibility	*Industry*
Low	Services, communications, textiles and apparel, and other
High	Chemicals, machine building, mining and ore processing, transportation, food processing, consumer goods

the case we tried to group and recode the industries into two groups (high/low) with regards to the CSR involvement for that particular industry. This has been done using the existing literature by Waddock and Graves (1997). They categorized firms within their sample from similar industries according to the average CSR in that particular industry. We have taken over their categorization and came with the division of industries that is stated in Table 8.4.

The variable size is measured by two questions in the questionnaire. The first item asked for actual revenue stated in US dollars (USD). The other question was on the number of employees present. A couple of problems arose with the question on the actual revenue for the responses given were not useful to interpret them correctly. The responses that the respondents gave were stated in numerous currencies next to the currency asked, namely USD. In the beginning we tried to recalculate the given answers to USD, but this became problematic when almost 35% of responses were in the wrong currency. Therefore, we choose to discard this variable, leaving the item on employees as the only one used for the size as a control variable.

The three different dimensions of CSR namely Environment, Labor, and Philanthropy are all measured by the 5-point Likert scale items. The dimensions or constructs Environment and Labor are measured through three questions each and the construct Philanthropy is measured with a single 5-point Likert scale item and two checklist questions on which the contributions areas were made by the organizations. To carry out the statistical analysis, the three items on Environment have been grouped and recoded into one variable (ENVtotal). This procedure has also been carried out for the labor dimension (LABOURtotal). The dimension Philanthropy, consisting of one 5-point Likert scale item and two checklist questions needed the most recoding work. The 5-point Likert scale item was recoded with scores ranging from zero to one (1=0, 2=0.25, 3=0.5, 4=0.75, 5=1). Afterwards, the two checklist questions in which respondents could answer yes or no to doing community work or making donations have been recoded (yes=1 and n =0). After this recoding, the three items were grouped together and recoded into one variable (PHILtotal). Furthermore, a new variable (CSR-total) is created by grouping all nine questions together. This has been done to test the hypothesis stated above.

Analysis of the data is done by a (M)ANOVA technique, which is aimed at detecting and examining differences in variances between groups. In this study, this entails the differences between the three ownership structure groups and how they vary on the implementation of CSR practices.

4. Analysis and Results

Ownership structure was normally distributed and is therefore suitable for the statistical analysis methods of (M)ANOVA and t-test. The respondents were asked to choose between three different ways their organization was owned. They were given the choice between state owned, mix, and privately owned. The scores on this particular question are listed in Table 8.9. This table shows us that the division of answers given is fairly equal. Thirty-five respondents were from state-owned companies, 42 were from privately owned organizations, and 34 were from mixed organizations. This equality in group sizes ensures that the independent variable ownership structure is suitable for an (M)ANOVA analysis.

Before starting the hypothesis testing, an overview of the CSR practices results is presented. The results of this study show that in the emerging economy of China for this particular sample, private companies implement the most CSR practices in total. Stock companies rank second, and SOEs rank third on the total mean scores on CSR. Also, the types of CSR practices implemented by Chinese organizations are mainly environmental 40%, followed by labor practices approximately 35%, and social at 25%. It is interesting to see that almost all organizations implement all three different types of CSR practices, but differ on the amount of effort they put into a particular practice type.

Table 8.5 shows the hypothesis accompanied by the method of analysis and the outcomes.

Thus, to examine if SOEs implement more CSR practices than stock or private companies (H1) and if private companies implement less CSR initiatives than other companies (H3), an ANOVA was conducted. The between-groups score, even though not significant, displays a trend, since 0.053 is close to being a significant difference ($p < 0.05$). To test between which groups a trend is visible, a post hoc analysis has been carried out by means of Tukey HSD test. This test confirms the visibility of a trend between SOEs and private companies.

To examine (H2) whether stock companies implement more CSR practices related to labor standards than to other CSR practices, a t-test was used. The outcomes show a significant difference between the variables related to labor practices and the variables related to environmental practices $t(33) = 4.38$, $p = 0.000$. To check whether the other values were also significant, a one-sample t-test was also conducted on the smallest value, namely the three questions on philanthropic contributions grouped

Table 8.5 Hypothesis With Outcomes

Hypothesis	*Measurement*	*Outcome*
Hypothesis 1: *State-owned enterprises in China implement more CSR practices than stock or private companies on all different types of CSR practices.*	ANOVA	F(2,103) = 3.03, p = 0.053 (not significant)
Hypothesis 2: *Chinese stock companies will implement more CSR practices related to labor standards than to other types of CSR practices.*	t-test	*t*(33) = 4.38 p= 0.000. (significant)
Hypothesis 3: *Private companies in China will implement less CSR initiatives than Chinese SOEs and Chinese stock companies in general.*	ANOVA	F(2,103) = 3.03, p = 0.053 (not significant)
Hypothesis 4: *Private companies in China will implement more social-related CSR practices than other types of CSR practices.*	t-test	*t(37)* = –50,33, p = 0.000 (significant, but negatively instead of positively)

together (PHILtotal) (1.38). The outcome also shows a significant difference $t(33) = 16.96$, $p = 0.000$.

To examine H4, whether private companies implement social-related practices more than other CSR practices, another one-sample t-test was performed. The first t-test between the philanthropic contributions (PHILtotal) and environmental CSR practices (ENVtotal) shows a significant difference $t(37) = -50.33$, $p = 0.000$. The second t-test between philanthropic contributions (PHILtotal) and the CSR practices related to labor (LABOURtotal) also shows a significant difference $t(37) = -61.34$, $p = 0.000$.

5. Discussion and Conclusions

This study focusses on the relationship between ownership structure and CSR practices in China. It has done so by investigating three different types of ownership structures most present in China, namely SOEs enterprises, stock companies, and private companies across ten industries. Through an e-mail questionnaire, middle and higher managers were asked how much their organization was involved in different types of CSR practices. Findings support that Chinese stock companies commit more to labor responsibilities and implement more CSR practices related to labor standards than to other types of CSR practices, such as philanthropic or environmental practices. Furthermore, private companies commit themselves more to labor and environmental responsibilities and less to philanthropic CSR. Finally, results show that no particular ownership types are dominant in the field of CSR in China and that different types of ownership structure elucidate different CSR commitments.

The model used in this study was based on four hypotheses, and this section will elaborate on the outcomes from the content point of view. It was argued that SOEs enterprises in China implement more CSR practices than stock or private companies. Although a positive trend, a weak positive relationship was visible between the groups SOEs and private companies, no significant association was found. A possible implication for this positive but weak trend could be that when gathering a larger sample, it will become significant, and the claims of Zu and Song (2019) would be justified. Another possible explanation for the weakness of this relation is that CSR is still in the early stage of development as Lin-Hi (2010) state, and no particular ownership types are dominant in the field of CSR in China.

The second hypothesis stated that Chinese stock companies will implement more CSR practices related to labor standards than to other types of CSR practices, such as philanthropic or environmental practices. This statement was confirmed by our empirical results, which show that Chinese Stock companies commit more to labor CSR rather than to philanthropic or to environmental CSR. To understand this trend, we must keep in mind that Chinese stock companies operate increasingly on the global arena and are therefore trying to meet the international standards that mostly developed institutions pressure them into upholding.

The results concerning the third hypothesis show no conclusive relationship regarding private companies in China and their CSR intensity as compared to Chinese SOE's and Chinese stock companies in general. Given the ownership structure of private companies, a possible reason for this finding might lie in a person's subjective view on CSR or the CSR desirability of that person. It might be plausible to argue that a person's desirability to implement CSR activities outweighs the influence the ownership structure has on this subject. However, this is just our speculation and authors' grasp on this relationship, and further research is necessary to make a conclusion.

The last hypothesis implied that private companies in China will implement more philanthropic practices related to CSR rather than other types of CSR practices, such as labor or environmental practices. A negative relation was found between private companies and the amount of social practices they implement in contrast to SOEs and stock companies. This means that private companies commit more to labor and environmental practices rather than to social practices. The outcome of this study contradicts on this particular part some views in mainstream literature of the behavior of private companies in this particular research setting. A possible reason for this could be that whilst private companies are in general smaller in size and have less resources available, they devote their resources on the practices which legislation pressures them into and do not have enough funds to address other more voluntary types of CSR such as social practices.

5.1. Theoretical Implications

This study contributes to the field literature by investigating the relationship between the ownership structure and CSR. As similar work has been done in other emerging countries, for example Mexico (Muller & Kolk, 2007), this study expands the existing field by adding the empirical data from China.

First, the claims that Zu and Song (2009) made in their studies that the Chinese government always had a tradition of taking social responsibility for their employees by providing safety nets and social protection does not find any conformation in this study as empirical results do not show any similar support. Even the argument of Bai et al. (2000) that the main task for governments is to create social stability and welfare for the society as a whole are not confirmed by this study. The results do not show that SOEs governed by the Chinese government are more actively involved in creating social welfare than other types of organizations. This also contradicts the vision of Lin-Hi (2010) that CSR initiatives are mostly controlled by the Chinese government.

Second, the outcome of this study strengthens the results by Xu and Wang (1999) on ownership structure and corporate governance. They state that stock companies must respond to shareholder and stakeholder pressure from outside China, that is international arena. This pressure is formed by the fact that most stock companies in China are multinationals and that they sell their products across the globe. Thus, Western society (governments) and other regulatory agencies (EU, US) put pressure on Chinese stock companies to implement CSR practices as this is a perquisite in order to be allowed onto the European and US markets. This study therefore provides empirical support for the claim that Stock companies are inclined to address labor standards first because developed countries and the international business partners expect them to do so.

Finally, this study does not show that private firms implement less CSR activities than other types of organizations in China or that they implement a particular type of CSR practice more than the other types of organizations investigated. In fact, the results show that private companies implement less CSR initiatives related to social practices. The statement by Xu and Wang (1999) that private organizations deal with a particular pressure from their local society to act in their best interest is not supported by this study.

This study therefore finds overlap with and contributes to existing literature on CSR in emerging countries (Xu & Wang, 1999; Bai et al., 2000; Lin-Hi, 2010) as it partly builds on those studies and contributes by providing empirical data and possibly support or elucidating some contradictory results for particular claims made in those studies.

5.2. Policy Implications

Firstly, policy makers or managers from Chinese stock companies operating abroad should broaden their attention on other CSR practices in addition to labor practices, for this is a way for those organizations to set themselves apart from the rest and attract positive attentions from customers.

Next, policy makers from SOEs should use the organizations deep pockets, which are provided by state funds, to create social stability and welfare for the society as a whole. In this ever-globalizing world, the Chinese government is being closely watched by other countries and institutions, and they could use SOEs to build a better image of China and Chinese organizations in particular.

Furthermore, it is possible for managers or policy makers to use these findings to search for compatible partners as CSR performance might be used as a criterion to find a suitable joint venture partner or any other type of partnership. This is particularly the case for policy makers or managers of multinationals from developed countries who are looking for a suitable acquisition or partnership possibilities in China.

Finally, managers or policy makers in Chinese private companies should focus more on their local society. The local markets are where they sell most of their products, and attention should be shifted to local CSR initiatives to improve the local community's welfare through community project and charity donations so they could use CSR as a marketing tool to their own benefit to improve their image and possibly increase their customer base.

5.3. Limitations

The results of this study should be interpreted with some caution, due to a number of reasons. First of all, the study has been executed with a rather small sample considering the vast amount of Chinese organizations. It is recognized that China is a country where research and surveys are often hard to conduct, which was experienced during our data collection. The response rate to the e-mail survey was very low, so a considerable amount of e-mails was send to attain a usable sample size. Second, there may be some problems with generalizability of the findings due to the fact that certain industries were overrepresented in the used dataset. Third, due to practical reasons, we decided not to test the respondents' social desirability, for this would lengthen the survey dramatically and decrease even more the response rate.

5.4. Future Research

This study used the ownership structure as a single determinant for the type of CSR practice organizations implement. It is very plausible to argue that there are more predictors that determine which type of CSR practice organizations undertake. Determinants such as different stakeholder pressures (Xu & Wang, 1999) or philosophical and managerial beliefs (Jensen & Meckling, 1976) are for instance worth researching in this particular setting. The contradictory debate between scholars on the effects and influence of ownership structures on CSR initiatives (e.g., Baskin, 2006; Jenkins, 2005), in which the results of this study show that ownership structure just has a small influence in certain cases, call for further research. These two views could for instance be studied on a larger scale in countries with similar characteristics opening up the possibility to compare the outcomes across countries. Another possibility is to conduct similar research in a qualitative fashion, by doing several case studies on the subject across different industries and countries.

Note

* *This research was conducted in collaboration with Bas Romein.*

9 A Topical Sustainability Issue
Recycling

1. Introduction

Recycling, recovery, treatment, and storage of waste are the main priorities of the European Union (EU) agenda. The Romania's environmental policy principles are in line with the European and international previsions, ensuring the protection and conservation of nature, biological diversity, and the sustainable use of its components.

Waste management is one of the major issues which Romania is facing in terms of environmental protection. Responsibility for waste management activities rests with its generators, according to the polluter-pays principle, or as the case may be, producers, according to the principle of manufacturer's responsibility.

Recycling is a topical issue and has a strong impact on society, waste collection, and disposal, being perceived as one of the basic elements that conditions the quality of life. This activity is ranked as the most important, after ensuring the conditions for a decent living life.

The European directives transposed into Romanian legislation have led to a new approach to the waste problem, paying attention to the need to protect and save natural resources, reducing management costs and finding effective solutions to reduce pollution.

The Romanian legislation on waste, harmonized with that of the European Union, has had a positive impact in the recent years, but considerable efforts are still needed to ensure compliance with the European standards.

The environmental protection is the duty and responsibility of the Romanian authorities, as well as of all natural and legal persons. The central and local authorities foresee in their budgets funds to meet the obligations arising from the implementation of the community environmental legislation and for the environmental protection programs.

Production and consumption of goods and services are also generators of waste that are often not recovered or unmined, and their treatment contributes to environmental pressures (transport, storage facilities, incinerators).

To encourage producers to improve the environmental performance of their products throughout their life cycle, the principle of extended producer responsibility should be recognized and applied as a general principle underlying the corporate legal responsibility.

The extensive responsibility of the manufacturer makes it financially responsible for the products that become waste, giving them an incentive to develop products that avoid unnecessary waste and can be used in recycling or recovery operations.

The industrial sector, through the exploitation of natural resources, energy consumption, and production processes generating both pollutants and waste, is the main cause that has led to environmental degradation. It is therefore necessary to take measures to ensure that the environmental impact of the product is as small as possible, that it will use advanced waste recycling technologies, tracking and measuring emissions of pollutants in the atmosphere and in waters.

Economic activity implies not only the concern to increase the volume and quality of material goods and services by ensuring a high economic efficiency, but also an increasing concern to protect the environment, which is the basic material condition of economic growth.

A report from the European Commission assessing the implementation of the EU environmental policies in the member states, published in 2015, shows that Romania has very low recycling levels.

In practice, there is no ideal solution to solve waste management problems. There are only a handful of measures that can be taken. One of them is recycling, processing of material for other products. Some materials are very good for recycling. Others theoretically can be recycled but require costly procedures.

The recycling strategy targets the following main objectives: prevention of waste generation through the promotion of clean technologies and green products; waste recovery by optimizing selective collection and sorting systems; the final disposal of waste for which a recovery solution has not been found.

Recycling can be done through two types of actions: reuse and recovery.

The advantages of recycling are conserving natural resources, reducing storage space and protecting the environment. However, the collection, transport, recovery, and final processing of materials require additional energy, and most recycling programs are subsidized economically. The fundamental issues in recycling materials are related to identification of recyclable materials; identifying opportunities for reuse and recycling; and identification of markets for redeemable materials.

In most cases, redeemable materials are inferior to the original ones, so the market prices must be attractive to prospective buyers.

Among the recycling materials is household waste. Other materials come from shops, hotels, canteens, public catering establishments, educational institutions, and any other public institutions, as well as from industrial enterprises, workshops, and commercial companies. Considering the possibility of utilization, household waste can be compostable (organic residues resulting from the preparation of food; wood, rubber, plastics) and recyclable.

The most important recyclable materials are paper, metals, plastics, and textiles.

Paper recycling. Newspapers, magazines, notebooks, cardboard packaging for food can be converted by recycling into writing paper or paper for magazines, books, and brochures. Paper bags, bags, paper towels, napkins, cards, and wrapping paper can also be obtained from the paper packaging waste. Paper cannot be recycled too often because the fibers break through during the recycling process and become worn out to be converted into paper.

Separate collection of paper and cardboard waste should also extend to the overall population (as compared to the current situation where it is only implemented at the level of economic agents/organizations/firms), as a very large amount of paper and cardboard can be recovered. By paper recycling, we save the forest, and for every ton of recycled paper, we save 30,000 liters of water, the energy consumption is reduced by about 25%, and atmospheric pollution by 80%, which is why paper and cardboard recycling is very important.

Recycling glass. Bottles of juice, beer, and glass jars can be recycled indefinitely without the resulting product losing its qualities. It is enough to have 5 grams of impurities (pebbles, ceramics, metals) in a tone of glass to compromise the recycling of the entire amount of glass. Recycled white glass can only be obtained from white glass waste, so it is very important to separate it from green and brown glass.

The recycling of PET bottles has become an increasingly important application as PET bottles are being introduced in an increasing number of countries, with the product application being very wide. In the recycling process, it is important that the bottles remain whole and that they can be separated into two categories, colored PET and colorless PET.

Recycling of metals. There are two categories of metal packaging: aluminum packaging and steel packaging. Aluminum is the most recyclable waste, and it can be recycled indefinitely without losing its qualities. Most aluminum packages represent aluminum cans for drinks. Steel as well as aluminum can be recycled without losing its qualities. With the energy required to get a new steel box, 4 packages of recycled steel can be manufactured.

Recycling of plastics. Since there are many types of plastics, each has to be recycled separately, through specific processes. Many packaging waste materials can be recycled: PET bottles, plates, glasses, jars, dishes, and so on.

Recycling of textiles. All textile objects are recycled and used for packaging non-food products.

Environmental protection activity raises its level of quality, and the prevention of environmental degradation is less costly than damage repair.

2. Priority Principles and Objectives in Waste Management

At the basis of the waste management activities, there are several principles set out in the Romanian management strategy and the community legislation. The principle of primary resource protection refers to the need to minimize and streamline the use of primary resources, focusing on the use of secondary raw materials. The principle of prevention means that the waste hierarchy is applied as a priority order in the waste prevention and management legislation and policy, as follows: prevention, preparation for reuse, recycling, other recovery operations, and ultimately disposal safety for the environment. The principle of substitution indicates the need to replace hazardous raw materials with non-hazardous raw materials, thus minimizing hazardous waste. Subsidiarity principle establishes the allocation of competences so that the decisions on waste management are taken at the lowest administrative level compared to the source of generation. The proximity principle establishes that waste should be treated and moved as close as possible to the source of generation. The principle of preliminary measures indicates the main aspects to be taken into account for any activity: the current stage of technology development, the requirements for environmental protection, and the choice and application of those economically feasible measures.

Priority objectives in waste management take into account the general principles underlying these activities: (a) prevention or reduction of waste production and the degree of danger through the development of clean technologies, low-consumption natural resources; the development of technology; and the marketing of products which, by way of manufacture, use, or disposal, do not have an impact or have the least possible impact on the increase in the volume or the danger of waste or the risk of pollution; the development of adequate technologies for the final disposal of hazardous substances from waste for recovery; (b) reuse, recovery of waste by recycling, recovery or any other process by which secondary raw materials are obtained, or the use of waste as a source of energy.

The main objective of the waste management provisions must be to protect human health and the environment from the harmful effects of waste collection, transport, treatment, storage, and disposal. Thus, the following necessary and mandatory conditions must be met: It must not present any risk to water, air, soil, fauna, or vegetation; it must not produce noise or unpleasant odor; and it must not affect landscapes or protected areas.

Romania has the obligation to create an adequate integrated network of waste disposal installations, taking into account the best available technologies, which do not involve excessive costs, while complying with the requirements of the Treaty of Accession of Romania to the EU.

In Romania, the types of generated waste are classified as:

- Municipal and assimilated waste—all waste generated in urban and rural areas by households, institutions, commercial units, and service providers (household waste), street waste collected from public areas, streets, parks, green areas, waste from construction and demolition, muds from urban waste water treatment

- Production waste—all waste generated by industrial activities; may be non-hazardous waste and hazardous waste
- Waste generated from medical activities—all waste generated in hospitals, polyclinics, and medical offices and is divided into two categories: hazardous medical waste and other that fall into the category of assimilable waste.

A particularly important aspect is the achievement of adequate and sustainable management, finding solutions to ensure that the final solution is final. Specific requirements for the authorization of waste management activities are therefore required.

3. Recycling Activities

As many other countries in Central and Eastern Europe, Romania has inherited from the communist period serious environmental problems, caused by the extensive industrial policy, that didn't take into account the impact on the environment and the health of the population. The most serious problems are encountered with regard to the water quality, waste management, and air and soil pollution.

The natural resources are an essential component of Romania's wealth. To improve the living conditions in Romania, these natural resources need to be exploited in a sustainable manner. The mission of sustainable development is to find ways for the economic growth and development, along with the rational use of the natural resources, so that renewable resources could be maintained and the non-renewable ones could be used at a peace that takes into account the needs of the future generation.

The waste transformation into a resource requires the full implementation of the EU waste legislation, which includes the waste hierarchy, the need to ensure separate waste gatherings, the objectives of avoiding landfilling of waste; reducing the waste generation per capita and absolute waste generation; limiting energy recovery to non-recyclable materials and phasing out gradually the storage of recycling or recoverable waste.

The issue of the negative impact on the environment and human health, as a result of the waste disposal by using some inappropriate methods and technologies stays a topical subject, especially in the context of the sustained upward trend in the amount of generate waste.

Waste is a vital environmental, social, and economic issue. Depending on how they are being handled, waste can have an impact on both the human health as well as the environment through emissions in air, soil, water surface, and underground water. However, they can also lead to the loss of the material resources, metals, and other recyclable materials, while also having an energy source potential.

Waste management is one of the concerning issues present in Romania nowadays.

In the civilized world, the technology and the industry have become so advanced that people are as hypnotized by their miracles, forgetting that a civilized world is first a clean world. Many enjoy the fact that they can find countless bagged products, bottles, or metal containers in the supermarket, but don't even think about the process by which that packaging goes through after the content is consumed.

First, that packaging will become a waste, like many other already existing types of waste, that must be collected in special containers for storage. A myriad of public awareness campaigns have been carried out so that the pre-selection and waste collection would take place selectively and effectively, thus removing the environmental contamination risk. Because the responsibility belongs not only to the citizens but also to the companies, the waste collection company must ensure that the waste collection and processing are done efficiently and in accordance with the rules set by the Ministry of the Environment and the National Agency for the Environment Protection.

The economic agents that carry out the recycling activities from natural private individuals may do so only on the basis of the collection authorization issued by the country prefecture, with the approval from the commune, city, or municipality town hall where they operate, on the grounds that they own the space and the appropriate facilities necessary for the storage of the collected waste and on the basis of the environmental permit issued by the territorial authority for the environmental protection.

It is mandatory to reintroduce in the productive cycle the recyclable waste collected by handing it over to the specialized economic agents, legally authorized for the recovery activity.

Waste management includes collecting, transport, recovery, and disposal, as well as overseeing these operations and taking care of the storage areas after their closing. In the hierarchy of waste management options, which is included both in the EU and national regulations, recovery holds the priority over the storage disposal. The necessary measures must be planned in such a way that they will reach the most efficient way of recycling and recovery, taking into account all types of waste, sources of waste, and different waste composition.

Sorting is the initial stage of recycling domestic waste. By sorting we mean the assortment of domestic waste in well-defined categories: paper, plastic, glass, organic waste, and metal waste to ease the collecting and recycling domestic waste activity of the companies. The quality and the way in which the collection takes place depends almost entirely on the quality and the stringency of the sorting process at the source.

Storing domestic waste, regardless of their mixed or stored nature is stored in specially designated places, called "ecological ramps." By an ecological ramp, we imply a site in which various types of waste are stored without affecting the environment.

The purpose of collecting waste is to collect it where it's produced in an organized and cost-effective manner, to prevent environment pollution and to allow the reuse and recycling as much as possible.

Waste recycling reduces the primary raw materials demand, and most often the usage of secondary raw materials is less costly than of the primary ones. Waste recycling and reuse can be done in two ways. The first one allows the sorting and dividing after the waste is fully collected. This can be done mechanically or manually. The dividing effectiveness can be significant, and it is an efficient way for some fractions. The main condition is that the recovered fraction can then be recycled: the quality of the divided waste fraction shouldn't be too affected by the full collection and the subsequent separation. For example, dividing the metals, wood, and PET packaging is relatively mild, and the recovered materials can still be used as secondary raw material. This is not the case of glass for example (which breaks while being collected and remains scattered in small fragments in the waste mass), paper (which is heavily polluted by the organic part of the waste that makes it less usable as a secondary source in the paper industry), and organic waste (which could be polluted with heavy metals if recovered entirely from the collected waste).

For each recovered and reused fraction, it is necessary to analyze the sorting effectiveness after collection or before, at the source. Sorting at the source generally allows the separation of some good quality waste fraction. To achieve a separate waste collection, the households must implicitly have the necessary means of sorting waste. This means that they need containers or other collecting means in which different fractions of waste can be stored separately and that these containers must be collected periodically. This complicates the organization of waste collection and can proportionally increase the collection expenses. However, these expenses can be partially offset by using the fractions thus separated as secondary raw materials. The containers with reusable materials are picked up and transported carefully through local administrations, to picking points where materials are sorted and delivered to the manufacturing companies. With regard to the selective collection, the first necessary action is to identify the container types that can be used for the selective waste collection (packaging, organic waste, and the rest of domestic waste), as well as the labeling or branding manner.

Regardless of the waste collection system, it is necessary to create or develop some sorting and processing facilities for recycling. Collected glass packages must be sorted to ensure that the glass sorted by color is free of contaminants. Paper and cardboard must be sorted to eliminate the impurities and to achieve the quality required for the paper and cardboard industry. For example, category sorting such as writing paper, cardboard, and low-quality paper in packages ensures that the necessary recycling quality is attained. To achieve the overall recovery/recycling targets and of biodegradable materials reduction sent for final storage, all possible measures for the recovery of biodegradable waste should be used.

The storage activity regulation aims to prevent or reduce the negative effects on the environment, the surface water pollution in particular, as well as underground water, soil, air, including the greenhouse effect, and any risk to the population's health throughout the warehouse lifetime and after it expires.

Recyclable waste holders, legal persons, are obliged to ensure their collection, sorting, and temporary storage, upholding the environment protection and norms and health standards of the population, as well as their reintroduction in the productive process through the reuse in their own production processes; valorization and commercialization of the secondary raw materials and the reusable products obtained by recycling; handing over to the specialized economic agents, authorized for recovery, of the recyclable waste based on the origin documents.

Romanians are acquainted with the recycling concept, which they most often associate with the environmental protection, but unfortunately, that's where they stop. There are just a few who act and see the divided collection as a necessity and make a habit out of it.

At this point, Romania has a low recycling rate out of the total waste generated, and for its growth, it needs the involvement of all market actors, the infrastructure, and awareness.

Poor waste collection in Romania has more profound economic implications than the payment of some possible penalties imposed by the European forums. Due to a low degree of waste collecting, the recycling industry in Romania has to resort to massive raw material imports to ensure its production and to keep the created workplaces, mostly in economically underdeveloped areas.

The Romanian authorities are responsible for the implementation of economic instruments that would boost the business environment from the value range. Preventing waste occurrence or reducing it at the source means using and throwing as few products and packaging materials as possible. Reducing at the source preserves the natural resources and reduces pollution, including the volume of greenhouse gases, one of the global warming causes.

Waste recovery involves costs due to the involved energy consumption, selective collection, transport, temporary storage, and at the same time, it can sometimes be polluting. It is obvious that avoiding the waste formation is referable than capitalizing on it.

In Romania, the 1989 political and economic change lead to a consumption increase and to an industry and trade restructuring. Currently, there is a wide range of offers, more expensive and with larger packaging, as well as short-term goods, meaning more waste. As a result, a greater emphasis should be placed on the prevention strategies and the implementations of incentives to prevent waste generating.

Waste avoidance strategies and the administrative tools that promote waste prevention aim at designing and manufacturing products that generate little waste, which would have a long life and can be easily repaired; the use of performing technologies for good production, which generate little waste; packaging systems that produce little waste when packaging products; educating the population to consciously adopt the decision to choose those products that generate minimum waste.

Appling a sustainable waste management system must involve significant changes in the current practices. The implementation of these changes requires the involvement of all segments of the Romanian society: individuals, social and economic institutions, research institutions, and nongovernmental organizations.

10 A Hermeneutical Approach to Sustainability Research and Practice Reflection by Ana Cristina Campos Marques

1. Introduction

"Know thyself," is an ancient aphorism that can inspire different perspectives to tackle the sustainability challenge. A challenge composed of many interdependent ones such as climate change, biodiversity loss, environmental degradation, geopolitical instability, refugees, poverty, and social inequality. It is a unique moment in the history of humankind, and because of the likely influence of humans on the planet's natural systems, this epoch was named as Anthropocene. Of course, there is no certainty about the amount of human influence on the planet. These are complex processes, not direct cause and effect, and scientific thinking is limited. It cannot be certain of everything. However, despite its limitation, there is a huge faith in technology. There is a hope that science will fast develop new technologies that will save the planet and humanity. The problem is that the same technology that can tackle the sustainability challenge can contribute to make it even worst. It all depends on the assumptions used to develop and to use that technology. The danger is that technology is moving faster than the human understanding about oneself and reality.

Developing technology with the certainty that everything can be predicted and controlled has proved to have catastrophic consequences. An example is the gases produced for the refrigeration systems that seemed so harmless, but then it was discovered that they destroyed the ozone layer. And not to mention fossil fuels, which seemed perfect to provide energy for the development of economy, but which is now known to be polluting and contributing to the global warming. There was a belief that these technologies would solve some problems without bringing major consequences. There were also other beliefs that today seem absurd, like being on a planet in the center of the universe and the Sun spinning around it. In a way, this belief is still there; sometimes the humankind seems to still believe to be the center.

In the meantime, the sustainability challenge can influence all life on the planet, including human. This complex challenge defies the humankind view on reality and its role in it. Therefore, it is time to reflect on more fundamental questions about reality and existence, that is, ontology. This study is a reflection on these fundamental questions in the context of the sustainability challenge. I reflect on questions related to the interplay about the assumptions on reality, being, and the tackling of the sustainability challenge. Accordingly, scholars argue that it is important to reflect on the philosophical assumptions of research and practice. An example is Maturana and Varela (1998), who argues that "scientists usually do not reflect upon the constitutive conditions of science" (p. 4). Another example is Vildåsen et al. (2017), who found that the majority of scientific publications on corporate sustainability are not transparently aware of their philosophical assumptions.

In the words of the philosopher Paul Ricoeur: "to understand myself is to make the greatest detour, via de memory which retains what had become meaningful for all mankind" (2016, p. 12). This study is personal, I use my own experience on sustainability of nearly 20 years working with sustainability issues in Brazil and Latin America. I disclose the changes in my sustainability narratives through the changes in my ontology. Furthermore, this study is based on hermeneutics, which is concerned with the process of understanding. In the hermeneutics of this study "understanding is not concerned with grasping a fact but with apprehending a possibility of being" (Ricoeur, 2016, p. 17), which I do by disclosing my own story. A contribution of this study is a call for reflection on the philosophical assumptions that underlie research and practice.

2. Philosophical Perspectives

> "I know that I know nothing."
>
> (Socrates, 470–399 BC)

2.1. Ontology and Epistemology

What is reality? Or more specifically, what are the philosophical assumptions about the nature of reality? These are questions of ontology, which is related to the "nature of reality and existence" (Easterby-Smith et al., 2012, p. 17). Then, how do these philosophical assumptions relate to the different sustainability narratives? To illustrate it, I share my own story that shows the interplay between ontology and sustainability narratives.

In the engineering college, I learned to calculate and control an objective reality, which seemed to exist independently of me. I was immersed in a world where the predominant ontology was realism where "an apprehendable reality is assumed to exist, driven by immutable natural laws and mechanisms" (Guba & Lincoln, 1994, p. 109). When I finished college, I went to work in industries in the area of sustainability, initially with more technical issues and then in management. The intersection of these two areas was important for the change of my ontology. A clear example for me was the decision-making process for purchasing a pollution control equipment at a company where I was the sustainability manager. All engineering calculations were made for the equipment, as well as calculations of technical and economic feasibility. So, in an ontology of realism where it is believed in a single truth, this would be enough for the decision-making process. But each person interpreted the same data completely differently from the others. The predominant ontology was relativism, where reality is subjective, therefore different for each person.

A few decades later, living in another country, in a "reality" different from the country where I was born, I keep asking the same questions about the nature of reality and existence. I now understand that this is a question that philosophers have been wondering for millennia. The answers vary according to different philosophical assumptions (ontologies), which determine how scientific research is conducted and interpreted. Then, epistemology can be defined as "a general set of assumptions about ways of inquiring into the nature of the world" (Easterby-Smith et al., 2012, p. 18). This study is based on the epistemology of social construction where the so-called reality is constructed individually and collectively. Therefore, in this study, reality is subjective and based in a dialectic of inner worlds (cognitions, feelings, intuitions, values) and outer worlds (interactions, relations, social practices) of people, through language. In the words of Maturana and Varela, we "exist as human beings in language using language for our explanations" (1998, p. 3). Therefore, this study is not about revealing an independent reality, but about exploring a subjective reality through the dialectic of my inner and outer worlds, shaped by language.

2.2. *Language and Reality*

In the postmodern view of social constructivism, language constructs reality. This is called the linguistic turn, which is "a philosophical change from viewing language as a medium for expressing a pre-given reality to viewing reality as being shaped by language" (Flory, 2008, p. 21). Some researchers go deep in this consideration, stating that language is the human domain of existence. One example is the biologist Humberto Maturana, who considers that language is what separates subjects from objects. In his words, "without language and outside language there are no objects, because objects only arise as consensual coordinations of actions in the recursion of consensual coordinations of actions that languaging is" (Maturana & Varela, 1998, p. 30). He complements it by adding that "for living systems that do not operate in language there are no objects; or in other words, objects are not part of their cognitive domains" (Maturana, 1998, p. 30). Therefore, as language is also the medium that reality is constructed, then maybe language cannot mirror reality. However, "science is not a manner of revealing an independent reality; it is a manner of bringing forth a particular one bound to the conditions that constitute the observer as a human being" (Maturana, 1998, p. 6). In this study, I analyze my own "reality" through personal experiences on sustainability narratives. Additionally, as language is also the human medium of communicating, social researchers (e.g., Alvesson & Kärreman, 2000; Alvesson & Sköldberg, 2009; Ricoeur, 2016) acknowledge the limits of language and emphasize the importance of reflection on its application during research. In this study, I use hermeneutics to be aware of the limits of language and to reflect on it.

2.3. Hermeneutics

Hermeneutics is concerned with the process of understanding. Alvesson and Sköldberg (2009) add that this process of understanding may be even more relevant than its results. Ricoeur (2016) complements it by stating that the "understanding ceases to appear as a simple way of knowing in order to become a way of being and a way of relating to beings and to being" (2016, p. 4). In this study, I describe my process of understanding the diversity of sustainability narratives, and how it changed my own way of being and the way of relating to myself and to others. My purpose, on exposing my own process of understanding, is to challenge and inspire people in their own processes. I agree with Klamer (2016b) that science has two main roles: therapeutic and edifying. In his words, "scientific work is therapeutic when it poses new questions, uncomfortable questions maybe, and makes people aware of certain phenomena" (Klamer, 2016b, p. XIV). He adds that "scientific work becomes edifying when it offers concepts, ways of thinking, models, insights and findings with which people can make sense of the questions they encounter and enables them to see their world in a different light and act accordingly" (Klamer, 2016b, p. XIV). I hope that this study can contribute to people in both therapeutic and edifying ways.

It is noteworthy that hermeneutics in this study is more related to ontology than to epistemology. Thus, "hermeneutics is not a reflection on the human sciences, but an explication of the ontological ground upon which these sciences can be constructed" (Ricoeur, 2016, p. 15). Additionally, there are different approaches in hermeneutics, and this study follows the alethic one. In alethic hermeneutics the focus is on "truth as an act of disclosure, in which the polarity between subject and object . . . is dissolved in the radical light of a more original unity" (Alvesson & Sköldberg, 2009, p. 91). Examples of scholars in alethic hermeneutics are Gadamer (2013), Heidegger (2010) and Ricoeur (2016).

As this study is personal, I disclose my process of understanding sustainability narratives. Then one could argue how objective and neutral I can be as researcher. However, "hermeneutics itself puts us on guard against the illusion or pretension of neutrality" (Ricoeur, 2016, p. 3). Therefore, for hermeneuticians social sciences are not value free, because "the subject and object are mutually implicated" (Ricoeur, 2016, p. 17). This means that there is a constant dialectic of inner and outer worlds of people, which is more fluid and permeable than concrete and separated. Additionally, I agree with Maturana and Varela (1998) that "science as the domain of scientific statements does not need an objective independent reality, nor does it reveal one" (p. 6).

3. The Narrative Approach

> *"In order to seek truth, it is necessary once in the course of our life, to doubt, as far as possible, of all things."*
>
> (René Descartes, 1644)

I have come across several methods during my scientific path. Initially, I learned to calculate a reality that seemed so objective out there. Then, I understood the qualitative way of developing scientific research. Now, I doubt everything, even the methods. However, I write this section because I agree with McCloskey (1983) that "nothing is gained from clinging to the Scientific Method, or to any methodology except honesty, clarity, and tolerance" (p. 482). Thus, for the sake of honesty, clarity, and tolerance, I present the foundations of this study, which is conducted through narratives.

Narrative is "the reflective product of looking back and making sense of stories constructed to make sense of life" (Flory, 2008, p. 70). Then, I look back to my own story to make sense of the sustainability narratives. Czarniawska (1997) suggests that the narrative approach is a "systematic reflection on a craft that we are practicing while doing re-search" (p. 77). This re-search is what I do when searching again and reflecting on the sustainability narratives in my story. Additionally, the narrative approach is different from the positivism approach, because "narratives exhibit an explanation instead of demonstrating it" (Czarniawska, 2004, p. 8). Then, following Ricoeur (2016) reasoning, in the narrative approach, understanding and explanation are fused in an interpretation of the text (Czarniawska, 1998). The sustainability narratives in my story exhibit themselves their explanation, what at same time leads to an understanding.

It is worth highlighting that narrative is different from story, because story is polyphonic (Boje, 2012). On the other hand, "narrative requires plot, as well as coherence" (Boje, 2001, p. 1). In this study, the plot is sustainability, which I attempt to make sense though my story. The coherence is through the understanding of my ontology in the narrated moment. Of course, stories are made up of innumerable narratives that intertwine in different contexts. So, my narrative in this study is partial. It would be impossible to make a precise picture of everything I experienced in the area of sustainability. Furthermore, one might ask: How this study about a personal narrative can be related to the societal ones? In the words of Czarniawska (2004): "to understand a society or some part of a society, it is important to discover its repertoire of legitimate stories and find out how it evolved" (p. 5). This study is a contribution to it.

3.1. Brazilian Context

Understanding and tackling the sustainability challenges is important worldwide. Although, as this is a personal study, related to my experiences on sustainability narratives, it is conducted through the Brazil context. The reason for it is that in Brazil, I had most of my experiences on sustainability. Additionally, it is important to point out that Brazil holds a substantial part of the planet's remaining natural systems, like Amazon forest and biodiversity. Brazil also faces complex sustainability challenges like deforestation, environmental degradation, the existence of large socio-economic differences, and the widespread political and business corruption. This all mixed with a diverse population, which can contribute to a broad range of perspectives.

4. Narratives on Sustainability

> *"The human being is the measure of all things, of what there is and that is there, and of what there is not and that is not."*
>
> (Protagoras, 490–415 BC)

How to tackle the sustainability challenge? I asked this question, directly or indirectly, the hundreds of people over 20 years of work in the area of sustainability, both in Brazil and in Latin America. I then witnessed countless narratives on sustainability. These narratives varied enormously. From specific technical issues to holistic human development. From greenwashing to consciously responsible organizations. From the need to predict and control the natural systems to consider these same natural systems as part of oneself. From the importance of control to the growth and development of the country's economy, to the importance of freedom for the growth of people and the natural systems of the same country. Why so much difference in these narratives? What could explain that? During all these years, I also asked myself the same question about tackling the sustainability challenge. My own responses varied, as I listened and saw different perspectives on this issue. It was a constant dance of my inner and outer worlds. So here I describe this process.

4.1. Sustainability Narratives Through the Ontology of Realism

There is an objective reality out there, and to predict and control this reality, it is enough to learn some technical fundamentals. So, we can predict everything and control the immutable natural laws and mechanisms. We can also objectively study and control people, individually (e.g., behavior) and collectively (e.g., economy). Additionally, we need to survive, and we also need to consume. So, the planet's resources have to meet our needs. After all, we are the most intelligent beings on this planet, so we can use and exploit all its resources, in the way that is most convenient for us. But, do not worry, because we can control the processes of nature. Then, tackling the sustainability challenges is mainly a way to make better use of technology (e.g., cleaner energy).

These were some of the narratives I have heard over so many years in the area of sustainability. Now I understand that they are part of an ontology of realism. This type of ontology was predominant in the college I attended, in chemical engineering. I learned chemical and physical principles from so-called objective reality, to then calculate and control a world out there. When I finished college, I went to work in industries, initially in the more technical area and then in the more managerial area. In the technical area, the realism ontology served me well, at least to predict and control the operation of industrial processes. After some time, I understood that I liked the environmental field, then I followed a master's degree in eco-design, in mechanical engineering. There I was again, learning to calculate a reality that seemed so objective. Due to the environmental issue, I considered nature in my calculations and predictions, but in an instrumental way. So, if I wanted to produce an "eco product," I would calculate and evaluate the materials and processes that would be most sustainable. Over time, due to my success in the technical area, I was invited to work in more managerial areas of sustainability. So, there were less calculations and less process control, but more people management. People with different ways of thinking and understanding their realities. In the world of people management, the ontology of realism did not seem to make much sense anymore. Then I asked myself: How to deal with people who understand reality in so different ways?

4.2. In Between

Gradually my ontology of realism was being transformed. At first the transformation was more instrumental; it was more to help me in meeting technical sustainability goals. I had to manage people from diverse cultures, social, and economic realities. Brazil is a diverse country. So, the way of talking, motivating, and managing were quite different from person to person. Additionally, since I was a sustainability manager in a large multinational industry, I had to manage several stakeholders, both internal and external. To help me in this task, I followed a MBA in one of the best business schools in Brazil. I thought: "Now I will learn the 'technique' to manage all these stakeholders and their various interests." The MBA has helped me to understand various technical issues (finance, accounting), as well as managerial issues (strategy, marketing). But I understood that there was no absolute truth for managing people. Additionally, the MBA did not teach me neither about people development, nor about self-development. Now I understand that the vast majority of MBA in the world are quite focused on an ontology of realism. Then, techniques are taught to predict and control a so-called objective external world. Personal development is not usually focused on MBA courses. This for me is quite strange, because the inner world of people is completely forgotten. Then, how a leader will become the very best he or she can be, for then to develop others for their maximum potential. I think that one cannot help others if one cannot help oneself. So how will this leader help people develop to make a real contribution to both company and society? How will this leader be able to motivate people? Only financially motivated strategies do not work so well in a broadly connected and competitive world. I have heard a lot of leaders that in fact this never worked, which only helped to make things worse, turned people into machines to achieve goals, regardless of the methods used. And that human beings are complex, good financial compensation is important, but most people want to contribute to something bigger than themselves, to be part of a larger purpose. I have heard from great leaders that their secret was something like integrating all the humanity of the people, helping them finding their own voices, that when this happens, the company, people, and society grow immensely, all together.

4.3. Sustainability Narratives Through the Ontology of Relativism

After working more than a decade in industries, I went to work in an international consultancy in the area of sustainability. So, I started to attend organizations all over Brazil and part of Latin America. At that time, I have heard so many different narratives in sustainability that I have lost count. I was talking to people from various functions ranging from CEOs, PhDs in the area, leaders of different spiritual traditions to machine operators and the so-called common people. Contexts varied from industries, universities, and communities to governmental agencies. The range of different narratives was enormous. During this time, I also participated in a transdisciplinary training course, taught by philosophers, psychologists, engineers, administrators, and leaders of various traditions in Brazil. The diversity of sustainability narratives has grown even more. All of these experiences have intertwined and strongly shaken the ontology of realism that I had previously learned. Objective and controllable reality was getting farther and farther away from my reality. Sustainability became for me less and less a way of "doing" to a way of "being." During that time, the sustainability narratives that challenged me the most are the following:

> Reality is subjective, and control is likely illusory. There is not a single reality, but several, which are constructed individually and collectively. So, predict and control of nature is more illusory than real. People are continuously constructing their realities, individually and collectively. We cannot objectively study, nor control people. Nature is part of ourselves, so an unlimited use of its resources directly affects us. Tackling the sustainability challenges is mainly about becoming aware of this subjective reality, then construct a more sustainable one.

Now, years after experiencing these narratives, I understand that they are part of the ontology of relativism. In this ontology "realities are apprehendable in the form of multiple, intangible mental constructions, socially and experientially based, local and specific in nature . . . and dependent for their form and content on the individual persons or groups holding the constructions" (Guba & Lincoln, 1994, p. 110).

I started this study full of certainties in sustainability. After all, a solid academic background combined with decades of hands-on experience in this area give the illusion that I already knew enough. However, after challenging experiences combined with reflection on fundamental philosophical questions, my certainties were dissolving, one by one. It was not an easy process, I metaphorically had to die along with some certainties, to reborn with new and more innocent views. This personal process of dissolution of certainties is still in progress. The words of Ubiratan D'Ambrosio, a Brazilian scholar, inspire me in this journey: "To evolve from the arrogance of knowledge to the humility of seeking" (Pozatti, 2007, p. 9). In what follows, I discuss more about sustainability narratives and make some propositions for research and practice.

5. Discussion and Implications

> *"As a human being, one has been endowed with just enough intelligence to be able to see clearly how utterly inadequate that intelligence is when confronted with what exists."*
>
> (Albert Einstein)

5.1. A Problem to Be Solved or a Paradox to Be Managed?

Perhaps realism and relativism are two states of the same thing. In the same way that light can be both particle and wave. The following quote relates to the apparent duality of light, as a particle and wave. However, it could also exemplify the apparent duality of ontologies of realism and relativism:

> It seems as though we must use sometimes the one theory and sometimes the other, while at times we may use either. We are faced with a new kind of difficulty. We have two contradictory pictures of reality; separately neither of them fully explains the phenomena of light, but together they do.
>
> (Einstein & Infeld, 1938, pp. 262–263)

Similarly, sometimes the realism ontology seems to make more sense, at other times the relativism ontology, while at times both. Additionally, as both realism and relativism seem to be contradictory pictures of reality, it is important to be aware that they are just limited representation of the so-called reality. A reality that we possibly cannot totally grasp. In the words of Maturana, "we shall put aside our daily tendency to treat our experience with the seal of certainty as though it reflected an absolute world" (1987, p. 25). So, to develop science on the assumption that we have a complete and true version of reality can lead to even more catastrophic results than we already have. If we continue to believe that we can certainly predict and control the entire reality of the planet, and further aggravated by the "advanced" technology for destruction we have today, we can destroy all life on the planet, including our own.

5.2. Beyond Realism and Relativism

Considering the limitations of both realism and relativism, if we look through realism or through relativism, we may see different, but limited perspectives. In the words of Gadamer (2013): "Every finite present has its limitations. . . . The horizon is the range of vision that includes everything that can be seen from a particular vantage point" (p. 313). However, a "person who has no horizon does not see far enough and hence over-values what nearest to him." On the other hand, "to have a horizon" means not being limited to what is nearby but being able to see beyond it" (p. 313). Hence, it would be important to not be limited by both realism or relativism, not over-valuing neither, to see beyond it.

Fusion of horizons is a Gadamer (2013) concept that can help to see beyond the limits of realism and relativism. It means that each person has a limited version of reality; this is because of one's filters through it like beliefs, preconceptions, prejudices, etc. There is a fusion of horizons when one is open to see through different perspectives. I think that this openness requires humility and courage, because to do this, one must detach from the absolute certainties, not being limited to a single vision of reality. Then, humility to accept that one has a partial and limited version of reality. In the words of Desiderius Erasmus (1466–1526): "No man is wise at all times, or is without his blind side." And courage to deconstruct one's own certainties at every moment, being in the empty space of not knowing, to look at the world with a more innocent gaze.

Only the fusion of horizons might not be enough for tackling the complex sustainability challenge. Then, *phronesis* (practical wisdom) can help to "figure out what is the right thing to do" (Klamer, 2016b, p. 25). *Phronesis* is a term from Aristotle (2009) who considers it the principal form of knowledge, before technical (*téchne*) and theoretical (*sophía*) knowledge. "*Phronesis* involves the weighing of values, conditions, interests and findings in order to do the right thing" (Klamer, 2016a, p. 372). Several other scholars (e.g., Heidegger, 2010; MacIntyre, 1981; McCloskey, 2007) also argue about the importance of *phronesis* in research and practice. *Phronesis* "is often a chaotic process with a lot of talk, a going back and forth, the making of mistakes, and more talk and deliberation" (Klamer, 2016a, p. 372). Then, *phronesis* is more than rational reflection. According

Heidegger (2010), it is a way of being-in-the world (*Dasein* in his words), concerning and caring for it.

5.3. Implications

In this study, I reflected on questions related to the interplay between the assumptions on reality and the tackling of the sustainability challenge. In terms of implications for research and practice, I suggest the following:

- Awareness that both realism and relativism are just limited interpretations of the so-called reality. A reality that is shaped by language (Flory, 2008; Maturana, 1978). Then, caution is important on sustainability research and practice, especially the ones related to the sustainability of the planet. Perhaps we do not know so much, perhaps our scientific methods are still rudimentary to understand all the complexity of the nature systems.
- Besides the limitations of realism and relativism, research and practice on sustainability generally draw from these philosophical assumptions without explicit awareness of it (Vildåsen et al., 2017). Then, it is valuable to reflect before taking for granted its results and narratives. Hermeneutical reflection can contribute to it.
- Fusion of horizons (Gadamer, 2013) can contribute to expand the limits of realism and relativism. For it, it is useful to be open to consider multiple perspectives, from different philosophical assumptions, asking different questions.
- However, even an amplified horizon may not be enough for tackling the sustainability challenges. Then, *phronesis* (Aristotle, 2009) can help to find the right thing to do (Klamer, 2016b), in a way of being-in-the-world with concern and care (Heidegger, 2010). For it, I also suggest including self-development in sustainability programs of organizations and business schools. Finally, to tackle the sustainability challenge might also be important to open space for uncertainty and doubt. In the words of Johann Wolfgang von Goethe (1749–1832):
  " *Only when we know little do we know anything. Doubt grows with knowledge.*"

References

Agle, B. R., Mitchell, R. K., & Sonnenfeld, J. A. (1999). Who matters to CEOs? An investigation of stakeholder attributes and salience, corporate performance, and CEO values. *Academy of Management Journal*, *42*(5), 507–525.

Aguilera, R. V., Rupp, D. E., Williams, C. A., & Ganapathi, J. (2007). Putting the S back in corporate social responsibility: A multilevel theory of social change in organizations. *Academy of Management Review*, *32*(3), 836–863.

Alvesson, M., & Kärreman, D. (2000). Taking the linguistic turn in organizational research: Challenges, responses, consequences. *The Journal of Applied Behavioral Science*, *36*(2), 136–158.

Alvesson, M., & Sköldberg, K. (2009). *Reflexive Methodology: New Vistas for Qualitative Research* (2nd edition). London: Sage.

Antoldi, F., & Todisco, A. (2007). *The Influence of Social Network in the Diffusion of CSR Practices Among SMEs: An Empirical Survey in the Industrial Districts of Lombardy*. Collana Working Paper, 1–26.

Aristotle. (2009). *The Nicomachean Ethics*. Translated by W. D. Ross. Oxford: Oxford University Press.

Arrow, K. (1963). Uncertainty and the welfare economics of medical care. *American Economic Review*, *53*, 941–973.

Ayres, I., & Braithewaite, J. (1992). *Transcending the Deregulation Debate*. New York: Oxford University Press.

Baarda, D. B., Goede, M. P. M. de, & Teunissen, J. (2005). *Basisboek voor Kwalitatief Onderzoek* (2nd edition). Groningen: Wolters-Noordhoff.

Babiak, K., & Trendafilova, S. (2011). CSR and environmental responsibility: Motives and pressures to adopt green management practices. *Corporate Social Responsibility and Environmental Management*, *18*(1), 11–24.

Bai et al. (2000). A multitask theory of state enterprise reform. *Journal of Comparative Economics*, *28*, 716–738.

Bansal, P., & Roth, K. (2000). Why companies go green: A model of ecological responsiveness. *Academy of Management Journal*, *43*(4), 717–736.

Baron, D. P. (1995). Integrated strategy: Market and nonmarket components. *California Management Review*, *37*, 47–65.

Baron, D. P. (2003). *Business and Its Environment*. Upper Saddle River, NJ: Prentice Hall.

Baron, D. P., & Diermeier, D. (2007). Introduction to the Special Issue on Nonmarket strategy and social responsibility. *Journal of Economics & Management Strategy*, *16*(3), 539–545.

Baskin, J. (2006). Corporate responsibility in emerging markets. *The Journal of Corporate Citizenship*, Winter.

Beddewela, E., & Fairbrass, J. (2015). Seeking legitimacy through CSR: Institutional pressures and corporate responses of multinationals in Sri Lanka. *Journal of Business Ethics*, *136*(3), 503–522.

Belal, A. R. (2008). *Corporate Social Responsibility Reporting in Developing Countries: The Case of Bangladesh*. Aldershot, UK: Ashgate Publishing, Ltd.

Belal, A. R., & Momin, M. (2009). Corporate social reporting (CSR) in emerging economies: A review and future direction. *Research in Accounting in Emerging Economies*, 9, 119–143.

Belu, C., & Manescu, C. (2013). Strategic corporate social responsibility and economic performance. *Applied Economics*, *45*(19), 2751–2764.

Bewley, K., & Li, Y. (2000). Disclosure of environmental information by Canadian manufacturing companies: A voluntary disclosure perspective. *Advances in Environmental Accounting and Management*, *1*(1), 201–226.

Blowfield, M., & Frynas, J. G. (2005). Setting new agendas: Critical perspectives on corporate social responsibility in the developing world. *International Affairs*, *81*(3), 499–513.

Boddewyn, J. J. (2003). Understanding and advancing the concept of "nonmarket." *Business Society*, *42*(3), 297–327.

Boeije, H. (2006). *Analyseren in Kwalitatief Onderzoek*. Utrecht: Boom Onderwijs.

Boje, D. (2012). Reflections: What does quantum physics of storytelling mean for change management? *Journal of Change Management*, *12*(3), 253–271.

Boje, D. M. (2001). *Narrative Methods for Organizational & Communication Research*. London: Sage.

Boli, J., & Hartsuiker, D. (2001). *World Culture and Transnational Corporations: Sketch of a Project*. Paper presented at the International Conference on Effects of and Responses to Globalization, Istanbul.

Bos, W., & Tarnai, C. (1999). Content analysis in empirical social research. *International Journal of Educational Research*, *31*(8), 659–671.

Bowen, F. E. (2000). Environmental visibility: A trigger of green organizational response? *Business Strategy and the Environment*, *9*(2), 92.

Bowen, H. R. (1953). *Social Responsibilities of the Businessman*. New York: Harper & Row.

Brammer, S., & Millington, A. (2003). The effect of stakeholder preferences, organizational structure and industry type on corporate community involvement. *Journal of Business Ethics*, *45*(3), 213–226.

Brammer, S., & Millington, A. (2006). Firm size, organizational visibility and corporate philanthropy: An empirical analysis. *Business Ethics: A European Review*, *15*(1), 6–18.

Brammer, S., & Pavelin, S. (2006). Voluntary environmental disclosures by large UK companies. *Journal of Business Finance & Accounting*, *33*(7–8), 1168–1188.

Branco, M., & Rodrigues, L. (2006). Communication of corporate social responsibility by Portuguese banks: A legitimacy theory perspective. *Corporate Communications: An International Journal*, *11*(3), 232–248.

Brønn, P., & Vidaver Cohen, D. (2009). Corporate motives for social initiative: Legitimacy, sustainability or the bottom line? *Journal of Business Ethics*, *87*, 91–109.

Buhmann, K. (2006). Corporate social responsibility: What role for law? Some aspects of law and CSR. *Corporate Governance*, 6, 188–202.

Bühner, R., Rasheed, A., Rosenstein, J., & Yoshikawa, T. (1997). *Research on Corporate Governance: A Comparison of Germany, Japan, and U.S.* Academy of International Business Annual Meeting, Monterrey.
Buhr, H., & Grafström, M. (2004). "Corporate social responsibility" edited in the business press. Paper presented at the conference on Corporate Social Responsibility in the Era of the Transforming Welfare State, Florence, Italy.
Buhr, H., & Grafström, M. (2006). The making of meaning in the media: The case of corporate social responsibility in the financial times, 1988–2003. In *Managing Corporate Social Responsibility in Action: Talking, Doing and Measuring*. Aldershot, UK: Ashgate Publishing.
Campbell, J. L. (2006). Institutional analysis and the paradox of corporate social responsibility. *American Behavioral Scientist*, *49*, 925–938.
Campbell, J. L. (2007). Why would organizations behave in socially responsible ways? An institutional theory of corporate social responsibility. *Academy of Management Review*, *32*, 946–967.
Campbell, J. T., Eden, L., & Miller, S. (2012). Multinationals and corporate social responsibility in host countries: Does distance matter? *Journal of International Business Studies*, *43*, 81–106.
Capriotti, P. (2009). Economic and social soles of companies in the mass media: The impact media visibility has on businesses' being recognized as economic and social actors. *Business and Society*, *48*, 225–242.
Carroll, A. B. (1979). A three-dimensional conceptual model of corporate performance. *Academy of Management Review*, *4*, 497–505.
Carroll, A. B. (1991). The pyramid of corporate social responsibility: Toward the moral management of organizational stakeholders. *Business Horizons*, *34*(4), 39–48.
Carroll, A. B. (1999). Corporate social responsibility: Evolution of a definitional construct. *Business & Society*, *38*, 268–295.
Carson, S. J., Madhok, A., & Tao, W. (2006). Uncertainty, opportunism, and governance: The effects of volatility and ambiguity on formal and relational Contracting. *Academy of Management Journal*, *49*(5), 1058–1077.
Chan, A. (2005). China says no to developed countries' corporate social responsibility. *International Union Rights*, *12*(1), 18–19.
Chandler, R. A., & Ku Ismail, K. N. I. (2005). Disclosure in the quarterly reports of Malaysian companies. *Financial Reporting, Regulation and Governance*, *4*(1), 1–25.
Chapple, W., & Moon, J. (2005). Corporate social responsibility (CSR) in Asia: A seven-country study of csr web site reporting. *Business & Society*, *44*(4), 415–441.
Chau, G. K., & Gray, S. J. (2002). Ownership structure and corporate voluntary disclosure in Hong Kong and Singapore. *The International Journal of Accounting*, *37*(2), 247–265.
Chen, C. J., & Jaggi, B. (2001). Association between independent non-executive directors, family control and financial disclosures in Hong Kong. *Journal of Accounting and Public Policy*, *19*(4), 285–310.
Cho, S. Y., Lee, C., & Pfeiffer, R. J. (2013). Corporate social responsibility performance and information asymmetry. *Journal of Accounting and Public Policy*, *32*(1), 71–83.
Cook, R., & Fox, D. (2000). Resources, frequency and methods: An analysis of small and medium-sized firms' public policy activities. *Business& Society*, *39*, 94–113.

Cormier, D., & Gordon, I. M. (2001). An examination of social and environmental reporting strategies. *Accounting, Auditing & Accountability Journal*, *14*(5), 587–617.

Cotter, J., Lokman, N., & Najah, M. M. (2011). Voluntary disclosure research: Which theory is relevant? *The Journal of Theoretical Accounting Research*, *6*(2), 77.

Cowan, S., & Gadenne, D. (2005). Australian corporate environmental reporting: A comparative analysis of disclosure practices across voluntary and mandatory disclosure systems. *Journal of Accounting & Organizational Change*, *1*(2), 165–179.

Crane, A., & Matten, D. (2007). Corporate social responsibility as a field of scholarship. In A. Crane & D. Matten (Eds.), *Corporate Social Responsibility, Volumes I, II & III*. London: Sage.

Czarniawska, B. (1997). *A Narrative Approach to Organization Studies*. Vol. 43. Thousand Oaks, CA: Sage.

Czarniawska, B. (2004). *Narratives in Social Science Research*. London: Sage.

Dacin, M. T. (1997). Isomorphism in context: The power and prescription of institutional norms. *Academy of Management Journal*, *40*, 46–81.

Dahan, N. (2005). A contribution to the conceptualization of political resources utilized in corporate political action. *Journal of Public Affairs*, *5*, 43–54.

Dahlsrud, A. (2006). How corporate social responsibility is defined: An analysis of 37 Definitions. *Corporate Social Responsibility and Environmental Management*, *15*, 1–15.

Davies, R. (2000).*Why Asian Business Has to Care About Poverty*. Retrieved on 3 May 2013, from: http:/pwblf.org/csr/csrwebassist.nsf/webprintview/f1d2b3u4.html

Davis, K. (1973). The case for and against business assumption of social responsibilities. *Academy of Management Journal*, *16*, 312–322.

Dawkins, J., & Lewis, S. (2003). CSR in stakeholder expectations: And their implication for company strategy. *Journal of Business Ethics*, *44*(2–3), 185–193.

De Bakker, F. G., Groenewegen, P., & Den Hond, F. (2005). A bibliometric analysis of 30 years of research and theory on corporate social responsibility and corporate social performance. *Business & Society*, *44*(3), 283–317.

Deegan, C., & Carroll, G. (1993). An analysis of incentives for Australian firms to apply for reporting excellence awards. *Accounting and Business Research*, *23*(91), 219–227.

Déjean, F., & Martinez, I. (2009). Environmental disclosure and the cost of equity: The French case. *Accounting in Europe*, *6*(1), 57–80.

Delmas, M. (2002). The diffusion of environmental management standards in Europe and the United States: An institutional perspective. *Policy Sciences*, *35*, 91–119.

Delmas, M., & Toffel, M. W. (2004). Stakeholders and environmental management practices: An institutional framework. *Business Strategy and the Environment*, *13*(4), 209–222.

Demsetz, H., & Lehn, K. (1985). The structure of corporate ownership: Causes and consequences. *Journal of Political Economy*, *93*(6), 1155–1177.

Den Hond, F., & De Bakker, F. G. (2007). Ideologically motivated activism: How activist groups influence corporate social change activities. *Academy of Management Review*, *32*(3), 901–924.

Dentchev, N. A., van Balen, M., & Haezendonck, E. (2015). On voluntarism and the role of governments in CSR: Towards a contingency approach. *Business Ethics: A European Review*, *24*(4).

Dharwadkar, B., George, G., & Brandes, P. (2000). Privatization in emerging economies: An agency theory perspective. *Academy of Management Review*, *25*(3), 650–669.

DiMaggio, P., & Powell, W. (1983). The iron cage revisited: Institutional isomorphism and collective rationality in organizational fields. *American Sociological Review*, *48*(2), 147–160.

Dobers, P., & Halme, M. (2009). Corporate social responsibility and developing countries. *Corporate Social Responsibility and Environmental Management*, *16*(5), 237–249.

Doh, J. P., & Teegen, H. (2003). Nongovernmental organizations as institutional actors in international business: Theory and implications. *International Business Review*, *11*(6), 665–684.

Doh, J. P., & Guay, T. R. (2006). Corporate social responsibility, public policy, and NGO activism in Europe and the United States: An institutional-stakeholder perspective. *Journal of Management Studies*, *43*(1), 47–73.

Doh, J. P., Lawton, T. C., & Rajwani, T. (2012). Advancing nonmarket strategy research: Institutional perspectives in a changing world. *The Academy of Management Perspectives*, *26*(3), 22–39.

Doh, J. P., Littell, B., & Quigley, N. R. (2015). CSR and sustainability in emerging markets: Societal, institutional, and organizational influences. *Organizational Dynamics*, *44*(2), 112–120.

Dögl, C., & Behnam, M. (2015). Environmentally sustainable development through stakeholder engagement in developed and emerging countries. *Business Strategy and the Environment*, *24*(6), 583–600.

Donaldson, T., & Preston, L. E. (1995). The stakeholder theory of the corporation: Concepts, evidence, and implications. *Academy of Management Review*, *20*(1), 65–91.

Dyer, G. (2007). China executes ex-chief of food and drug watchdog for bribery. *Financial Times*, *11*.

Easterby-Smith, M., Thorpe, R., & Jackson, P. R. (2012). *Management Research*. London: Sage.

Einstein, A., & Infeld, L. (1938). *The Evolution of Physics: From Early Concepts to Relativity and Quanta*. New York: Touchstone.

Eng, L. L., & Mak, Y. T. (2003). Corporate governance and voluntary disclosure. *Journal of Accounting and Public Policy*, *22*(4), 325–345.

European Commission. (2000). *Commission of the European Communities, Promoting a European Framework for Corporate Social Responsibility, Green Paper*. Brussels: European Commission.

European Commission. (2002). *Corporate Social Responsibility: A Business Contribution to Sustainable Development*. Retrieved on 29 February 2016, from: http://trade.ec.europa.eu/doclib/docs/2006/february/tradoc_127374.pdf

Fama, E. F., & Jensen, M. C. (1983). Separation of ownership and control. *The Journal of Law and Economics*, *26*(2), 301–325.

Fetscherin, M., Li, S., Alon, I., Lattemann, C., & Yeh, K. (2010). Corporate social responsibility in emerging markets: The importance of the governance environment. *Management International Review: Journal of International Business*, *50*(5), 635–654.

Field, A. (2009). *Discovering Statistics Using SPSS*. New York: Sage Publications.

Fields, T. D., Lys, T. Z., & Vincent, L. (2001). Empirical research on accounting choice. *Journal of Accounting and Economics*, *31*(1), 255–307.

Figar, N., & Figar, F. (2011). Corporate social responsibility in the context of the stakeholder theory. *Economics and Organization*, *8*(1), 1–13.

Flory, M. (2008). *The Never-Ending Story: Narrating the Paradox of Self-Management in Organizations*.

Fombrun, C., & Shanley, M. (1990). What's in a name? Reputation building and corporate strategy. *Academy of Management Journal*, *33*(2), 233–258.

Freeman, R. E. (1984). *Strategic Management: A Stakeholder Approach*. Marshfield, MA: Pittman.

Friedman, M. (2007). The social responsibility of business is to increase its profits. In *Corporate Ethics and Corporate Governance* (pp. 173–178). Heidelberg, Berlin: Springer.

Frooman, J. (1999). Stakeholder influence strategies. *Academy of Management Review*, *24*(2), 191–205.

Gadamer, H.-G. (2013). *Truth and Method* (2nd revised edition). London: Bloomsbury Academic. First published in 1975.

Galaskiewicz, J. (1991). Making corporate actors accountable: Institution-building in Minneapolis—St. Paul. In W. W. Powell & P. J. DiMaggio (Eds.), *The New Institutionalism in Organizational Analysis* (pp. 293–310). Chicago: University of Chicago Press.

Gamerschlag, R., Möller, K., & Verbeeten, F. (2011). Determinants of voluntary CSR disclosure: Empirical evidence from Germany. *Review of Managerial Science*, *5*, 233–262.

Gamson, W. A., & Modigliani, A. (1989). Media discourse and public opinion on nuclear power: A constructionist approach. *American Journal of Sociology*, *95*(1), 1–37.

Gardberg, N., & Fombrun, C. (2006). Corporate Citizenship: Creating intangible assets across institutional environments. *The Academy of Management Review*, *31*, 329–346.

Garriga, E., & Melé, D. (2004). Corporate social responsibility theories: Mapping the territory. *Journal of Business Ethics*, *53*(1–2), 51–71.

Gefei, Y., Zhihong, Y., & Yibo, D. (2008). *Corporate Social Responsibility*

Giannarakis, G. (2014). The determinants influencing the extent of CSR disclosure. *International Journal of Law and Management*, *56*(5), 393–416.

Ginsberg, M. (1931). The concept of evolution in sociology. *Proceedings of the Aristotelian Society*, *31*, 201–224.

Global Reporting Initiative. (2016). *What Is GRI?* Retrieved on 19 January 2016, from: www.globalreporting.org/information/about-gri/what-is-GRI/Pages/default.aspx

Goktan, M. S., & Ucar, E. (2012). Public vs. private: Characteristics of the companies backed by listed private equity. *Journal of Accounting and Finance*, *12*(5), 11.

Gond, J. P., Kang, N., & Moon, J. (2011). The government of self-regulation: On the comparative dynamics of corporate social responsibility. *Economy and Society*, *40*(4), 640–671.

Gray, R. (2000). Articles review. *Social and Environmental Accounting*, *20*(2), 26.

Gray, R. (2010). Is accounting for sustainability actually accounting for sustainability . . . and how would we know? An exploration of narratives of organizations and the planet. *Accounting, Organizations and Society*, *35*(1), 47–62.

Gray, R., Javad, M., Power, D. M., & Sinclair, C. D. (2001). Social and environmental disclosure and corporate characteristics: A research note and extension. *Journal of Business Finance & Accounting*, *28*(3–4), 327–356.

Gray, R., Owen, D., & Maunders, K. (1987). *Corporate Social Reporting: Accounting and Accountability*. London: Prentice-Hall.

Greening, D. W., & Gray, B. (1994). Testing a model of organizational response to social and political issues. *Academy of Management Journal*, *37*(3), 467–498.

Greenwood, R., Li, S., Prakash, S., & Deephouse, D. (2005). Reputation, diversification, and organizational explanations of performance in professional service firms. *Organization Science*, *16*, 661–673.

Greenwood, R., Suddaby, R., & Hinings, C. R. (2002). Theorizing change: The role of professional associations in the transformation of institutionalized fields. *Academy of Management Journal*, *45*(1), 58–80.

Guba, E. G., & Lincoln, Y. S. (1994). Competing paradigms in qualitative research. In N. K. Denzin & Y. S. Lincoln (Eds.), *Handbook of Qualitative Research* (pp. 105–117). London: Sage Publications.

Guler, I., Guillén, M. F., & Macpherson, J. M. (2002). Global competition, institutions, and the diffusion of organizational practices: The international spread of ISO 9000 quality certificates. *Administrative Science Quarterly*, *47*(2), 207–232.

Gulyás, Á. (2009). Corporate social responsibility in the British media industries—preliminary findings. *Media Culture Society*, *31*, 657–668.

Haberberg, A., Gander, J., Rieple, A., Martin-Castilla, J., & Helm, C. (2008). *Patterns in the Adoption of Corporate Social Responsibility Practices*. Corporate Responsibility Research Conference, Queen's University Belfast.

Hair, J. F., Black, W. C., Babin, B. J., & Anderson, R. E. (2014). *Multivariate Data Analysis* (Vol. 7). Essex: Pearson Education Ltd.

Haniffa, R. M., & Cooke, T. E. (2005). The impact of culture and governance on corporate social reporting. *Journal of Accounting and Public Policy*, *24*(5), 391–430.

Healy, P. M., & Palepu, K. G. (2001). Information asymmetry, corporate disclosure, and the capital markets: A review of the empirical disclosure literature. *Journal of Accounting and Economics*, *31*(1), 405–440.

Heidegger, M. (2010). *Being and Time*. A revised edition of the Stambaugh translation. New York: State University of New York. First published in 1953.

Hillman, A., and Hitt, M. (1999). Corporate political strategy formulation: A model of approach, participation and strategy decisions. *The Academy of Management Review*, *24*, 825.

Ho, L. C., & Taylor, M. E. (2007). An empirical analysis of triple bottom-line reporting and its determinants: Evidence from the United States and Japan. *Journal of International Financial Management & Accounting*, *18*(2), 123–150.

Ho, S. S., & Wong, K. S. (2001). A study of the relationship between corporate governance structures and the extent of voluntary disclosure. *Journal of International Accounting, Auditing and Taxation*, *10*(2), 139–156.

Hoffman, A. J., & Ventresca, M. J. (2002). *Organizations, Policy and the Natural Environment*. Stanford, CA: Stanford University Press.

Hond, den F., & Bakker, de F. G. A. (2007). Ideologically motivated activism: How activist groups influence corporate social change activities. *Academy of Management Review*, *32*(3), 901–924.

Husted, B. (2001). *Toward a Model of Corporate Social Strategy Formulation*. Paper presented at the Social Issues in Management Division, Academy of Management.

Husted, B., & Allen, D. (2007). Strategic corporate social responsibility and value creation among large firms lessons from the Spanish experience. *Long Range Planning*, *40*(6), 594–610.

Husted, B., & Salazar, J. (2006). Taking Friedman seriously: Maximizing profits and social performance. *The Journal of Management Studies*, *43*(1), 75–91.

Igalens, J., & Gond, J. P. (2005). Measuring corporate social performance in France: A critical and empirical analysis of ARESE data. *Journal of Business Ethics*, *56*(2), 131–148.

Inchausti, B. G. (1997). The influence of company characteristics and accounting regulation on information disclosed by Spanish firms. *European Accounting Review*, *6*(1), 45–68.

International Chamber of Commerce (ICC). (2016). *Business in Society: Making a Positive and Responsible Contribution*. Retrieved on 29 February 2016, from: www.iccwbo.org/products-and-services/trade-facilitation/9-steps-to-responsible-business-conduct/

Ioannou, I., & Serafeim, G. (2010). *What Drives Corporate Social Performance? International Evidence from Social, Environmental and Governance Scores*. Harvard Business School Accounting and Management Unit Working Paper No. 1507874, Harvard University, Cambridge, MA.

ISO 14001. (2013, April 19). Retrieved from: http//www.iso14000.nl/

Jackson, G., & Apostolakau, A. (2009). Corporate social responsibility in Western Europe: An institutional mirror or substitute? *Journal of Business Ethics*, *94*(3), 371–394.

Jain, A., Keneley, M., & Thomson, D. (2015). Voluntary CSR disclosure works! Evidence from Asia-Pacific banks. *Social Responsibility Journal*, *11*(1), 2–18.

Jamali, D. (2010). The CSR of MNC subsidiaries in developing countries: Global, local, substantive or diluted? *Journal of Business Ethics*, *93*, 181–200.

Jamali, D. R., El Dirani, A. M., & Harwood, I. A. (2015). Exploring human resource management roles in corporate social responsibility: The CSR-HRM co-creation model. *Business Ethics: A European Review*, *24*(2).

Jenkins, R. (2005). Globalization, corporate social responsibility and poverty. *International Affairs*, *81*(3), 525–540.

Jensen, M. C., & Meckling, W. H. (1976). Theory of the firm: Managerial behavior, agency costs and ownership structure. *Journal of Financial Economics*, *3*(4), 305–360.

Jones, M. T. (1999). The institutional determinants of social responsibility. *Journal of Business Ethics*, *20*, 163–179.

Karnani, A. (2010, August 23). The case against corporate social responsibility. *Wall Street Journal*. Retrieved on 1 May 2013, from: Google Scholar.

Kavitha, W., & Anita, P. (2011). Disclosures about CSR practices: A literature review: IUP. *Journal of Corporate Governance*, *10*(1), 45.

Kemp, M. (2001).*Corporate Social Responsibility in Indonesia: Quixotic Dream or Confident Expectation?* Geneva, Switzerland: United Nations Research Institute for Social Development.

Khan, H. U. Z. (2010). The effect of corporate governance elements on corporate social responsibility (CSR) reporting: Empirical evidence from private commercial banks of Bangladesh. *International Journal of Law and Management*, *52*(2), 82–109.

King, A. A., Lenox, M. J., & Terlaak, A. (2005). The strategic use of decentralized institutions: Exploring certification with the ISO 14001 management standard. *Academy of Management Journal*, *48*(6), 1091–1106.

Klamer, A. (2016a). The value-based approach to cultural economics. *Journal of Cultural Economics*, 40, 365–373.
Klamer, A. (2016b). *Doing the Right Thing: A Value Based Economy*. London: Ubiquity Press.
Klein, J. G., Smith, N. C., & John, A. (2004). Why we boycott: Consumer motivations for boycott participation. *Journal of Marketing*, *68*(3), 92–109.
Kolk, A. (2003). Trends in sustainability reporting by the Fortune Global 250. *Business Strategy and the Environment*, *12*(5), 279–291.
Kolk, A. (2005). Environmental reporting by multinationals from the Triad: Convergence or divergence? *MIR: Management International Review*, 145–166.
Kolk, A., Hong, P., & Van Dolen, W. (2010). Corporate social responsibility in China: An analysis of domestic and foreign retailers' sustainability dimensions. *Business Strategy and the Environment*, *19*(5), 289–303.
Koppell, J. G. S. (2008). Global governance organizations: Legitimacy and authority in conflict. *Journal of Public Administration Research Theory*, *18*(2), 177–203.
Kostova, T., & Zaheer, S. (1999). Organizational legitimacy under conditions of complexity: The case of the multinational enterprise. *Academy of Management Journal*, *24*(1), 64–81.
Lader, C. (2008). *Barron's AP United States Government & Politics*. New York: Barron's Educational Series.
Lee, P. M. (2008). A review of the theories of corporate social responsibility: Its evolutionary path and the road ahead. *International Journal of Management Reviews*, *10*, 53–73.
Lépineux, F. (2004). Stakeholder theory, society and social cohesion. *Corporate Governance: The International Journal of Business and Society*, *5*(2), 99–110.
Levy, D., & Kaplan, R. (2008). CSR and theories of global governance: Strategic contestation in global issue arenas. In Andrew Crane, Dirk Matten, Abagail McWilliams, Jeremy Moon, & Donald S. Siegel (Eds.) *The Oxford Handbook of CSR* (pp. 432–451). Oxford: Oxford University Press.
Lexisnexis. (June 2013). Retrieved from: http//www.lexisnexis.nl/
Li, Q., Luo, W., Wang, Y., & Wu, L. (2013). Firm performance, corporate ownership, and corporate social responsibility disclosure in China. *Business Ethics: A European Review*, *22*(2), 159–173.
Lin-Hi, N. (2010). The problem with a narrow-minded interpretation of CSR. Why CSR has nothing to do with philanthropy. *Ramon Llull Journal of Applied Ethics*, *1*(1), 75–95.
Lynes, J., & Andrachuk, M. (2008). Motivations for corporate social and environmental responsibility: A case study of Scandinavian airlines. *Journal of International Management*, *14*, 377–390.
Lyon, T. P., & Maxwell, J. W. (2008). Corporate social responsibility and the environment: A theoretical perspective. *Review of Environmental Economics and Policy*, *2*(2), 240–260.
MacIntyre, A. (1981). *After Virtue*. Paris: Notre Dame University Press.
Mahoney, L. S., Thorne, L., Cecil, L., & LaGore, W. (2013). A research note on standalone corporate social responsibility reports: Signaling or greenwashing? *Critical Perspectives on Accounting*, *24*(4), 350–359.
Maignan, I., Ferrell, O. C., & Ferrel, L. (2005). A stakeholder model for implementing social responsibility in marketing. *European Journal of Marketing*, *39*(9–10), 956–977.

Mănescu, C. (2011). Stock returns in relation to environmental, social and governance performance: Mispricing or compensation for risk? *Sustainable Development*, *19*(2), 95–118.

Margolis, J. D., & Walsh, J. P. (2003). Misery loves companies: Rethinking social initiatives by business. *Administrative Science Quarterly*, *48*(2), 268–305.

C:\Users\cvo\AppData\Local\Microsoft\Windows\Temporary Internet Files\Content.Outlook\M3815695\15032-1202-Ref Mismatch Report.docx - LStERROR_55Marquis, C., Glynn, M. A., & Davis, G. F. (2007). Community isomorphism and corporate social action. *Academy of Management Review*, *32*(3), 925–945.

Mathews, M. R. (1995). Social and environmental accounting: A practical demonstration of ethical concern? *Journal of Business Ethics*, *14*(8), 663–671.

Matten, D., & Moon, J. (2004). Corporate social responsibility education in Europe. *Journal of Business Ethics*, *54*(4), 323–337.

Matten, D., & Moon, J. (2005). *Pan-European Approach*. Berlin, Heidelberg: Springer.

Matten, D., & Moon, J. (2008). 'Implicit' and 'Explicit' CSR: A conceptual framework for a comparative understanding of corporate social responsibility. *Academy of Management Review*, *33*(2), 404–424.

Maturana, H. R. (1978). *Biology of Language: The Epistemology of Reality*.

Maturana, H. R. (1987). *The Tree of Knowledge: The Biological Roots of Human Understanding*. Boston, MA: Shambhala Publications.

Maturana, H., & Varela, F. (1998). *The Tree of Knowledge*, revised edition. Boston and London: Shambhala.

Mazda.com. (2013, April 19). Retrieved from: www.mazda.com/csr/csr_vision/respect/

McBarnet, D. (2007). *Corporate Social Responsibility Beyond Law, Through Law, for Law: The New Corporate Accountability*. Oxford: Cambridge University Press.

McCartney, J. D., McPhail, C., & Smith, J. (1996). Images of protest: Dimensions of selection bias in media coverage of Washington demonstrations, 1982 and 1991. *American Sociological Review*, *61*(3), 478–499.

McCloskey, D. N. (1983). The rhetoric of economics. *Journal of Economic Literature*, *21*(2), 481–517.

McCloskey, D. N. (2007). *The Bourgeois Virtue: Ethics for an Age of Commerce*. Chicago: University of Chicago Press.

McWilliams, A., Siegel, D. S., &Wright, P. M. (2006). *Corporate Social Responsibility: International Perspectives*. Working Papers in Economics, 1–13.

Meek, G. K., Roberts, C. B., & Gray, S. J. (1995). Factors influencing voluntary annual report disclosures by US, UK and continental European multinational corporations. *Journal of International Business Studies*, 555–572.

Meyer, J. W., & Rowan, B. (1977). Institutionalized organizations: Formal structure as myth and ceremony. *American Journal of Sociology*, *83*(2), 340–363.

Michelon, G., Pilonato, S., & Ricceri, F. (2015). CSR reporting practices and the quality of disclosure: An empirical analysis. *Critical Perspectives on Accounting*, *33*, 59–78.

Mitroff, I., Pauchant, T. C., & Shrivastava, P. (1989). Crisis, disaster, catastrophe: Are you ready? *Security Management*, *33*(2), 101–108.

Mitton, T. (2002). A cross-firm analysis of the impact of corporate governance on the East Asian financial crisis. *Journal of Financial Economics*, *64*(2), 215–241.

Moon, J., & Shen, X. (2010). CSR in China research: Salience, focus and nature. *Journal of Business Ethics*, *94*, 613–629.
Muller, A., & Kolk, A. (2009). CSR performance in emerging markets evidence from Mexico. *Journal of Business Ethics*, *85*(2), 325–337.
Muller, A., & Kolk, A. (2010). Extrinsic and intrinsic drivers of corporate social performance: Evidence from foreign and domestic firms in Mexico. *Journal of Management Studies*, *47*(1), 1–26.
Myers, M. (2000). Qualitative research and the generalizability question: Standing firm with Proteus. *The Qualitative Report*, *4*, 5–16.
Ng, E. J., & Koh, H. C. (1994). An agency theory and probit analytic approach to corporate non-mandatory disclosure compliance. *Asia-Pacific Journal of Accounting*, *1*(1), 29–44.
Nidasio, C. (2004). *Implementing CSR on a Large Scale: The Role of Government*. Paper presented at the research track 7, 'Policy making and the Role of Government' in 3rd Colloquium of the European Academy of Business in Society, Ghent.
Nikolaeva, R., & Marta, B. (2011). The role of institutional and reputational factors in the voluntary adoption of corporate social responsibility reporting standards. *Journal of the Academy of Marketing Science*, *39*(1), 139–157.
Oi, J. (1995). The role of the local state in China's transitional economy. *The China Quarterly*, *144*, 1132–1149.
Oliver, C. (1992). The antecedents of deinstitutionalizaiton. *Organization Studies*, *13*, 563–588.
Oliver, C. (1999). Strategic responses to institutional processes. *The Academy of Management Review*, *16*, 145–179.
Orlitzky, M., Schmidt, F. L., & Rynes, S. L. (2003). Corporate social and financial performance: A meta-analysis. *Organization Studies*, *24*(3), 403–441.
Palazzo, G., & Scherer, A. G. (2006). Corporate legitimacy as deliberation: A communicative framework. *Journal of Business Ethics*, *66*(1), 71–88.
Peinado-Vara, E. (2004). *Corporate Social Responsibility in Latin America and the Caribbean*. Sustainable Development Department Technical Papers Series, 1–10.
Peloza, J. (2009). The challenge of measuring financial impacts from investments in corporate social performance. *Journal of Management*, *35*, 1518–1541.
Peng, M. W. (2003). Institutional transitions and strategic choices. *The Academy of Management Review*, *28*, 275–296.
Peng, M. W., & Heath, P. (1996). The growth of the firm in planned economies in transition: Institutions, organizations, and strategic choice. *The Academy of Management Review*, *21*, 492–528.
Perrini, F. (2007). *Encouraging CSI in Italy: The Enabling Role of Government in Mandating, Motivating, and Supporting Responsible Business Practices*. Working Paper for the Corporate Social Responsibility Initiative, 35, 1–31.
C:\Users\cvo\AppData\Local\Microsoft\Windows\Temporary Internet Files\Content.Outlook\M3815695\15032-1202-Ref Mismatch Report.docx - LStERROR_60 Perrini, F., Russo, A., & Tencati, A. (2007). CSR strategies of SMEs and large firms: Evidence from Italy. *Journal of Business Ethics*, *74*(3), 285–300.
Peters, S., Miller, M., & Kusyk, S. (2011). How relevant is corporate governance and corporate social responsibility in emerging markets? *Corporate Governance: The International Journal of Business in Society*, *11*(4), 429–445.
Pirsch, J., Gupta, S., & Grau, S. L. (2007). A framework for understanding corporate social responsibility programs as a continuum: An exploratory study. *Journal of Business Ethics*, *70*(2), 125–140.

Polit, D., & Hungler, B. (1991). *Nursing Research: Principles and Methods*. New York: JB Lippincott.

Porter, M. E. (1980). *Competitive Strategy*. New York: Free Press.

Porter, M. E. (1990). *The Competitive Advantage of Nations*. New York: Free Press.

Portney, P. R. (2008). The (not so) new corporate social responsibility: An empirical perspective. *Review of Environmental Economics and Policy*, 2, 261–275.

Pozzati, M. (2007). *Buscando a inteireza do Ser: Proposições para o desenvolvimento sustentável da consciência humana*. Porto Alegre: Gênese Editora.

Prencipe, A. (2004). Proprietary costs and determinants of voluntary segment disclosure: Evidence from Italian listed companies. *European Accounting Review*, *13*(2), 319–340.

Preuss, L., Haunschild, A., & Matten, D. (2006). Trade unions and CSR: A European research agenda. *Journal of Public Affairs*, *6*(3–4), 256–268.

Prieto-Carrón, M., Lund-Thomsen, P. E. T. E. R., Chan, A., Muro, A. N. A., & Bhushan, C. (2006). Critical perspectives on CSR and development: What we know, what we don't know, and what we need to know. *International Affairs*, *82*(5), 977–987.

Qu, R. (2007). Effects of government regulations, market orientation and ownership structure on corporate social responsibility in China: An empirical study. *International Journal of Management*, *24*, 582–591.

Reverte, C. (2009). Determinants of corporate social responsibility disclosure ratings by Spanish listed firms. *Journal of Business Ethics*, *88*(2), 351–366.

Ricoeur, P. (2016). *Hermeneutics and the Human Sciences*. Edited and translated by J. B. Thompson. Cambridge Philosophy Classics edition. New York: Cambridge University Press. First published in 1981.

Roberts, R. W. (1992). Determinants of corporate social responsibility disclosure: An application of stakeholder theory. *Accounting, Organizations and Society*, *17*, 595–612.

Rowley, J. (2002). Using case studies in research. *Management Research News*, *25*, 16–27.

Said, R., Hj Zainuddin, Y., & Haron, H. (2009). The relationship between corporate social responsibility disclosure and corporate governance characteristics in Malaysian public listed companies. *Social Responsibility Journal*, *5*(2), 212–226.

Scharmer, C. O. (2009). *Theory U: Learning from the Future as It Emerges*. San Francisco, CA: Berrett-Koehler Publishers.

Schultz, F., & Wehmeier, S. (2010). Institutionalization of corporate social responsibility within corporate communications. *Corporate Communications: An International Journal*, *15*(1), 9–29.

Scott, W. R. (1995). *Institutions and Organizations*. Thousand Oaks, CA: Sage Publications.

Shenkar, O., Luo, Y., & Yeheskel, O. (2008). From "distance" to "friction": Substituting metaphors and redirecting intercultural research. *Academy of Management Review*, *33*(4), 905–923.

Shenkar, O., & Yadong, L. (2008). *International Business*. Chicago: Sage Publications.

Shipan, C. R., & Volden, C. (2008). The mechanisms of policy diffusion. *American Journal of Political Science*, *52*(4), 840–857.

Siegel, P. H., Agrawal, S., & Rigsby, J. T. (1997). Organizational and professional socialization: Institutional isomorphism in an accounting context. *The Mid-Atlantic Journal of Business*, *33*, 49–68.

Silverblatt, A. (2004). Media as social institution. *American Behavioral Scientist*, *48*, 35–41.

Sohn, H. (1982). Prevailing rationales in the corporate social responsibility debate. *Journal of Business Ethics*, *1*, 139–144.

Spar, D. L., & Mure La, L. T. (2003). The power of activism: Assessing the impact of NGOs on global business. *California Management Review*, *45*(3), 78–101.

Stanwick, P. A., &. Stanwick, S. D. (1998). The relationship between corporate social performance and organizational size, financial performance and environmental performance: An empirical examination. *Journal of Business Ethics*, *17*(2), 195–204.

Stellner, C., Klein, C., & Zwergel, B. (2015). Corporate social responsibility and Eurozone corporate bonds: The moderating role of country sustainability. *Journal of Banking & Finance*, *59*, 538–549.

Steurer, R. (2010). The role of governments in corporate social responsibility: Characterising public policies on CSR in Europe. *Policy Sciences*, *43*, 49–72.

Stevens, R., Loudon, D., Wrenn, B., & Cole, H. (2006). *The Concise Encyclopedia of Church and Religious Organization Marketing*. New York: Haworth Press.

Stoian, C., & Zaharia, R. M. (2012). CSR development in post-communist economies: Employees' expectations regarding corporate socially responsible behavior—the case of Romania. *Business Ethics: A European Review*, *21*(4), 380–401.

Story, J., & Neves, P. (2015). When corporate social responsibility (CSR) increases performance: Exploring the role of intrinsic and extrinsic CSR attribution. *Business Ethics: A European Review*, *24*(2).

Strang, D., & Soule, S. (1998). Diffusion in organizations and social movements: From hybrid corn to poison pills. *Annual Review of Sociology*, *24*(1), 265–290.

Suchman, M. (1995). Managing legitimacy: Strategic and institutional approaches. *The Academy of Management Review*, *20*, 571–610.

Tagesson, T., Blank, V., Broberg, P., & Collin, S. O. (2009). What explains the extent and content of social and environmental disclosures on corporate websites: A study of social and environmental reporting in Swedish listed corporations. *Corporate Social Responsibility and Environmental Management*, *16*(6), 352–364.

Tan, J., & Litschert, R. (1994). Environment-strategy relationship and its performance implications: An empirical study of the Chinese electronics industry. *Strategic Management Journal*, *15*, 1–20.

Tran, T. K. (2008). *Growth of Joint Stock Companies in the Seventeenth Century*.

Trevino, L. J., Thomas, D. E., & Cullen, J. (2008). The three pillars of institutional theory and FDI in Latin America: An institutionalization process. *International Business Review*, *17*(1), 118–133.

Tsui, A. S., Schoonhoven, C. B., Meyer, M. W., Lau, C. M., & Milkovich, G. T. (2004). Organization and management in the midst of societal transformation: The People's Republic of China. *Organization Science*, *15*(2), 133–144.

Van Marrewijk, M. (2003). Concepts and definitions of CSR and corporate sustainability: Between agency and communion. *Journal of Business Ethics*, *44*(2–3), 95–105.

Vildåsen, S. S., Keitsch, M., & Fet, A. M. (2017). Clarifying the epistemology of corporate sustainability. *Ecological Economics*, *138*, 40–46.

Walsh, J. P., Weber, K., & Margolis, J. D. (2003). Social issues and management: Our lost cause found. *Journal of Management*, *29*(6), 859–881.

Wartick, S. L. (1992). The relationship between intense media exposure and change in corporate reputation. *Business & Society*, *31*, 33–49.

Waddock, S. A., & Graves, S. B. (1997). The corporate social performance-financial performance link. *Strategic Management Journal*, *18*(4), 303–319.

Wartick, S. L., & Mahon, J. F. (1994). Toward a substantive definition of the corporate issue construct: A review and synthesis of the literature. *Business and Society*, *33*(3), 293–311.

Waddock, S., & McIntosh, M. (2009). Beyond corporate responsibility: Implications for management development. *Business and Society Review*, *114*(3), 295–325.

Wartick, S. L., & Wood, D. J. (1998). *International Business and Society*. Malden, MA/Oxford, UK: Basil Blackwell.

Watson, A., Shrives, P., & Marston, C. (2002). Voluntary disclosure of accounting ratios in the UK. *British Accounting Review*, *34*(2), 289–313.

Watts, R. L., & Zimmerman, J. L. (1978). Towards a positive theory of the determination of accounting standards. *Accounting Review*, 112–134.

Webb, E. (2004). An examination of socially responsible firms' board structure. *Journal of Management and Governance*, *8*(3), 255–277.

Weber, M. (2008). The business base for corporate social responsibility: A company-level measurement approach for CSR. *European Management Journal*, *26*, 247–261.

Weber, R. P. (1990). *Basic Content Analysis* (2nd edition). Newbury Park, CA: Sage Publications.

Weigelt, K., & Camerer, C. (1988). Reputation and corporate strategy: A review of recent theory and applications. *Strategic Management Journal*, *9*, 443–454.

Weldon, E., & Vanhonacker, W. (1999). Operating a foreign invested enterprise in China: Challenges for managers and management researchers. *Journal of World Business*, *34*, 9–94.

Welford, R. (2004). Corporate social responsibility in Europe and Asia: Critical elements and best practice. *Journal of Corporate Citizenship*, *13*, 31–47.

Welford, R., Chan, C., & Man, M. (2008). Priorities for corporate social responsibility: A survey of businesses and their stakeholders. *Corporate Social Responsibility and Environmental Management*, *15*(1), 52–62.

Welford, R., & Peiyuan, G. (2005). Corporate environmental reporting and disclosure in China. *CSR Asia: Hong Kong*.

Whetten, D. A., Rands, G., & Godfrey, P. (2002). What are the responsibilities of business to society. *Handbook of Strategy and Management*, 373–408.

Windsor, D. (2001). The future of corporate social responsibility. *The International Journal of Organizational Analysis*, *9*(3), 225–256.

Wirtz, B. W. (2011). *Media and Internet Management*. Wiesbaden: Gabler.

Wood, D. J. (1990). Corporate social performance revisited. *The Academy of Management Review*, *16*, 691–718.

Wu, X. (2001). Foreign direct investment, intellectual property rights and wage equality in China. *China Economic Review*, *11*, 361–384.

Xu, S., & Yang, R. (2010). Indigenous characteristics of Chinese corporate social responsibility conceptual paradigm. *Journal of Business Ethics*, *93*, 321–333.

Xu, X., & Wang, Y. (1999). Ownership structure and corporate governance in Chinese stock companies. *China Economic Review*, *10*(1), 75–98.

Yang, H. (2011). Business implications of corporate sustainability in an emerging country: Evidence from China. *International Review of Business Research Papers*, *7*(1), 77–89.

Young, M. N., Peng, M. W., Ahlstrom, D., Bruton, G. D., & Jiang, Y. (2008). Corporate governance in emerging economies: A review of the principal—principal perspective. *Journal of Management Studies*, *45*(1), 196–220.

Zappalà, G. (2004). Corporate citizenship and human resource management: a new tool or a missed opportunity?. *Asia Pacific Journal of Human Resources*, *42*(2), 185–201.

Zenisek, T. J. (1979). Corporate social responsibility: A conceptualization based on organizational literature. *The Academy of Management Review*, 4, 359–368.

Zhang, K. (2006). *China as the World Factory*. Oxon, UK: Routledge.

Zhu, Q., & Sarkis, J. (2007). The moderating effects of institutional pressures on emergent green supply chain practices and performance. *International Journal of Production Research*, *45*(18–19), 4333–4355.

Zu, L., & Song, L. (2009). Determinants of managerial values on corporate social responsibility: Evidence from China. *Journal of Business Ethics*, *88*, 105–117.

Zucker, L. G. (1987). Where do institutional patterns come from? Organizations as actors in a social systems. In: *Institutional Patterns and Organizations: Culture and Environment*. Cambridge, MA: Ballinger.

Index